MERGERS

and

ACQUISITIONS

STRATEGY

for

CONSOLIDATIONS

Roll Up, Roll Out, and Innovate for
Superior Growth and Returns

NORMAN W. HOFFMANN

New York   Chicago   San Francisco   Lisbon   London
Madrid   Mexico City   Milan   New Delhi   San Juan
Seoul   Singapore   Sydney   Toronto

1 2 3 4 5 6 7 8 9 0   DOC/DOC   1 8 7 6 5 4 3 2

ISBN: 978-0-07-179342-1
MHID: 0-07-179342-9

e-ISBN: 978-0-07-179343-8
e-MHID: 0-07-179343-7

This publication is designed to provide accurate and authoritative information in regard to the subject matter covered. It is sold with the understanding that neither the author nor the publisher is engaged in rendering legal, accounting, or other professional service. If legal advice or other expert assistance is required, the services of a competent professional person should be sought.

      —*From a Declaration of Principles Jointly Adopted by a Committee of the American Bar Association and a Committee of Publishers and Associations*

Library of Congress Cataloging-in-Publication Data

Hoffmann, Norman.
  Mergers and Acquisitions Strategy for Consolidations: Roll Up, Roll Out, and Innovate for Superior Growth and Returns / by Norman Hoffmann.— 1st ed.
    p. cm.
  ISBN 978-0-07-179342-1 (alk. paper)—ISBN 0-07-179342-9 (alk. paper)
    1. Market segmentation. 2. Consolidation and merger of corporations. 3. Success in business.   I. Title.
  HF5415.127.H64 2012
  658.1'62—dc23
                                                      2012004963

For Sue, Loren, and Wyatt

Contents

Acknowledgments

Gathering the insights for this book required my patient tutelage under four extraordinarily capable and ingenious business leaders over more than two decades.

Following a conscientious 1979 letter-writing campaign, I persuaded Kelso Gillenwater to ignore the assessment of a personnel director who had determined me unsuited for a summer internship with Landmark. An electric personality, Kelso immediately captured people's attention and inspired their enthusiastic participation in whatever effort he chose. Recruited by Frank Batten and Bill Diederich to continue a rollup of desirable community newspapers, Kelso subsequently appointed me to assist with due-diligence evaluations and strategic planning; and, while mentored by him, I gained an understanding of the practical applications of many of the techniques described in this book. Kelso understood, however, that I needed years of field experience to become a truly effective manager; and, before leaving Landmark, he reassigned me to one of Landmark's small daily newspapers.

As general manager of New Mexico's *Los Alamos Monitor*, I reported to another remarkable leader, Larry Coffey, divisional president of Landmark Community Newspapers, Inc. Unlike Kelso, Larry's unassuming, quiet demeanor caused many to underestimate his abilities and skills as a business operator and cost-conscious manager. Larry believed in strict accountability, but he managed with a velvet glove and an intense devotion to doing what was right. Those were personal traits that I sought to cultivate, and from him I learned the merits of focusing on critical operational metrics, measuring their achievement, employing those metrics to guide performance, and holding staff accountable for producing a high quality news product. After Larry appointed me to identify and acquire niche publications, fate directed that his car should be wrecked and its repairs delayed by a dawdling relative. Over the following months, I therefore enjoyed an uninterrupted hour of his advice and critiques as I chauffeured him on our daily commute to and from work. Such guidance was further burnished during shared lunches each day with his key managers, Larry Paden, Max Heath, Randy Mast, and Gary Miller—all of whom contributed to developing my skills as a manager.

Throughout those early years, Bill Diederich was a constant presence, offering periodic guidance and the occasional motivational push. Following the Winston-Salem *Trading Post* acquisition, Bill became my direct supervisor as I assisted with the classified publication rollup; and I discovered just how much time there was in each day. Though separated by hundreds of miles, I began anticipating the phone ringing around 5:30 p.m. for the commencement of a sometimes two-hour conversation to review everything in excruciating detail. And, following a late dinner on the road, I'd arrive at my motel with the obligation to call Bill for a debriefing, which would last past midnight. From Bill, I learned the importance of careful examination of all assumptions, the means to accumulate obscure information, the techniques to uncover critical details and find meaning beneath the surface, and the tactics of successful negotiations. Somehow, he also instilled within me an ability to differentiate between an ordinary deal and an extraordinary opportunity.

During those earlier years, I had not known Conrad Hall particularly well. I first discovered his magic when his promotion led to his relocating two of us so our offices could be remodeled for his use. He was such a charming man and so considerate as he helped arrange alternative space for us. What spell made us smile and follow him blindly, we wondered as we resituated ourselves at desks in the microwave transmitter room, replete with its concrete floors and gray cinderblock walls. When Landmark's newly acquired classified papers were reorganized as a separate division led by Conrad, I came to truly appreciate not just his charm as a polished southern gentleman but also his acumen as a business leader. The integration of the dozens of disparate acquisitions required an insightful conductor who could orchestrate the hundreds of tasks necessary to succeed; and Conrad's training as a VMI engineer was brilliantly displayed as he multitasked us through the process. Moreover, while his intelligence guided our success, his sincere devotion to the interests of his team and the community inspired an unparalleled loyalty during those evolutionary years. Fundamental to our impressive development were the daily lunches during which he encouraged debate and perpetual assessment of our operations' performance relative to the critical success factors underlying our industry. Regular lunch mates during that era were Britt Reid, Mitch Brooks, Sunny Sonner, and George Brooks—Trader's key management team, which participated vigorously in the iterative assessments to enhance decision making and the implementation processes. But more than dedicated executives whose advice and devoted involvement were fundamental to my development, these were my friends, despite our sometimes heated exchanges: "Are you hallucinating?!"

Of course, all these people were among the chosen leaders enlisted by Frank Batten, the inspirational and visionary owner of Landmark Communications, whose success was very much predicated upon his ability to attract such talent and inspire their devotion to Landmark's development. Their contributions were mirrored by others in allied divisions, including Dick Roberts and Rex Bradley at TeleCable, Carl Mangum and Bob Benson at the metropolitan newspapers, and Dick Fraim and Lem Lewis at the broadcast operations. And, from Cox Enterprises, I am particularly grateful for the involvement of its chairperson, Jim Kennedy, and its executives, including Bob Musselman, Jay Smith, David Easterly, and Bill Disbrow. From each of these people, I observed comparable skill and dedication to improving operations; and they served to re-emphasize the lessons offered by my direct superiors. I'll never forget that it was Frank who addressed me by name as he introduced himself on an elevator ride during my first week's employment; and, if it were not for his enthusiasm, interest, support, and guidance, none of us would have enjoyed such a thrilling ride during our careers with Landmark. Frank Batten, Jr., continued that legacy, and we appreciated his sincere efforts throughout.

In addition, I am particularly grateful to Dick Barry, President of Landmark Communications during most of my tenure. Not only was he a constant advocate of Trader's development, but he was particularly helpful in providing me encouragement and enhanced details about our efforts as I wrote this book.

Similarly, I am grateful to others who contributed information for this book, including Macon Brock, founding CEO of Dollar Tree, Inc.; Chip Perry, President of AutoTrader.com, LLC; Jim McKnight, former COO of AutoTrader.com, LLC; Dick Roberts, retired President of TeleCable, Inc.; and entrepreneurs Mike Nenni and Wayne Moriarity. Contributions were also gratefully received from Trader's Jack Ross, Bill Rieth, Richard Jamin, Bill Dorsey, Jeff Moore, Ernie Blood, Peter Ill, Rick Murchake, Jim Shumadine, Joe Fuller, Rusty Friddell, Terry Blevins, and Tom Malone-Povolny. I also appreciated the help of Alexis Davis and Becky Robinson, my administrative assistants, who kept me and all my materials organized, thereby facilitating the compilation of the materials for this book.

After I completed my first draft, Rosemary Hoffmann provided the cirtical, most appreciated first review, offering valuable comments and recommendations before submission to the publisher. To guide my way during the publishing process, I thank Lynne Rabinoff, my agent who introduced me to the fine people at McGraw Hill, including Jennifer Ashkenazy, Mary Glenn, Scott Kurtz, and Maureen Harper—all of whom demonstrated sincere interest in this project and who provided able assistance in polishing the work. I also thank Brigitte Gabriel, who encouraged Lynne to take me on as her client.

Finally, I thank all the staff members of Trader Publishing Company and Dominion Enterprises—each of whom contributed measurably to the success we all engineered. To those still involved, I wish you the very best of future success.

Trader Publishing Company Acquisition and Development Timeline

Year	Landmark Communications	Trader Publishing Company	Cox Enterprises
1985	Winston-Salem Trading Post		
1986	Tradin' Times		
1987	Buffalo/Rochester Swap Sheet		
1988	7 acquisitions		Auto Trader licensor and 10 licensees
1989	8 acquisitions		3 acquisitions
1990	5 acquisitions		
1991		Founding with merger of Cox/Landmark subsidiaries	
1992		Diablo Dealer free photo guide	
1994		Auto Mart launches 1 acquisition	
1995		6 acquisitions	
1996		National Media Systems (distributor) 4 additional acquisitions	
1997		Employment Guide 5 additional acquisitions	
1998		CareerWeb acquisition 3 additional acquisitions	
1999		Dealer Specialties (data collection) 4 additional acquisitions Spin-off of AutoTraderOnline.com	
2000		Roomsaver travel guides United Advertising Publications 8 additional acquisitions	
2001		5 acquisitions	
2002		12 acquisitions	
2003		15 acquisitions	
2004		Homes.com and Boats.com 12 additional acquisitions	
2005		5 web hosting acquisitions 13 additional acquisitions	
2006		eNeighborhoods 4 additional acquisitions	
	Creation of Dominion Enterprises	Partnership termination	Creation of Cox Auto Trader

Introduction

"There's a human dynamic about the M&A thing. It's like sex. M&A is fun. It's one of those things that's fun even when done badly. Hence, you have everyone trying it."[1]

Thus spoke Dave Roux, cofounder of Silver Lake Partners, a private equity firm that manages over $13 billion in assets. Few truer words have been expressed about the intoxicating appeal of merger and acquisition activity among inhabitants of the executive suite.

In completing 145 self-funded acquisitions from 1985 to 2006, the leadership of Trader Publishing Company was similarly exhilarated by the thrill of the chase and the euphoria of striking deals. If done well, such acquisition efforts will succeed the way Trader did in growing to $1.3 billion in annual revenue while paying its investors over $1 billion in dividends over its 20-year history. Trader's strategy of buying and consolidating (rolling up) small value-priced niche publishers achieved impressive returns by capturing efficiencies, leveraging scale, and implementing best practices to accelerate the growth of previously underdeveloped businesses. In turn, those transactions formed the model for creating similar products and services through their rollout to new markets to produce even better returns. Then, as fast-evolving markets and technology demanded, Trader identified and exploited transformative innovations to evolve into an increasingly Internet-oriented provider of advertising portals and web-hosting services, a transformation that was critical to ensuring long-term profitability and success.

The relatively unheralded lessons of this case study of Trader and its antecedents stand in sharp contrast to the stories trumpeted by the media. Headlines appear daily about enthralling big-money transactions resulting from a dashing suitor pursuing a beguiling industry beauty, promising a marriage of joyous potential and fruitful procreation. Occasionally, the right of conquest is spiced with the drama and tension of a ravenous battle between virulent fiends and noble white knights, and on a rare day a white squire magically appears to save the corporate damsel from wedding an unsavory brute. All too often, however, once the merger's wedding bells ring, the promise fades to a grim reality of disappointment and despair. What appeared an attractive marriage is transformed into a nightmare, frequently leading to an expensive divorce, the banishment of the fading beauty to a harem of neglected anonymous hags, or, worse, murder:

- Daimler-Benz acquires Chrysler for a value of $37 billion in 1998, experiences debilitating losses, and eventually sells the company to a private equity firm for $1.4 billion while agreeing to absorb preclosing losses and other expenses, thereby consuming the proceeds and producing a net additional Daimler payout of $650 million in 2007.[2]
- Yahoo acquires Broadcast.com in July 1998 for $5.7 billion, subsequently concludes that its business model as a video portal is untenable, and, while simply redirecting the URL's traffic to Yahoo.com, puts lipstick on the pig by alleging that it provided a valuable backbone for its media businesses.[3]
- Circuit City pays $300 million for InterTan in 2004, battles unwanted takeover initiatives from Highfields Capital in 2005, but then experiences competitive and financing difficulties during the financial debacle of 2008 as it collapses into bankruptcy and liquidation after Blockbuster abandons its own proposal for a merger.[4]

So compelling are the stories of disastrous acquisitions that conventional wisdom supports the assertion that most transactions destroy rather than create value. No less an authority than Warren Buffett routinely decries the rampant examples of foolhardy executives bidding adieu to their shareholders' equity on unconscionable transactions:

The sad fact is that most major acquisitions display an egregious imbalance: They are a bonanza for the shareholders of the acquired; they increase the income and status of the acquirer's management; and they are a honey pot for the investment bankers and other professionals on both sides. But, alas, they usually reduce the wealth of the acquirer's shareholders, often to a substantial extent.[5]

Buffett shamefacedly admits to periodic failures such as his acquisition of Dexter Shoes and Berkshire Hathaway's original core textile business, now shuttered.

But acquisitions through his Berkshire Hathaway have made Buffett one of the richest men in the world, and his uniquely successful investment record since 1965 underscores the rational appeal of a well-managed acquisition program. During the succeeding 40 years, his 20 percent-plus compounded annual return handily beat the S&P 500 Index's less than 11 percent growth.[6] His experience demonstrates that successfully run companies can reinvest their profits in other businesses with promising growth prospects to build future wealth.

Theoretically, there are at least five advantages that encourage a shareholder to invest in companies that do acquisitions. Compared with the average investor, (1) a successful company's leadership should have superior investment and management acumen to assess, negotiate, and manage investments in allied businesses, (2) the acquirer's core business should have marketing, administrative, or other "synergistic" resources to enhance results, (3) the company can depreciate the values acquired in asset deals, thereby obtaining tax savings and effectively discounting the purchase price, (4) the benefits of scale should reduce financing and operating costs, increasing profitability and investment returns, and (5) a company can invest more because the alternative investor dividends are diminished by 20 percent state and federal income taxes.

Unfortunately, as Buffett asserted, the record of corporate acquisitions is at best discouraging. In his sobering book *Deals from Hell*, Robert Bruner analyzed 10 particularly horrific transactions, prefaced by his scholarly analysis of more than 130 studies of the success of acquisition throughout the last several decades. In that overview, however, he persuasively argued that merger and acquisition activity does indeed pay:

> These studies show that the shareholders of the selling firms earn large returns from M&A, that the shareholders of the buyers and sellers *combined* earn significant positive returns, and that the shareholders of buyers generally earn about the required rate of return.[7]

Some may debate Bruner's conclusions by observing that most of the studies merely extrapolate their assessment of success from comparisons of shareholder value as implied by comparatively short-term reactions to stock price. Unfortunately, the vagaries of accounting and the dearth of broad samples make it infeasible to measure value creation and destruction accurately from the perspective of return on the equity employed for the acquisition over the long-term ownership period. This calculation is further complicated by the acquiring entities' efforts to integrate the acquired businesses into their own operations, making it virtually impossible to assess whether value creation is attributable to a specific acquisition.

Regardless, it is certain that some acquisitions do pay, and they can pay big. Accordingly, a prudent M&A practitioner will strive to avoid the mistakes demonstrated by failed deals and subscribe to practices that have produced superior returns. In particular, an intelligent practitioner will try to avoid transactions that are merely seductively glamorous and focus instead on those which offer a compelling opportunity to build substantial value through increased profits produced by leveraging complementary assets to reduce costs and increase combined revenues.

There remains, however, a formidable barrier to success among those deals trumpeted by the *Wall Street Journal* or touted by the talking heads on CNBC. The fact that those transactions are sufficiently large to attract media attention ensures that they will also have captured the attention of the hordes of investment bankers, private equity managers, and stock analysts who will stimulate the competitive pricing battles expected in efficient financial markets. In fact, every sell-side investment banker who fails to engender bids beyond the seller's own valuation risks dismissal for his incompetence.

A prudent investor understands that rarely will a good deal be captured in a well-attended auction led by investment bankers. The auction's usual competition produces the intended bidding frenzy to produce tippy-top prices, undermining the opportunity to earn superior returns. The adrenaline rush and the psychological need to win, coupled with the limited time to develop and interpret critical information to measure intrinsic value, lead to a sale price set by the bidder who most overestimates the financial benefits of acquisition. As was noted in a recent study, megamergers (those representing the top 1 percent in acquisition price) accounted for 43 percent of all acquisition outlays for public companies from 1980 to 2007, and they destroyed value for the acquirers, producing on average a strongly negative return on investment.[8]

Even in privately negotiated transactions, good values are difficult to find among the large transactions. When an acqustion is initiated by a buyer, the offer needed to motivate acceptance must be so compelling that the seller rationally concludes that he can make more by selling than by holding on to the beloved company. In essence, the people most knowledgeable about the business and presumably most capable of cultivating its value must be convinced that the buyer's price is greater than the discounted value of the profits most likely to be produced by themselves as the current operators. Alternatively, the buyer has evidently concluded that the synergistic opportunities produced by the merger will generate the substantial incremental profits necessary to warrant the compelling price.

In cases in which the seller initiates a private transaction, there may be a greater opportunity to negotiate a favorable price, but again, in large transactions, it is almost inevitable that the sellers will be represented by advisors who will guide valuations to higher levels. Arguably, those advisors should discourage selling unless the price exceeds the discounted value of the cash flows anticipated from the business. However, incentive pay encourages their advocacy of completing a deal at any price, and they usually have been enlisted by owners who have already decided to sell. Accordingly, they will be motivated to support a sale while being generally guided by both professional ethics and the need to fulfill their contracted duty to provide their client with a realistic understanding of fair market value (not intrinsic value) to be used as the baseline for a sale.

Of course, most years we hear about a handful of good big deals. When market panics ensue, bargains materialize when a distressed seller is forced into an emergency transaction, as the shareholders of Bear Stearns discovered in 2008 when that year's economic collapse forced its sale to JPMorgan Chase for $10 per share, a 94 percent discount from its $170 price a year earlier.[9] There are also examples of poorly run businesses whose acquisition produced superior returns for those who successfully streamlined costs, sold off unproductive assets, captured actual benefits of scale, and/or focused their efforts on the most profitable activities. Warren Buffett has repeatedly astonished the efficient market theorists by routinely acquiring well-run companies for fair prices below intrinsic value that subsequently delivered superior returns with their required margin of safety.

However, truly attractive big deals are rare among those getting the most publicity. When we read about InBev's further consolidation of the beer industry with its 2008 acquisition of Anheuser-Busch for almost $52 billion (about 26 times the company's trailing 12 months' earnings of $2 billion), we scratch our heads, wondering about the rationality of the deal. Will it really be possible to reduce the price substantially by selling off unrelated assets such as Busch Gardens while cutting an astonishing $1.5 billion in annual operating costs from the core business, as promised by InBev?[10] Even if those actions are successful, will the resulting growth and after-tax earnings produce a return on investment sufficient to reward the shareholders for the implied risk of the transaction? Although this was certainly appealing to Anheuser stockholders who saw their shares leap more than 50 percent from their low three months before the deal, it is hard to conclude from the visible evidence that the transaction will produce a compelling long-term return for InBev's owners.

An inevitable conclusion is that too many deals are struck without regard to their financial prudence. Usually appointed for marketing or operational savvy instead of investment acumen, CEOs on the acquisition trail are often like children in a candy store after they've been given their allowance. Money is burning a hole in their pocket, and they can't wait to spend it on some tasty treat to satisfy their appetite for a sugar rush. Why not spend it on a gigantic hoard of Gummi Bears and peanut butter cups and make all the other kids envious of their enticing assortment? Handing money back to their daddy (the shareholders) certainly has no appeal.

Alternatively, a visionary CEO gets some strategic initiative embedded in his psyche and is driven to acquire a company that promises an avenue to the fulfillment of that illusory dream. What else could possibly explain eBay's 2005 acquisition of the $60 million *revenue* Skype for $3.9 billion?[11] You'd hope a company's board of directors would provide the critical investor mentality to counter the delusions of the CEO or chair who suddenly pursues some harebrained scheme, but few risk the consequences arising from their assertion that the emperor has no clothes. Better to say, "Let our boy do the deal. He's passionate. He's done okay so far. Besides, it's only the shareholders' money," thereby producing another example of rich executives playing recklessly with other people's money. Sadly, after the departure of the sponsoring CEO (but not before absorbing eight- and nine-figure annual losses), eBay sold Skype for a $2.75 billion valuation in 2009.[12] Less than two years later, the roulette wheel spun once more when Microsoft dramatically raised the ante by announcing its $8.5 billion acquisition of the still less than $1 billion revenue, cash-flow-negative Skype, and the pundits launched into another round of rolled eyes and head scratching over a suspiciously absurd valuation.[13]

When it comes to acquisitions, successful deal makers must think like investors. With a tip of their hat to Benjamin Graham, they pay homage to the precepts outlined in his *Security Analysis* and *The Intelligent Investor* and will pursue only an acquisition that "upon thorough analysis, promises safety of principal and a satisfactory return."[14] To calculate that return, they must realistically assess the probable cash flows arising from the business; only then can they determine whether it can be acquired for a price that will produce a return sufficient to compensate for the risks. Inevitably, the best returns will flow from companies that can be acquired for prices substantially lower than their intrinsic values.

But finding large acquisitions below intrinsic value is difficult. Sophisticated advisors, competitive bidding, and reluctant sellers represent the realities that provoke higher prices. And with the increasingly abundant resources of the burgeoning crowd of private equity investors, the competition for attractive large acquisitions will almost certainly drive the vast majority of all future transactions into the overpriced zone.

Fortunately, independent investors never have a realistic prospect of acquiring one of the companies profiled in the media. They have neither the capital nor the gall to expend their energies on the pursuit of the big-money deals. That relegates them to transactions that in reality have a far greater possibility of generating superior returns.

To succeed, an entrepreneurial investor needs to take the advice of baseball's Wee Willie Keeler, who despite his 5-foot 4-inch stature and 29-ounce bat posted Major League's fourteenth best batting average over his 18-year career. In his immortal words: "Keep your eye clear, and hit 'em where they ain't."

A clear eye implies an unobscured insight into the realistic opportunities arising from a prospective investment, and where they (the smart, big-time, big-money acquirers) ain't, of course, is in the realm of small-scale transactions. It is rarely worth the energy of a sophisticated private equity investor or corporate strategic buyer to evaluate $50 million transactions, and considering something less than $5 million is usually dismissed as ludicrous. They rightly assume their hourly compensation alone would wipe out the annual profits of small acquisitions in a matter of days. That assessment, however, has been proved shortsighted by energetic deal makers who have bought into a new market in the early stages of a product's life cycle or assembled a group of small existing companies to serve a dynamically growing market segment.

Small opportunities are also abundant. While the big boys of private equity and corporate acquisition efforts focus on the approximately 12,000 companies and subsidiaries with over $50 million in sales, there is a happier hunting ground for the meaty opportunities offered by well over 5 million smaller companies plus another 13 million proprietorships. It is estimated that at any given moment there are typically 1.7 million businesses for sale in the United States, and experience demonstrates that at the right price, even businesses that are not on the market can be acquired by someone willing to make a compelling offer.

Most important, a long, fabled history demonstrates that the choicest of these small opportunities are where the big upside financial returns lie:

- An energetic milk shake machine salesperson buys a fast-food franchise for a few thousand and then a couple of years later scrounges the capital from lenders to buy the franchisor for $2 million. By replicating the concept through thousands of start-ups and buying up several other franchisees, Ray Kroc lays the foundation to transform a San Bernardino hamburger joint with his innovative training, marketing, and product extensions into the $95 billion market cap McDonald's Corporation.[15]

- Former cottonseed salesman Bob Magness acquires a tiny community antenna television company in Memphis, Texas, and then somehow cobbles together a string of similar operations throughout the United States by finagling deals and borrowing money. By 1972, the $19 million revenue company has $132 million in debt, and Magness recruits 31-year-old John Malone to step up acquisition activity, new launches in larger markets, and innovation to transform the company into Tele-Communications, Inc., which AT&T acquires in 1998 for $30 billion in stock and $16 billion in assumed debt.[16]
- A child from the projects of New York City grows up to work for a successful coffee shop but becomes frustrated when he fails to persuade the owners to modify their product line. He starts his own store, and in two years Howard Schultz eventually buys his former employer's business, introduces espresso drinks such as café latte, replicates the concept through thousands of other start-ups, buys up similar competitors, and creates the $31 billion market cap Starbucks.[17]

In innumerable cases like these, a poorly capitalized individual with boundless energy, passionate commitment, a stomach for risk, and creative talent identifies an existing enterprise, sees a future upside that has not been exploited by others, and successfully negotiates to acquire it on very attractive terms. In an environment where companies are valued on the basis of their profitable earnings before interest, taxes, depreciation, and amortization (EBITDA or cash flow), the large investors routinely cough up prices with cash flow multiples stretching from eight times to infinity. Small transactions, however, are routinely completed for three to six times cash flow. With comparatively little invested to acquire proven cash flows, the small acquirer then aggressively transforms the business into a huge corporation by enhancing its products, replicating its business model in new geographic markets, and acquiring comparable underdeveloped businesses for integration under a unified brand.

In the vernacular of organizational development, the transformation engineered by these originally small-time M&A artists is a combination of the processes of rollup, rollout, and product innovation.

Rollup (also known as buy-up or niche consolidation) is the process of acquiring roughly identical businesses that serve a specific market and product segment to build a competitive mass and gain economies of scale to accelerate profits while improving the efficiencies of operations, promotion, and centralized administration. The tactic arose during the earliest days of commerce when some budding capitalist persuaded his competitor to sell out, but the practice reached a fevered pitch during the era of the nineteenth-century robber barons. With people such as Andrew Carnegie consolidating the heavy industries and John D. Rockefeller aggregating the oil industry, others were buying up consumer goods manufacturers, such as James B. Duke, whose American Tobacco gained control of close to 80 percent of the national tobacco business and a huge share of the international market. Their abuses and the political necessity to mitigate the resulting monopolistic ills led to the trust-busting of the early 1900s.

Rollout is the more genteel process of replicating the business model in new geographic territories or market segments, thereby leveraging the infrastructure and increasing the economies of scale. Without the baggage of anticompetitive, sometimes destructive consolidation, it is rightfully lauded as it introduces the availability of valued products and services to adjacent markets while simultaneously creating new employment to enhance the public welfare.

Innovation is the too frequently missed characteristic of the rollup practitioners who gained notoriety in the 1990s. In anticipation of the rewards of a bountiful initial public offering, hundreds of venture capital–fed deal makers went on acquisition sprees to consolidate almost any market segment: funeral homes, auto dealers, office supply stores, software developers, heating and air-conditioning contractors, temporary staffing agencies, and so on. However, simply acquiring like businesses to gain critical mass and then integrating their administration through a more efficient infrastructure will only lay the groundwork for success. Without the start-up opportunities and an innovative component, product, or service to enhance the integrated operations, there is substantial risk of failure. After four years of effort to complete 23 acquisitions in the semiconductor industry, Brooks-PRI Automation was compelled to write off $624 million of its over $800 million in investments because the consolidation failed to capture and perpetuate the innovative culture necessary to forestall impending obsolescence in its fast-changing industry.[18]

To ensure long-term success and superior investment returns, it is critical to have leadership capable of (1) identifying enhancements to existing products and business practices and then (2) implementing them aggressively to the market to strengthen their bond with old patrons while producing a tantalizing reputation that will draw new customers.

In 1950, Joseph Schumpeter observed that capitalism in the modern world is driven by a "perennial gale of creative destruction" that is "incessantly revolutionizing the economic structure from within, incessantly destroying the old one, incessantly creating a new one."[19] Over a half century later, the accuracy of that assessment is underscored by the dramatically accelerating turbulence creating perpetual upheaval in business. In the 1990s, Yahoo left in its wake the detritus of such search engines as Excite!, Altavista, Lycos, and Prodigy, but now, despite previously establishing a presumably indomitable lead, it finds itself struggling against the growing dominance of Google, which is now falling under the shadow of Facebook.

Accordingly, simply acquiring and integrating a bunch of like businesses will not lead to enduring success. Enduring success will be assured only by the continuing capacity to identify and implement transformative innovations that will improve efficiencies, adapt to changing market needs, and resonate with clients and consumers who cough up more money to boost revenues profitably.

Fortuitously, the acquisition targets of a rollup usually prove to be a fertile source for innovative ideas. Just as there are no two identical snowflakes, there are no two identical entrepreneurs; each one has achieved his or her level of success through the application of a personal vision in the development of the business. A smart M&A practitioner will be conscientious in assessing each prospective acquisition to identify best practices and product innovations for potential replication within the existing units:

- Twenty-nine-year-old John Y. Brown and his partners transformed Colonel Sanders's formula for a sit-down restaurant into a stand-up Kentucky Fried Chicken take-out business, rolling out nationally such franchisee-generated ideas as the bucket of take-out chicken originated by Salt Lake's Pete Harmon.[20]

- Santa Barbara franchisee Herb Peterson loved eggs Benedict and wanted something similar to ignite his restaurant's breakfast sales. The resulting Egg McMuffin was introduced in 1972 and quickly became McDonald's signature breakfast product, which alone grew to contribute approximately $5 billion in annual sales 20 years later.[21]
- After a rollup of comparable retailers (including Dollar Bills, Dollar Express, Only $One, and Greenbacks), Dollar Tree learned valuable lessons about urban marketing, the importance of high-turn consumables, and warehousing and distribution. With insights from its acquisitions, it reinvigorated previously stagnating same-store sales by rolling out some of its acquisitions' practices, including installation of freezers and coolers to sell refrigerated products, widened acceptance of debit and credit cards, and automated store replenishment.[22]

On the basis of the success of so many historical examples, there is compelling justification to pursue an acquisition and development strategy that is focused on the rollup of comparatively small businesses whose business models are then rolled out to new markets and enhanced with innovative products and services. Whether a poorly capitalized entrepreneur, a growth-oriented CEO, or a private equity investor, an astute leader can employ this strategy of acquiring small "best of breed" enterprises, integrating them within a business segment, and leveraging their core strengths to exploit innovations that will produce astonishing returns far exceeding the investment yields possible from big transactions. The acquisition by Cox Enterprises and Landmark Communications of several auto advertising guides provided the basis for the profitable consolidation and extraordinarily profitable rollout of a nationwide family of localized *Auto Trader* magazines in most major metropolitan markets. The icing on the cake, however, was the launch of AutoTrader.com, with the transformative innovation producing not only a stellar return on investment but also the metamorphosis necessary for the survival and prosperity of the brand in the Internet era.

This strategy, however, is not one that can be implemented with ease. To achieve success, it is critical to identify the right opportunity, formulate the best development strategy, execute adroitly, and nurture innovative product, operation, and service extensions throughout. Most important, it is critical to pursue the implementation with passion, skill, and focused dedication. The investor will be sorely disappointed in the belief that it merely takes clever deal making followed by a delegation of responsibility to a centralized backbone staffed by ordinary administrators. The last two decades are littered with examples of failure, most attributable to mismanagement: great prospects but horrible execution in terms of both excessive prices paid during the rollup and poorly implemented business plans after acquisition.

Finally, success generally comes only after patient, aggressive, and intelligent development. The market may be slow to recognize a business's value, it usually takes time to define and institute the important tactical components for success, and organic expansion may take a decade or more to complete. In the words of *Let's Make a Deal's* Monty Hall, "I'm an overnight success, but it took 20 years." This is particularly the case with entrepreneur-led enterprises that don't have massive reserves of capital or human resources to invest in the opportunity, but it is also true for large enterprises that do have the resources.

Trader Publishing Company's creation of a half-billion-dollar group of *Auto Trader* publications started in 1985 with Landmark's acquisition of the less than $1 million revenue Winston–Salem *Tradin' Post*, and it wasn't until 2000 that Trader completed the acquisition of its last *Auto Trader* licensee in San Diego. In contrast, it spent just four years to complete the national rollup of 12 acquisitions and the simultaneous rollout of 51 start-ups to create the almost $100 million revenue *Employment Guide* business. That, however, was the exception rather than the rule, and the prosperity of both brands became very much dependent on their ability to exploit the transformative innovations of the Internet by leveraging their content and sales organizations to launch online services. Nonetheless, over almost two decades, Trader completed a self-funded series of nine separate rollup/rollout initiatives while paying over $1 billion in dividends to its owners, spinning out the now $1 billion revenue AutoTrader.com as an independent entity, and producing a residual enterprise valued by investment bankers at both Lehman Brothers and Morgan Stanley at over $4 billion in 2006.

Like Starbucks' Howard Schultz and Trader's management, the independent entrepreneur, the corporate acquirer, and the private equity investor can earn impressive returns by shunning the pursuit of large acquisitions and concentrating instead on ferreting out usually unnoticed and undeveloped small opportunities. Those acquisitions can be astutely integrated in an efficiently executed rollup and then rolled out to new markets on a national scale under a unified brand while pursuing a policy of focused innovation. If the serial acquirer is particularly fortunate, he will discover an ability to consolidate units while engineering their evolutionary, innovative transformation to exploit the opportunity for exponential growth and outstanding investment returns.

Chapter 1

The Acquisition Imperative

"By the year 2023, newspapers will cease as a mass medium," said Bill Diederich, chief financial officer of Landmark Communications, on a cloudy autumn afternoon in 1983.

"That's preposterous," said a newspaper executive. "That's just 40 years from now, and it's absurd to believe that could ever happen. Newspapers have never been stronger than they are today. Reaching almost every household, they are the most efficient advertising medium within local markets. Frankly, our industry's profits are almost embarrassingly robust, and that kind of decline is simply unimaginable in such a short period of time. How could you possibly assert such an outrageous idea?"

"Just look at the circulation trends," Diederich said with a serious glint. "In 1950, newspaper household penetration was over 110 percent because the average homeowner subscribed to both the morning and afternoon newspapers. By 1960, that figure had dropped to something under 100 percent, and it dropped again to less than 90 percent in 1970. Today, it is less than 80 percent, and, one could argue, there's nothing to stop it from declining further. With broadcast, cable, and other media, younger people just aren't developing the newspaper-reading habit of their parents."

"Oh, those declines are just occurring because people are giving up their afternoon newspaper."

"True. Even the parents are satisfying their appetite for the day's events by tuning in to the evening news broadcasts on television. That transition will continue unabated, particularly with the development of Cable News Network and more comprehensive local news broadcasts."

"Well, there's some truth to that, but there's nothing to replace the morning newspaper. We're conscientiously tailoring our content to appeal to younger readers already. Your own group has done a marvelous job of creating neighborhood-zoned editions to ensure their local relevance and compelling consumer appeal. Hell, Bill, newspapers have thrived in this country since colonial days, and I figure they've got another 300 years in them."

"I wish you were right, but unfortunately, you're not."[1]

The need to reinvest in new products and services to ensure an organization's future is one of the fundamental justifications underlying the acquisition imperative. The modern world is fast-paced and ever-changing, and today's successful business will fall prey to the erosion of its core if it fails to respond to competitive pressures and the evolving demands of constantly shifting consumer preferences and needs. To survive in this increasingly turbulent environment, businesses must invest to adapt, creating or acquiring new products and services to satisfy changing social and customer needs.

In the newspaper industry, profits were substantial in the late twentieth century, sometimes exceeding 30 percent of revenues before taxes, and needs for capital expenditures were few. Newspapers therefore represented a herd of milkable cash cows, generating a bountiful flow of capital to pay dividends or fund an aggressive acquisition strategy. Founded in 1905 as Norfolk Newspapers by Samuel L. Slover, Landmark Communications, Inc., became one of the many that did both, and its acquisitions and development efforts were characterized by the practice of making seminal investments that, through conscientious development and innovation, led to the creation of an enterprise that thrust its entrepreneurial leader, Frank Batten, firmly into the ranks of the Forbes 400.

Stepping into the leadership role at age 27 in 1954, Batten leveraged the resources and talent of the company's *Virginian-Pilot* to create a media group composed of metropolitan newspapers in Norfolk and Roanoke, Virginia, and Greensboro, North Carolina; community newspapers in over a dozen states; the eighteenth largest cable TV operation; The Weather Channel; and several radio and television stations. In 1985 Landmark made its first acquisition of classified advertising publications such as *Tradin' Times* and *Auto Trader*, and in 1991 it used those publications to create Trader Publishing Company with Cox Enterprises, Inc., as its equal partner. Trader in turn continued the growth pattern to post 2006 revenues of $1.3 billion. At that time, the partners' interests diverged, and the company was split, with more than half the revenues and company returning to the Landmark fold as the newly renamed Dominion Enterprises.

In a private company owned primarily by the Batten family and its key managers, Landmark's owners were driven to create value. From its genesis, its profit-rich *Virginian-Pilot* newspaper did pay out handsome dividends to its owners, but its leaders understood there was more to be gained by reinvesting the funds in other businesses. Dividends, after all, are taxed a second time when the recipient receives them, and they therefore contain an element of wealth destruction. That was particularly the case during the 1950s and 1960s with their confiscatory tax rates, but even with today's less onerous capital gains taxes of approximately 20 percent (combined state and federal), every dollar paid out in dividends nets to just $0.80 remaining for reinvestment by the individual. Since a substantial share of the free cash flow was retained within the company, wealth could be conserved, and by reinvesting it in the acquisition of high-potential businesses, it theoretically could be redeployed into value creation activities, further benefiting the owners. This is the same rationale exploited by Warren Buffett, whose Berkshire Hathaway has never paid a dividend but has produced exemplary double-digit annual returns over almost five decades.

Moreover, the profits arising from investments in acquired businesses could be partially shielded from taxes by the depreciation and amortization write-offs accruing from acquisitions. Before the adoption of the Tax Reform Act of 1986, corporate acquirers were permitted to step up the tax basis of acquired assets to reflect the full premium paid in a stock acquisition. In effect, the government tax structure subsidized the purchase by permitting subsequent profits to escape taxation to the extent that they were so covered: $1 million of depreciation sheltered $1 million of profits, saving the company and its owners $400,000 in taxes (assuming combined state and federal rates of 40 percent). Although the generous step-up provision no longer exists for stock transactions, the opportunity to shelter profits remains for asset transactions. By buying the assets of a company instead of its stock, the acquirer can depreciate their values and amortize the full premium paid for goodwill over 15 years as tax write-offs, capturing tax savings that produce the approximately 40 percent acquisition subsidy. Notably, such tax benefits are not obtainable by an individual who invests in stocks and bonds.

Though cognizant of the tax benefits, Batten and his key managers were emboldened to acquire attractive companies because they had confidence in their managerial skills. They understood that Landmark's human and operational resources were valuable assets they could leverage in concert with astute acquisitions to produce superior profits. With those resources, they believed they could prudently invest the cash better within the company, producing better returns than they could earn as individuals.

There are, of course, scores of other justifications for merger and acquisition activity, and the academic journals are filled with commentary analyzing those motivations.[2] Hubris, the excessive pride and self-confidence of the Greek tragedy's protagonist, has often been identified as the driving force that compels leaders to pursue acquisitions.[3] To justify their megalomania, consolidators rationalize their actions by insisting that there are compelling benefits. Asserting the value of vertical integration efforts, they insist that the acquisition of components of a business's supply chain is necessary to ensure the timely availability of materials and services while capturing the target entity's profit margin. Noting the savings and efficiencies of scale, they argue that consolidation of similar businesses over broader geographic markets rationalizes horizontal integration. Acquired product line extensions better satisfy customer needs and strengthen leverage with vendors and over distribution outlets, offering synergistic savings and benefits. Tactical advantages of strategic importance are gained by acquiring scarce or proprietary resources, and regulatory or competitive issues are overcome through the judicious acquisition of companies that contain their solution and cure.

Courtesy of Oliver Stone's 1987 film *Wall Street*, Gordon Gekko has entered the business lexicon as the name most synonymous with greed as the motivation behind the break-up artists who unlock value by acquiring depressed businesses and reselling their constituent assets for huge profits after purging their weak managers and inefficiencies. As Gekko grandly proclaims:

> Greed, for lack of a better word, is good. Greed is right. Greed works. Greed clarifies, cuts through, and captures the essence of the evolutionary spirit. Greed, in all of its forms: greed for life, for money, for love, knowledge, has marked the upward surge of mankind; and greed, you mark my words, will not only save Teldar Paper but that other malfunctioning corporation called the U.S.A.[4]

Greed can also explain the actions of the rollup architects of the 1990s who cobbled together dozens of small companies within niche industries for a spectacular initial public offering as a newly formed über-consolidator. Perhaps valued at no more than eight times earnings before the IPO, the soaring stock of the newly public company rocketed to a multiple of 70 as the market became exuberant with expectations of continued rapid earnings growth fueled by promised efficiencies and compounding acquisitions. Those lucky enough to time their sales at the top escaped with a handsome profit, leaving the rest to experience losses as the stock lost trajectory and crashed downward when earnings growth sputtered or turned negative.

To some extent, including Dave Roux's simple explanation that it's "fun," one or more of these factors can explain almost all merger activity. But the only ones that make actual sense for a prudent investor are the ones that lead to value creation, that is, the ones that produce incremental benefits to the investors at rates of return superior to their alternatives. That commitment to value creation remained at the core of Landmark's, and subsequently its progeny Trader's, acquisition efforts.

Unfortunately, continued investment in the successful businesses of the past does not necessarily produce those long-term returns if their futures are fading. With his focus on circulation declines, Landmark's Bill Diederich was appropriately concerned about the future of the newspaper business, and as a key manager influencing and helping implement the investment and development strategy of Landmark, he perceived that the newspaper industry was fading despite the fact that others, such as the

Gannett and New York Times companies, were spending huge amounts in bidding wars to acquire metropolitan dailies in Des Moines, Louisville, and Boston.

In fact, in the 1980s, Landmark's newspapers represented the primary source of its bountiful cash flow, and acquiring more newspapers in the increasingly competitive arena of accelerating cash flow valuation multiples was deemed an imprudent option. The high acquisition prices undermined the opportunity to earn superior returns and placed the company in the precarious position of having all its eggs in one frail basket, subject to a single industry segment's cyclical or structural declines.

Traditional newspapers, broadcast media, and cable TV certainly had become very popular as acquisition targets at that time. They had prestige, high visibility, strong growth, and impressive cash flows, all of which led to high valuations exceeding their intrinsic ability to produce compensating future profits. Having acquired several such companies in the decades before they had grown so popular, Batten and Diederich knew that continuing to acquire those traditional media at their current high prices would produce less desirable returns than had been the case in the past. They considered it preferable to invest in some barely recognized high-growth opportunities that could be acquired for smaller cash flow multiples. Ideally, they should be businesses that were at the beginning of their product life cycle, capable both of exponential growth and of establishing a foundation for future development.

Walter Gretzky's mantra to his young son Wayne was "Don't go where the puck is. Go where the puck is going to be." That is particularly true in the media business, whose competitive landscape experiences a particularly rapid, unrelenting pace of change and new competition:

> The essential point to grasp is that in dealing with capitalism we are dealing with an evolutionary process. The fundamental impulse that sets and keeps the capitalist engine in motion comes from the new consumers' goods, the new methods of production or transportation, the new markets, the new forms of industrial organization, that capitalist enterprise creates. ... The opening up of new markets, foreign and domestic, and the organizational development from the craft

shop and factory to such concerns as U.S. Steel illustrate the same process of industrial mutation—if I may use that biological term—that incessantly revolutionizes the economic structure from within, incessantly destroying the old one, incessantly creating a new one. This process of Creative Destruction is the essential fact about capitalism. ... Every piece of business strategy acquires its true significance only against the background of that process and within the situation created by it. It must be seen in its role in the perennial gale of creative destruction.[5]

Written by Joseph Schumpeter in 1950, those words succinctly describe the forces underlying the turbulence and transformation of the media market during the last century.

Starting even before the days of Peter Zenger (the defendant in a 1733 landmark case establishing the foundation for American freedom of the press), the influence and success of American newspapers remained undisputed for a quarter of a millennium. But with the dawn of the twentieth century, radio reared its head, and unlike newspapers with their overnight delays, it instantaneously broadcast news (not to mention baseball's World Series) free from arbitrary production and distribution deadlines. More important, it could transmit the emotion and power of the personally spoken word. From Franklin Roosevelt's fireside chats to Hitler's galvanizing harangues, political leaders worldwide exploited radio's advantages, sometimes courageously and sometimes shamelessly. So too did the marketers of Madison Avenue who fueled the growth of that new medium.

Then, with the dawn of the television age, the "gale of creative destruction" began to loom larger for the newspaper industry. A snowstorm of black-and-white visual broadcasts quickly transformed into vivid living color programs appearing in the dens and eventually the kitchens and bedrooms of almost every home in the developed world, first by transoceanic cable and then by satellite. Cable television further catalyzed the growth of broadcast as a disruptive medium, accelerating the creation and dissemination of ever more detailed information and diverse programming with the launch of CNN, ESPN, the Financial News Network, C-SPAN, and other specialized channels. By 2011, newspaper household penetration declined to less than 44 percent while cable and satellite TV exceeded 85 percent penetration, and the typical home boasted almost three television sets (but less than half a newspaper).[6]

The advent of the Internet in the mid–1990s, of course, dramatically accelerated the erosion of the newspaper's primacy so that most pundits today would suggest that Landmark's Diederich had been overly optimistic, insisting instead that newspapers will experience their demise as a mass medium perhaps a decade sooner.

Arguably, the founders and leaders of Landmark Communications were among those at least intuitively aware of the imperatives of creative destruction. As the owner of Norfolk's market-leading *Ledger-Dispatch* afternoon newspaper, Sam Slover had pursued his own rollup strategy by acquiring a handful of Virginia newspapers, but he also bought the Depression-ravaged WTAR radio station for $15,000 in 1932 to support his competitive battle against the Norfolk *Virginian-Pilot*. After his acquisition of that morning newspaper in 1933, Slover retired from managing his small media group. Yet he had the prescience to apply for a television license in 1948 to facilitate the April 1950 launch of WTAR-TV, Virginia's second television station.

In 1954, at age 81, Slover appointed his 27-year-old nephew Frank Batten to lead Landmark. An aggressive, visionary leader driven to build the company, Batten was hesitant to overpay for increasingly pricey newspaper and broadcast properties and sought alternative, undiscovered media opportunities that would flourish in later years. As described in greater detail in Chapter 3, that quest led Batten to become one of the pioneer investors in the Community Antenna Television (CATV) business, now called cable television. After the research efforts of Diederich and eventual TeleCable president Dick Roberts, Landmark acquired its first cable franchise in Roanoke Rapids for $15,000 in 1964. At that time, there were almost no media companies making investments in the industry, though Cox Enterprises was one of the few. Consequently, Landmark had a large number of early opportunities to acquire franchises and launch systems in distinct localities on a nationwide basis without substantive competition from the big media players; despite the explosion of acquisition interest in cable properties after 1970, its TeleCable business grew to be the eighteenth largest in the United States in 1995 when it was acquired by John Malone's Tele-Communications, Inc.[7]

In 1979, when Landmark's Diederich began voicing his gloomy forecast of the demise of metropolitan newspapers, media companies such as Gannett and Tribune were bidding up the prices of metropolitan newspapers, pushing them beyond reasonable values, typically exceeding three times revenues or over 12 times EBITDA. In search of better values, Landmark had earlier turned its attention to acquiring smaller community newspapers serving small towns and more rural markets. In the early 1970s, they could be acquired for as little as one times revenue or six to eight times cash flow, and the largest of the successful weeklies had the potential for conversion into more profitable dailies. They also were likely to thrive longer than metropolitan papers because those smaller markets held little attraction for the alternative broadcast media that were steadily eroding the newspapers' prospects in larger cities.

However, by the end of the 1970s, competitive acquirers such as Thomson Newspapers and Park Communications had ignited a price war over almost every substantive paper and shopper serving the counties of America's hinterlands, and it was time to look to new opportunities.

Arguably, rather than acquire an existing company, particularly insightful leadership should pursue the course of the entrepreneur or venture capitalist. If it can truly see where the puck is going to be, why not focus on an innovative idea and start a new business from scratch?

When ABC's star weatherman of the 1970s, John Coleman, came knocking with his idea to launch the 24-hour Weather Channel, among the few to listen were Batten, Diederich, and John Wynne, Landmark's broadcast division president. Dozens of other media companies and venture capitalists had rejected Coleman's idea as ludicrous, but Batten and Landmark's management were inspired, confident that the venture could leverage Landmark's television broadcast experience while providing valuable content for its cable TV operations. When it was announced in 1981, the idea was roundly criticized as a niche network with improbable appeal to either advertisers or viewers. Sure enough, its first years produced frightening losses that almost precipitated its closure, but the Weather Channel eventually proved its merit, achieving breakeven in 1986 while commencing a meteoric rise till its sale in 2008 for $3.5 million to NBC and two private equity firms.[8]

The difficulties and risks of start-ups were made painfully clear during the early years of The Weather Channel. Studying some of the original financial forecasts, the cynical Batten suggested that projected revenues be halved and expenses doubled. But even those modified estimates proved woefully optimistic once the venture was launched, and the ensuing losses, operational strains, and battles over management practice and strategic direction produced a stressful environment that culminated in a distracting lawsuit and the contentious buyout of Coleman. Nevertheless, The Weather Channel proved successful whereas the majority of new business initiatives collapse in failure.

Before the Internet bubble burst in 2000, the late 1990s unleashed a torrent of new venture Internet start-ups. Venture capitalists backed hundreds of glittering ideas and took many of them public to capitalize on the bewilderment of the public markets. At their peak after their IPOs, Webvan traded at 48 times sales, Stamps.com traded at 83 times sales, and Akamai Technologies traded at 509 times sales.[9] But by 2005, the ensuing paper losses on publicly traded stocks for just those companies based in California's Silicon Valley totaled an incredible $2 *trillion*.[10]

Promising new business concepts are difficult to identify and even more difficult to develop profitably. Moreover, the necessary operational model critical for their success is typically developed through the crucible of trial and error. Edison spent 26 years experimenting before figuring out how to manufacture electric lightbulbs with tungsten filaments, and rather than working patiently like Edison on a start-up, there is a compelling appeal to acquiring existing companies whose budding success can be developed and integrated with others. Their demonstrated success provides proof of concept, a template for operations and market development, management talent to lead the effort, and in many cases profitable cash flow to fund future expansion. For return-oriented shareholders, it is most comforting to see management acquiring proven businesses that add accretive profits to the company immediately.

As Landmark's management struggled with the turnaround of The Weather Channel, it simultaneously continued its pursuit of value-priced media properties. After acquiring some advertising shoppers and a variety of specialty publications serving the nursing and senior citizen markets, it stumbled upon the opportunity to acquire the Winston–Salem *Trading Post* and its companion photo ad auto guide, *Wheels & Deals*. For more than a decade, Diederich had been a fan of similar publications distributed in Landmark's Norfolk home, and Batten's son had been impressed by a comparable publication in London. When they were offered the opportunity to acquire them along with a printing plant and two associated buildings for a price less than four times cash flow, the opportunity was too attractive to turn down despite their small size, and within six months their profits and growth proved so attractive that Diederich championed the initiative to acquire as many similar publications as possible throughout the United States.

Within six years, that single acquisition led to the creation in 1991 of Trader Publishing Company, whose fundamental development model over the next 15 years was predicated on the concept of rollup, rollout, and innovation, replicating in many respects Landmark's experience with the development of its TeleCable cable TV company. From 1986, Trader and its predecessors[11] pursued the strategy to fruition with nine separate initiatives, including the national rollup and rollout of the following:

- *Auto Trader* magazine and its ancillary titles (*Truck Trader, Boat Trader, Cycle Trader, RV Trader*, etc.), serving over 200 markets and leading to the launch of the innovative AutoTraderOnline.com and TraderOnline.com websites for vehicle sales
- *Auto Mart* magazine, a group of over 70 localized free distribution weekly magazines advertising the inventories of commercial car dealerships and eventually leading to the launch of AutoMart.com
- *The Employment Guide*, a group of approximately 50 free distribution weekly tabloids that give employers an efficient medium to recruit nonexempt employees (followed by the addition *of locally organize*d recruitment job fairs and EmploymentGuide.com)
- *Dealer Specialties*, a provider of used car (1) point-of-purchase descriptive window stickers, (2) data distribution services to facilitate the delivery of used car listings to over 2,300 Internet websites, and (3) car dealers web-hosting and Internet marketing services

- *Roomsaver,* a group of free distribution motel promotion guides offering coupon savings to lodgers (coupled with its online component, Roomsaver.com)
- *For Rent Magazine,* a group of over 50 localized free distribution monthly and bimonthly magazines promoting apartment rentals (and its ForRent.com website)
- *Dominion Homes Media,* including (1) *Harmon Homes,* a group of over 200 localized free distribution monthly magazines promoting residential real estate sales, and (2) Homes.com and a dozen other Internet services providing web-hosting services, residential data, and residential multiple listing services to real estate agents and consumers
- *Parenting,* a group of over 20 localized free distribution monthly tabloids targeted to growing families
- *Vehicle Web Services,* a family of web-hosting and Internet data distribution and marketing services to support commercial dealerships for motorcycles, recreational vehicle, boats, trucks, and heavy equipment

Tracing its roots to a tiny Landmark Communications division with 1985 revenues of less than $100,000, Trader pursued its serial program of rollups and rollouts to transform itself by 2006 into a $1.3 billion revenue company that the investment bankers at both Lehman Brothers and Morgan Stanley valued at $4 billion to $6 billion. Most significantly, after Trader's 1991 spin-off from its corporate parents as a $150 million revenue independent entity, its management built Trader and funded its acquisition program with the strength of its own balance sheet while simultaneously (1) paying its corporate investors over $1 billion in dividends and (2) spinning out the key assets and URL for the independent Internet service AutoTrader.com, which itself was valued at more than $1 billion in 2006.

The Landmark and Trader examples are particularly instructive for small entrepreneurial acquirers, corporate business developers, and private equity investors. Like Landmark, successful companies produce profitable cash flow that should be invested in opportunities that promise high returns. They should do this not just to consume cash that could otherwise be paid to appreciative shareholders. Instead, they should invest in opportunities that will build shareholder value because they can produce the higher returns made possible by financial leverage, astute management, and tax policy.

More specifically, Landmark's and Trader's development demonstrates that capable leadership can produce superior returns by identifying unnoticed opportunities, acquiring small well-run businesses for bargain prices in favored segments, and subsequently developing those opportunities through adoption of best practices, implementation of efficient processes, and introduction of innovative products and services. Unlike the transactions trumpeted in the media that require billions to conclude, Trader established its roots with a single company acquired for about $1 million, and the cash flow of that acquisition and subsequent transactions, coupled with a modest debt load, funded over 100 subsequent acquisitions.

The comparatively little capital employed by Trader further demonstrates that a small entrepreneurial businessperson can pursue the same strategy to build a successful large enterprise. Of course, so too can venture capitalists and private equity funds that can attract and retain the right leadership to manage acquisition, integration, and development.

Chapter 2

The History of Rollups

A glance at some of the news articles and magazine stories of the 1990s creates the impression that the rollup was a brand-new business development phenomenon in that decade. However, its roots stretch back to the earliest days of commerce when Ug clubbed Urk on the head to eliminate a competitor and gain control over another piece of the woolly mammoth meat market.

Economic historians blithely attribute the expansionist efforts of Alexander the Great and Genghis Khan to their compulsion to capture markets. In essence, the argument asserts that their conquering crusades were the manifestation of their rollup strategies to gain control of the surrounding sources of raw materials, production resources, and capacity for their own economic benefit. They were motivated by their compulsion to amass power and wealth over an increasing amount of territory, and they achieved that goal by means of force and aggression. They destroyed competitors, assimilated their human and natural resources, and integrated control over a wide dominion.

But long before them, around 3150 BCE, the Egyptian ruler based in Abydos (perhaps called Horus Scorpion) successfully unified the three principal social centers of Upper Egypt, the lush Nile Valley south of Memphis. Heralded in Egypt's first historical document, he achieved a critical military victory over his last remaining rival, thus culminating a millennium-long process during which the economic, political, and cultural character of the region became integrated. That rollup led to the three-millennium era of the Pharaohs and the construction of the Pyramids.[1]

Beginning in 1550 BCE, the Phoenicians pursued their own maritime version of the rollup by gaining control of and integrating the trade routes and commercial ports of the Mediterranean, and Marco Polo, almost 3,000 years later in the fourteenth century, gained his fame through his book popularizing his integration of trade associations to capitalize on the trade potential between Europe and China along the Silk Road.

Robber Baron Rollups

Although characterizing historical military and political consolidations as rollups may appear a stretch to business scholars, there can be no question of the importance of rollups as a building block of modern organizational development during the nineteenth century. With his partners in 1870, John D. Rockefeller founded Standard Oil, providing the base for his consolidation of the petroleum industry. Through aggressive tactics roundly criticized for their anticompetitiveness, he bought up or destroyed competititors and assimilated their operations into his own corporation. When states began legislating restrictions on the scale and scope of corporations, he engineered the "trust" form of enterprise to create and control his giant organization through a unified board exercising authority over scores of companies across multiple states. By 1890 Standard Oil controlled 88 percent of the refined oil flows of the United States, and by 1904 it controlled 91 percent of the production of oil and 85 percent of its final sales.[2]

So successful was the trust form of operation that it was quickly mimicked in other industries. Andrew Carnegie consolidated the steel industry, and J. P. Morgan finished the effort with the creation of U.S. Steel. However, Morgan stumbled badly when he attempted to capture control of the shipping industry through the International Mercantile Marine Co. Overestimating the potential profits from consolidation, Morgan and his partners grossly overpaid to acquire several shipping companies, and the leverage became untenable when the projected benefits failed to materialize. Three years after its *Titanic* luxury liner went down, the company sank into receivership in 1915, shortly after Morgan died.[3]

James Buchanan "Buck" Duke pursued a similar tack with his consolidation of the tobacco industry in the late nineteenth century through actual mergers rather than through trusts. While acquiring competitors with both cash and through predatory practices, he revolutionized the tobacco market when he gained control of the Bonsack cigarette rolling machine, which was capable of duplicating the production of 48 hand rollers.[4] Though originally frowned upon as inferior, Bonsack cigarettes were promoted heavily by Duke through innovative marketing techniques to accelerate their acceptance. Distributing samples to immigrants as they came off ships on New York docks, he also advertised them aggressively through billboards, posters, magazines, and newspapers, and he inserted collectible coupons and cards as premiums in his branded cigarette packs (his Piedmont brand included the Honus Wagner baseball card that was sold in auction for $2.35 million in 2007[5]). To reduce costs, Duke bypassed the leaf dealers and speculators (the middlemen between growers and cigarette manufacturers) by buying tobacco directly from farmers at warehouse auctions. Those innovations catapulted the business into a high growth trajectory, providing him with the cash and market muscle to continue his market consolidation. In 1890, he merged the five largest U.S. tobacco companies to create the American Tobacco Company, consolidating control of 40 percent of the domestic market. With that formidable foundation, he continued on the acquisition trail, buying at least 250 companies to monopolize the industry worldwide, capturing over 80 percent of the domestic cigarette market and more than 75 percent of all other forms of tobacco use (except cigars).[6]

Ironically, the year of American Tobacco Company's founding, 1890, was also the year the United States enacted the Sherman Antitrust Act. However, it wasn't until the Teddy Roosevelt trust-busting era that Duke was confronted by serious governmental opposition. In 1907 American Tobacco Company was charged with antitrust violations that inhibited free trade and competitiveness, and in 1911 the company was ordered to disband. Duke became one of the earliest large-scale practitioners of the spin-out (the split-off of a corporation's division as an independent company) when he engineered

American Tobacco Company's divestiture of approximately 60 percent of its operations with the re-creation of the Lorillard, R.J. Reynolds, and Liggett & Myers tobacco companies.

In 1907, Theodore Vail arose as another enterprising entrepreneur, leading the charge to roll up the nascent telecommunications industry. After the expiration of Alexander Graham Bell's original patents in 1893 and 1894, hundreds of small entrepreneurs had begun wiring their local towns for telephone service. There were, however, dozens of other patents, including those critical to long-distance transmission, and those patents provided American Telephone & Telegraph (successor to the American Bell Telephone Company) with a substantial advantage. With those patents, Vail, as manager of AT&T, aggressively acquired the independents, employing lower rates and better transmission service as his primary weapons. Those who didn't sell for an attractive price faced AT&T's launch of a competitive service that, once established, depressed the value of their original businesses, encouraging a sale before their collapse. To mitigate problems with community advocates and political leaders, Vail "agreed to give local governments a portion of the affiliate's operating profits, in this way making certain the political authorities had a stake in the company's future."[7] That cooptation of the local authorities, coupled with Vail's persuasive efforts to demonstrate the cost and service benefits of a unified telecommunications utility, helped pave the way for AT&T to establish itself as a "natural monopoly." By his death in 1920, Vail had established the company as the dominant telephone service in the United States, with assets of over $1 billion.[8]

News Media Rollups/Rollouts

While the yellow-journalists were decrying the evils brought upon the populace by the nefarious trusts, their employers were busy completing their own rollups and rollouts within the burgeoning media business.

Quickly getting in trouble for pranksterism, William Randolph Hearst departed Harvard a year later while on academic probation, eventually landing in California in 1887. The indisputable inspiration for Orson Welles's *Citizen Kane*, Hearst took charge of the *San Francisco Examiner* (acquired by his father in settlement of a gambling debt), transforming it into a circulation success with carnival journalism featuring headlines such as "BUTCHERED AS THEY RAN: The Fearful Climax to a Land Dispute in Texas." Simultaneously, he modernized the production systems and recruited the best editorial talent to leapfrog the paper to prominence by emphasizing a populist agenda. Attacking even companies owned by his father, he gained dominance in the highly competitive newspaper market by exposing corruption among corporations, politicians, and government entities. Growing in both his personal wealth and his ability to expand, he acquired the *New York Journal* in 1895 with financial assistance from his mother. Its eventual success led to Hearst's acquisition or start-up of an additional 26 newspapers and 18 magazines, including the *Los Angeles Examiner*, the *Detroit Times*, the *Boston American*, and the *Washington Times*. By 1928, Hearst's publishing group was delivering the daily news to 10 percent of Americans on weekdays and 20 percent on Sunday.[9]

But it was Hearst's New York venture that made the biggest headlines because he took the previously money-losing *Journal* into head-to-head competition with another media conglomerator. Much earlier, in 1878, Joseph Pulitzer, a formerly destitute Hungarian émigré, had acquired the *St. Louis Dispatch* for $2,500 and merged it with the *St. Louis Post*. Among those first capitalizing on the model of crusading journalism, Pulitzer transformed his struggling paper into a publishing phenomenon by attacking the railroads, prostitution, gambling, and government corruption. By 1883, his success gave him the capital to take his model to New York, where he acquired the *New York World* for $346,000 (ironically, from the railroad magnate Jay Gould, whom the paper subsequently lambasted for financial manipulation and skullduggery). Adjusting the editorial focus and employing the marketing techniques he'd honed in St. Louis, Pulitzer increased circulation from about 15,000 to 150,000 in two years, making the *World* the city's dominant paper. He innovated further by introducing the first color supplement, composed of reprints from humor magazines, and in 1885 he published "Hogan's Alley," the newspaper industry's first comic strip, featuring the Yellow Kid.

Though considering Pulitzer his mentor, Hearst hired away the *World*'s key staff and dropped the *Journal*'s price to a penny to take away readership. While beating the drum to command popular attention with headlines such as "Remember the *Maine!*" Hearst's *Journal* climbed to popularity and is credited with introducing the term *bulldog edition*, in reference to Hearst's famous admonition to his editors to grab readers by writing headlines that would "bite the public like a bulldog."

Despite the aggressive marketing battles, Pulitzer's *World* continued to flourish, and it laid the groundwork for the expansion of Pulitzer Publishing by his sons and grandsons into a substantial enterprise with over 14 newspapers and a dozen broadcast properties.[10]

The Conglomerate Kings

By the middle of the twentieth century, another rollup model began to rise in popularity in the form of the broadly diversified conglomerate. Today's General Electric is the most notable example, but in the 1960s James Ling became notorious as the era's consummate conglomerator as he built Ling-Temco-Vought (LTV Industries).

A 33-year-old high school dropout with a master electrician's certification, Ling acquired L.M. Electronics in 1956 and then the stereo maker Altec in 1959. In 1960 he bought the missile and defense contractor Temco, and a year later he acquired Chance Vought, an aerospace firm. In that era of low interest rates, Ling discovered that he could acquire companies whose cash flows could easily cover the interest charges associated with the acquisition debt. Then, because the transactions added to the profits of his core company, they helped create the illusion of faster earnings growth, encouraging investors to bid up the stock price to an impressive price-earnings (PE) multiple. Now characterized as momentum investing, Ling's practice produced a rapidly growing market capitalization for LTV as he acquired companies for low PEs that disproportionately added to the value of LTV's stock when their earnings were multiplied by LTV's larger, rapid growth in PE. For example, he could acquire $1 in earnings at a 12 PE, which would be transformed into twice the incremental value when multiplied by LTV's own 25 PE. LTV's market capitalization soared as Ling bought up disparate businesses such as Wilson & Company (meatpacking and sports equipment), Greatamerica Corp. (Braniff Airways and National Rental Car), and Jones & Laughlin Steel, and that high capitalization fueled larger and more frequent acquisitions. From a 1965 revenue base of just $36 million, LTV grew 100 times to establish its place as number 14 on the Fortune 500 with $3.75 billion in revenues in 1969.[11]

But Ling was merely following in the footsteps of Royal Little, the acquisitive founder of Textron Inc., who is often considered the pioneering innovator of the conglomerate. With $10,000, Little and his investors began acquiring textile firms in the 1920s, and he subsequently discovered that he could shelter profits from the era's confiscatory excess profits taxes by purchasing unrelated but attractive (and loss-ridden) companies that had tax benefits that often exceeded the acquisition price. With the substantial cash flows from one business segment, he acquired a diversity of businesses, which mitigated the cyclical declines of the textile industry. As a result of his opportunistic pursuit of bargains of any type, Little earned the reputation as "the junkman of American Industry, casting about for underpriced and ailing firms he could turn around."[12]

Decades later, others pursued comparable acquisition programs, including Harold Geneen, president of International Telephone & Telegraph. From a foundation of $766 million in revenues in 1959, ITT leaped to $17 billion in 1970 sales by acquiring approximately 350 companies in the insurance, hotel, real estate management, and other industries.[13]

Before Geneen took the reins of ITT, Tex Thornton was building Litton Industries. Having made his first real estate deal at age 14 and having acquired a gas station and car dealership by 19, Thornton was already an experienced deal maker when he paid $1.5 million for Litton in 1954. After a steady stream of acquisitions in the electronics field, Litton posted sales of $120 million in 1960 and then $500 million in 1963 when its stock was regularly trading at a 33 PE (it peaked at 75 times earnings).[14] From the ranks of Litton flowed a stream of management clones who left to assemble their own conglomerates, including Harry Gray, who built United Technologies, and Henry Singleton, who engineered a similar success at Teledyne. Each used the same technique of borrowing heavily to acquire quality businesses whose earnings could support the new debt while hyping the apparent earnings growth of the acquirer.[15]

By the end of the 1960s, however, the investing public began to wise up to the fact that little value creation or earnings benefit was arising from the combinations. While the government demonstrated its antitrust concerns by litigating over LTV's acquisition of Jones & Laughlin, the slowing economy produced a series of earnings disappointments among the conglomerates, revealing the reality that those companies could not compound infinitely. Stratospheric stock prices plummeted back to earth as conglomerate PEs fell to the levels of their underlying businesses, and several conglomerates began spinning off a variety of laggard subsidiaries as separate entities. Accordingly, after the 1968 peak of 207 mergers with an aggregate valuation of $13 billion, volume in 1970 dropped to just 70 deals with $2 billion in asset values.[16]

The high inflation of the 1970s and the more pedestrian investment environment of the 1980s failed to quell business combinations, but they did become more focused with an orientation toward combining similar businesses. Rather than seeing a mishmash of electronics companies buying steel mills or phone companies acquiring motel and insurance companies, there was a return to acquisition efforts within industry segments.

Niche Industry Rollups

While Jerry Ling and Harold Geneen were assembling their conglomerates of disparate businesses, others were turning their attention to the development and integration of new enterprises.

Bill Daniels, a former New Mexico Golden Gloves champion, was astonished in 1952 as he sat in Murphy's Bar in Denver watching New

York's Wednesday night fights. "My God, what an invention this is," he recalled, thinking about his first exposure to television. "I couldn't get it out of my mind, how do you get that great invention to a small town that didn't have any TV stations."[17] Back at his Casper home, there was a mountain range blocking transmission of television signals. Undaunted and with an innovative idea, he persuaded several oilmen to back the construction of the first microwave transmitters dedicated to carrying television signals to a community antenna system so that Casper's residents could view broadcasts from Denver, almost 300 miles away. That success led to his launching and acquiring other systems, and in 1955 he relocated to Denver, where he founded Daniels & Associates three years later to provide consulting and brokerage services to the budding industry. By 1965, with a growing reputation as the "Father of Cable TV," Daniels and his firm handled the sale of cable TV systems valued at over $100 million, representing 80 percent of all such transactions in that year; in 1989, his company brokered 55 deals totaling $1.9 billion.[18]

In 1954, a few years after the Casper launch, Jack Crosby was working at his father's appliance store in Del Rio, Texas, and became inspired to sell television sets. Unfortunately, there was no broadcast signal to provide programming to anyone buying a set, so he scrounged $10,000 to construct a 450-foot antenna to bring in programming from San Antonio, 255 miles away. That represented the beginning of his efforts to acquire and build other cable systems. Over the next 10 years, he joined with other pioneering partners such as Fred Lieberman, Ben Conroy, Gene Schneider, Richard Schneider, and Tubby Flynn to roll up and roll out Telesystems and Gencoe, Inc. (which became United Cable TV). Ultimately, his efforts led to the creation of eight major multi-location cable TV systems, including Communications Properties, Inc., and Telesystems International, Sweden's second largest cable TV company.[19]

Cox Enterprises subsequently became enthralled with the promise of cable TV, and its management began its own rollup of acquisitions and rollouts by winning franchises in 1964, ultimately leading to its establishment as the third largest U.S. cable TV operator.

While Daniels and Lieberman were leading the Pied Piper call to construct and consolidate the nascent cable TV industry, others were turning their attention to merging and modernizing old-line businesses. In 1968, Illinois's Dean Buntrock and Florida's Wayne Huizenga combined their garbage collection companies to create Waste Management, Inc. With first-year revenues of $5.5 million, the companies began methodically acquiring other firms, creating a critical mass by 1971, when they went public. With the public offering's fresh capital, the company splurged with an acquisition binge, completing 75 transactions in the next 18 months. Though slowing in later months, the acquisitions continued, driving almost 50 percent annual growth during the company's first 10 years.[20]

However, rather than simply combining operations, Waste Management introduced a variety of innovations that both supported growth and established its reputation as a professional, reliable lower-cost service. Striking a chord with a society celebrating the first Earth Day in 1969, the company positioned itself as proficient, safe, and environmentally responsible. Its standardized branded trucks were kept clean, and it provided cities and clients with safe, responsible chemical and toxic waste treatment and disposal. To support its myriad acquisitions, it developed and implemented centralized management information systems and operational procedures to improve efficiency and administration, all of which helped it provide superior service at rates as much as 30 percent lower than those of alternative or city-owned services.[21]

This approach of a focused rollup of similar businesses to expand market coverage represented a return to the earlier practices of the industrialists of the prior century. Yet because Waste Management's efforts were geographically dispersed and the company conscientiously avoided market dominance by leaving some competitors in place, it did not run afoul of antitrust legislation. Instead, Waste Management's dedication to its innovative practices and assiduous emphasis on efficiency permitted it to thrive in the presence of the smaller, less integrated competitors, producing 2008 earnings of $1.1 billion and average compounded annual revenue growth of 15 percent from $82 million in

1972 to $13.4 billion in 2008.[22] Today, Waste Management is North America's largest integrated provider of collection, disposal, recycling, and waste-to-energy services, and it has a market capitalization of over $16 billion and an enterprise value of almost $30 billion.

With examples such as Waste Management, venture capitalists and other deal makers began to take notice of the prospects for rollups in scores of fragmented business segments in the late 1980s and 1990s. During those two decades, individuals, companies, and venture capitalists sponsored countless initiatives to roll up small, fragmented businesses in almost every segment imaginable:

- Sonus Corp. began acquiring dozens of regional audiology clinics to serve the hearing aid market.
- Service Corp. International and Stewart Enterprises competed to consolidate the funeral home business.
- Telespectrum, Inc., attempted to buy a nationally significant share of U.S. telemarketing firms.
- U.S.A. Floral Products became a consolidator of small floral shops and distributors.
- Coinmach Laundry Corp. began acquiring scores of independent laundry equipment and service providers to the multifamily apartment industry.
- U.S. Office Products and Corporate Express simultaneously led the charge to acquire a large share of significant independent office supply stores.

In the 1990s, in fact, aggregators and investment bankers launched over 100 rollup companies through initial public offerings; that activity climaxed in 1998, when an average of five IPOs per week made their appearance on the public markets.[23] Simultaneously, large public and private companies such as Landmark and Cox were completing hundreds more rollups such as those creating TeleCable and Trader Publishing Company, and enterprising individuals were assembling their own smaller proprietary rollups.

One of the most notable rollup engineers of the 1990s was Steven Harter, who gained fame as an architect of smaller-scale consolidations. A childhood victim of a home foreclosure, Harter started his career as an accountant with a local environment services company that subsequently became the target of a rollup. Thus inspired, Harter orchestrated numerous rollups in several industry segments by employing the tactics of the "poof IPO," the pundits' playful term for the era's practice of combining several small companies and then magically, through the miracles of Wall Street, "poof," those companies are transformed into a public company. Harter first persuaded several owners to merge their independent businesses into a single entity with sufficient consolidated revenues to justify investment bankers' launch of the integrated company as an initial public offering. Upon completion, the participating founders earned a mix of cash and equity in the new company. Shares of the public company were then used to acquire perhaps dozens more small niche players, and their incremental cash flows perpetuated the appearance of impressive growth.[24] Through his Notre Capital Ventures fund, Harter completed at least nine separate public offerings, including the stock flotations for US Delivery Systems, Coach USA, Comfort Systems USA, Physicians Resource Group, HomeUSA, Transportation Components, NetVersant Solutions, and Metals USA.

Wayne Huizenga was inspired to reenter the fray after his 1984 retirement from Waste Management. In 1987, he and other investors acquired control of David Cook's money-losing Blockbuster Entertainment Corp. and changed its focus from that of a franchising operation to that of an acquirer of dozens of independent videocassette rental stores, rebranded as Blockbuster Video.[25] He did it again in 1995 when he acquired Republic Industries to form the foundation of another company devoted to waste disposal and security systems.[26] After the 1996 acquisition of National Car Rental, Huizenga merged that entity's used car sales business with his newly launched AutoNation stores to provide the base to acquire dozens of independent car dealerships to create a national organization.[27]

So exuberant was the enthusiasm for rollups that investors plowed $30 billion of capital into companies or funds making serial acquisitions in targeted business segments. By the mid–1990s, public companies pursuing the strategy saw their stock prices skyrocket into the stratosphere. Putting the impressive 1995–1996 S&P gain of 54 percent to shame, the stock of Stewart Enterprises leaped 115 percent, U.S. Office Products grew 137 percent, and AutoNation soared 1,651 percent.[28]

But alas, market directions change, particularly when the dimwitted herd of Wall Street's animal farm finally sees the light, inevitably discovering that the current investment fad is not the haven of the goose laying golden eggs. In fact, like that produced by the conglomerators of the 1960s, the growth of these rollups was often accomplished with massive assumption of debt combined with shareholder dilution precipitated by premium-priced stock-for-stock acquisitions. Like Jerry Ling of LTV, this new crop of rollup engineers was capitalizing on the buoyant market for high-growth stocks. While paying lip service to the concept of merging allied operations to leverage a more efficient administrative and marketing infrastructure, the founders of these companies were most often simply conglomerating a bunch of businesses to produce the critical mass necessary for an IPO. Upon flotation, the sheeplike public promptly bid up the shares to impressive PE multiples, bleating with growing enthusiasm as rapid acquisitions produced stellar growth rates. Those higher stock prices, of course, provided an overvalued currency to complete even more stock-for-stock deals while motivating subsequent public offerings to raise even more cash to fund more deals.

Unfortunately, to satisfy the market's continued expectation of comparable growth rates, that momentum investing strategy required more and larger transactions, yet it became increasingly difficult to identify and complete those deals. Coupled with the mounting difficulty of managing the expense and complexity of the increasingly unwieldy group of loosely confederated entities, earnings disappointments inevitably materialized as each subsequent transaction produced smaller incremental gains, and the stocks began to fall like stricken cattle. From January 1997 to the end of 1999, as the S&P index soared an astonishing 98 percent, U.S. Office Products dropped 89 percent,

Stewart Enterprises declined 72 percent, and AutoNation fell 70 percent. According to a Booz Allen Hamilton study of the concluding 18 months of the millennium, most shares of publicly traded rollup firms plummeted, with almost half losing at least 50 percent of their value,[29] and that study did not include all the firms that had collapsed and disappeared during the decade.

Reality had come home to roost. Moreover, those acquisition binges were accompanied by a severe case of indigestion as the acquirers attempted to integrate the pieces. In less than three years after its 1995 public offering, U.S. Office Products completed over 200 separate acquisitions in rapid-fire succession. On December 12, 1995, it announced a baker's dozen of 13 deals on that day alone, and seven months later it crowed about its "June class of deals totaling $775 million," composed of 48 separate acquisitions. But the complexity and cost of the deals had grown unmanageable for its chairman, Jonathan Ledecky, the former Steelcase manager who masterminded the company's creation, and the results began to falter.

As a columnist for the Internet's Motley Fool wrote: "One problem with rollups is that they're often run by people more adept at sales and promotion than at running large and growing businesses. Management may have little experience in the industry or with managing full-scale operations of dozens of companies. Integrating the businesses can be extremely difficult."[30] That was definitely the case for Ledecky, who had adopted a decentralized management strategy that permitted broad latitude and authority among the leadership of the newly acquired affiliated units. That independence not only reduced the potential to harvest synergistic savings but also increased the probability that the entities would operate at cross-purposes, undermining the results.

Further depressing U.S. Office Products' ability to produce enhanced profits was Ledecky's eclectic acquisition strategy. In addition to office supply firms, his company acquired Mail Boxes Etc., coffee and beverage services, and dozens of companies in disparate segments such as school supplies, corporate travel, print management, and technology solutions. By 1997, the company's operations were so cumbersome and its debt so onerous that U.S. Office Products was faced with the "restructuring imperative." With Ledecky's departure in January 1998, it spun off 40 percent of its least related businesses to shareholders as a separate unit, and it brought in adult supervision with a $240 million capital infusion from the private equity firm Clayton Dubilier & Rice, which acquired a quarter of the business.[31]

Undeterred, Ledecky went on to champion the launch of U.S.A. Floral Products as a rollup of floral shops, importers, and wholesalers. However, less than four years after its 1997 public offering to supply capital for its feeding frenzy, that company was in liquidation mode. At the end of 2000, it sold off its seven North American wholesale units at a substantial loss, and it tried desperately to sell its international Florimex division, which it had acquired two years earlier for $90 million. However, it was too late. Three months later, it filed for bankruptcy protection as it sold off all its other assets. The Florimex business was one of the last to go at a price of approximately $29 million.[32]

Many rollups of that decade experienced the same fate as U.S.A. Floral, and others struggled for survival. Reborn after a 1989 management buyout from the earlier Fleet Aerospace Corp. rollup of the 1980s, Brooks Automation transitioned to high acquisition mode in the late 1990s, using $700 million of its stock and about $107 million in cash on an acquisition binge to buy PRI Automation for $440 million along with 22 other software and technology companies. Four years later, in 2002, it was still struggling with its hangover as it took a $623 million write-off of its assets while attempting to find a focus and eliminate its horrendous cash drain.[33] It took another six years for it to recover, a process complicated by the indictment of its CEO for tax evasion, the departure of most of its board, and a 2008 SEC settlement to resolve a complaint of an earnings overstatement of $54.5 million from 1996 to 2005 related to employee stock options.[34]

Underlying the implementation of momentum investing strategies is the probability that the acquirer will fall into the trap of making foolish deals in the rush to buy more revenue and earnings. In the process of purchasing that growth, even bad acquisition targets begin to look appealing, and with money burning a hole in their pockets (or an overpriced stock), momentum investors rationalize that buying any growth is better than not buying at all. Only after the excitement of completing another deal does it become apparent that the newly acquired company is a dog, and the disappointed deal maker has to confront the truth of Bobby Bare's country music lament that "I've never gone to bed with an ugly woman, but I've sure woke up with a few."

Just as problematic is the fact that the acquirer finds herself across the negotiating table from the owners of attractive companies demanding prices in excess of intrinsic value. Eager to put another notch on his handle, the gunslinging rollup cowboy fires away with ever-increasing offers until he hits the seller's target. Instead of thinking dispassionately as a prudent investor should, the wheeler-dealer CEO lets her ego take over "to get the deal done," not worrying whether the price is so high that it will destroy the opportunity to earn a reasonable return on investment relative to the associated risk.

Even those rollup artists who won early accolades saw their sterling images tarnish with the passage of time. The rollup and subsequent 1996 sale of U.S. Delivery Group to Corporate Express in a 23.4-million-share stock swap established Steven Harter as one of the strategy's stars,[35] and he duplicated that feat with the $1.94 billion sale of his Coach USA to the British Stagecoach Group in 1999. However, three of Harter's other rollups filed for bankruptcy, and another came close. In fact, his two successes may have been attributable more to timing than to brilliant integration. Corporate Express subsequently saw its value collapse as problems surfaced, and Stagecoach's CEO was later to claim, "We bought the wrong company," asserting that they discovered serious problems within six months after the acquisition of Harter's group.[36]

Rollup Lessons

In reviewing the last 150 years of rollup history, several fundamental lessons emerge.

Industry consolidations in the late nineteenth century were driven by the robber barons' understanding that monopolization provided not just a larger enterprise but also powerful market control over resources, products, and pricing that created massive individual wealth. Their efforts, moreover, gave a kick-start to the creation of huge new industries, including AT&T's telecommunications business. Monopoly profits provided the capital necessary for the subsequent rollout and development of those industries, and centralized control allowed the concentrated focus of that investment on the innovations driving the industry to lofty new levels of success. Buck Duke's efforts with American Tobacco Company created a massive new industry from a comparatively small agrarian-based foundation as he revolutionized consumer marketing and drove the innovative development and adoption of automated cigarette production and packaging. However, though they initially produced the benefits of a faster, more efficient expansion of production and services over a much broader base, those consolidations came with severe social and economic costs. Abusive pricing exacted a huge toll, undermining general business development and society's economic welfare, and the intoxicating profits had the potential to lull management into complacency, discouraging new innovation arising from competitive initiative. The consequence, of course, was legislation outlawing the previously legal monopolization tactics and structures that permitted those abuses.

Still, the nonmonopolistic benefits of rollups remained. Shared infrastructure, cooperative and coordinated market development, unified promotion, and dissemination and adoption of a business sector's best practices can lead a consolidator to greater profits and market power, but only if pursued and realized. If realized, those benefits provide the knowledge, capital, and incentive to expand more aggressively, as demonstrated by the examples in the news media, cable TV, and waste collection industries.

The conglomerators of disparate businesses, however, provided few benefits unless they delivered efficiencies engineered by their leadership's focus on integrating operations to leverage best practices, enhance production processes, capitalize on the marketing and cost benefits of scale, and eliminate administrative and operational duplication. Without those factors, the rollups driven by the financial engineers rarely endured. The intoxicating allure of momentum investing's manufactured earnings growth ultimately led to collapses such as that of Jerry Ling's LTV when its added acquisitions ceased producing expected earnings growth. Success endured only for those organizations which, like General Electric, were blessed with insightful leadership relentlessly focused on the actual development of their individual businesses. Moreover, when they lost their adroit leadership focus, they ran into trouble, as did ITT when its mastermind, Harold Geneen, departed.

As subsequent chapters will demonstrate, the unsuccessful rollup artists of the last few decades failed to focus on continued business development, relying instead on the public market's temporary and often misguided fascination with momentum investing. Moreover, their deals were often completed without sufficient regard to either the probable success of eventual integration or management's ability to execute hypothetical business plans. Finally, in their euphoric rush to conclude deals at any price, they too often overpaid even for businesses that did make sense, and those overpayments produced a financial burden that undermined the ability to generate the needed return on investment.

The stock market's heady exuberance accompanying the rollups' early stock flotations inevitably turned to derisive scorn when, a few years later, its overblown expectations confronted the reality of those companies' actual operational results. Almost every example, the good and the bad, skyrocketed to irrational valuations such that even the best-managed consolidations disappointed investors when their stock prices returned to normality. The response among the investment Brahmins and academic analysts was to discredit the rollup strategy. As two noted business scholars observed, "a deep look into rollups shows the real issue often is fundamentally flawed strategies."[37]

However, discarding the whole concept as unworthy is akin to throwing the baby out with the bathwater. There are too many success stories like those of Landmark's TeleCable and Trader. Their impressive and often unheralded achievements demonstrate that there is a compelling strategy, but it is very much dependent on a comprehensive approach that emphasizes the implementation of astute integration tactics during the more complex and arduous consolidation period. Significantly, the most successful strategies are those which subsequently replicate their business models in new markets and capitalize on the innovative opportunities they later discover.

Chapter 3

Landmark Communications Rollups and Rollouts

"There will be plenty more deals to do even when the money runs out," said Frank Batten, suddenly casting his gaze out the office window on a warm spring day in 1973.

"But if we don't meet their demands, we'll lose it," said Diederich. "They're great cable properties."

"So they are, but the sellers want too much. We'll have to pass," said Batten blithely but with finality.[1]

Landmark Communications' Frank Batten well understood that when prospectors began panning for acquisition treasures, they would quickly scoop up scores of opportunities. Some would be valueless fool's gold, most would command investment stakes well in excess of their probable returns, but a very few would represent attractive strikes acquirable for reasonable capital and capable of producing impressive returns. He therefore repeatedly cautioned his acquisitive managers to conserve Landmark's limited financial resources for the most compelling, lowest-risk, highest-return transactions. If sellers demanded too much, he would not step up to the demanded price, recommending instead that the prospect be abandoned, with efforts redirected toward alternatives.

Moreover, Batten understood a fundamental lesson underlying business development: Growth comes through change and causes change. Learned while he was an undergraduate economics major at the University of

Virginia, that adage was a frequently quoted refrain of his professor, the much-admired scholar David McCord Wright, and it became an axiom for Batten as he expanded and transformed Landmark.[2]

Cable TV Rollups/Rollouts

A decade earlier, in 1963, Batten had been seeking attractive alternative media businesses that could be acquired economically, when his Norfolk, Virginia, radio station manager, Campbell Arnoux, encouraged him to consider the community antenna business. Finding the concept interesting, he enlisted the efforts of his research director, Dick Roberts, and his controller, Bill Diederich, to evaluate the opportunity. They arranged a visit by Bill Daniels to provide a seminar on the profit potential and pitfalls of the business, and they were quickly persuaded that it offered substantial upside opportunity with comparatively few risks. They then met with Fred Lieberman, who had assembled his own collection of properties with Jack Crosby and others. But Lieberman and his partners were stretched, and he offered to sell Landmark the franchise he'd acquired in Roanoke Rapids, North Carolina, for $15,000. That led to Lieberman suggesting further purchases in Beckley and Princeton, West Virginia. Landmark snapped them up, and, on the basis of those early efforts, Batten concluded that this would be a focus of Landmark's growth plans. Soon, after successfully developing and integrating a few attractive properties, Landmark gained the operational expertise and confidence necessary to roll out the concept to new markets. In fact, Batten concluded, it was better to build than to buy:

> Together, we learned that building cable systems could be an outstanding investment, particularly for private companies like ours that had the benefit of other profitable businesses. The reason was simple: Cable was a capital-intensive business that could produce high tax losses in early years through accelerated depreciation of construction costs. We could write off those losses immediately against our newspaper profits, and as a private company, we were not concerned about recording high book losses. As a result, our strategy was to concentrate

on getting franchises and building our own systems, rather than buying going concerns that might have used up most of their tax write-offs.[3]

Leading the charge was Rex Bradley, recently appointed divisional president of Landmark's new TeleCable business, and his team quickly initiated an organized effort to expand. Focusing on small outlying communities that did not have their own television stations, TeleCable won franchises in places such as Columbus, Georgia; Spartanburg, South Carolina; and Racine, Wisconsin, and acquired undeveloped systems in locales such as Kokomo, Indiana, and Bloomington–Normal, Illinois.

However, just 10 years after getting its start in cable, Batten's Landmark Communications was offered the opportunity to acquire one of the premier groups of cable TV properties, a group that represented the foundation of what was to become Viacom, and the price wasn't much more than $200 per subscriber. Although that represented a premium price compared with earlier transactions in the late 1960s, the values increased faster over the next 15 years until they exceeded $2,500 to $3,000. But Batten rejected the price as too rich. As he was to write many years later, "Throughout this period, we were bargain hunters, which I realized was a mistake. Our estimates of subscriber penetration, revenue growth, and final value turned out to be far too conservative."[4]

However, it wasn't a fatal mistake. Batten was right. There will always be a plethora of deals to do, and there is limited capital to complete them. It is impossible to do every one. Most important, to be a good steward of a company's resources, one must be ever prudent with its capital, striving to allocate it only to those investments which will produce superior returns and ensure the company's future. As Batten concluded, "I've always resisted the impulse to second-guess these kinds of missed opportunities. In fact, the same price discipline that kept us out of good deals kept us out of many more bad deals."[5]

From Batten's perspective, cable TV companies weren't the only investment opportunity. Like broadcast properties and metropolitan newspapers, their values had skyrocketed, increasing their risk and undermining an investor's potential return. Batten knew that winning franchises and developing new markets would yield a superior result, and there were bound to be alternative investments in other business sectors that had not been bid up beyond their apparent intrinsic values. Like all great investors, Batten was insistent on acquiring businesses that had substantial upside potential and could be purchased at a value price.

With the conglomerators and rollup artists rabidly bidding up prices just to get deals done, Batten insisted on directing Landmark's acquisition strategy with a strong emphasis on earning a high return on investment. As the owner of a privately held company, he avoided being deluded by a skyrocketing public stock price into pursuing a momentum investment strategy. Instead, his mission continued to be founded on the principle of building wealth through investment in companies whose earnings would grow at superior levels relative to their capital demands. When other acquirers began to bid up prices on metropolitan newspapers and broadcast properties, he perceived that the companies' prospective cash flows would fail to generate sufficient returns on the winning bids, and he insisted that his staff begin looking for other sectors for investment.

Community Newspaper Rollup

As part of Landmark's 1967 acquisition of the *Roanoke Times & World News*, it acquired the affiliated twice-weekly community newspaper, the *Galax Gazette*, about 100 miles away. Producing generous cash flows, the Galax, Virginia, newspaper proved highly rewarding, and it led Landmark's leaders to consider acquiring similar small newspapers serving the county seats in markets distant from large city metros. Their evaluation led them to investigate a Kentucky company called Newspapers, Inc.

Including more than a dozen weekly and semiweekly newspapers, the Kentucky company had been stitched together for bargain prices by Bill Matthews, an energetic entrepreneur who recognized that efficiencies could be produced by acquiring the independent newspapers in contiguous markets and managing and printing them from a centralized location. Though it took a lot of small markets to generate the revenues of a single metropolitan newspaper, the weeklies could be acquired for much lower earnings multiples. In fact, whereas some large city papers were selling for

as much as three or four times revenues, the weeklies were typically selling for something close to one times, and remarkably, those weeklies often
posted operating margins equivalent to those of the papers in big cities.
With dispatch, Diederich negotiated the purchase of Matthews's company,
employing it as the locus for further acquisitions and management of
Landmark's growing stable of community newspapers in county seats such
as Shelbyville, Kentucky; Red Oak, Iowa; New Albany, Mississippi; and
Los Alamos, New Mexico.

Another appealing characteristic of the community newspapers was
the fact that many of their smaller markets were experiencing faster
growth than were papers in urban areas, and faster market growth was the
prime criterion for Landmark as it began to evaluate community newspaper acquisition targets. Those markets, it concluded, could present an
enticing opportunity to transform the larger weeklies into small daily
newspapers to capture a much larger, more profitable share of the advertiser and subscriber dollar. More important, very few of those markets had
been discovered by the acquirers of large dailies and therefore could be
acquired more cheaply.

In the economic turmoil of the early 1970s, with wage and price controls and commodity disruptions, there was a brief period when newsprint
was in exceedingly short supply. Those printers and publishers that failed
to contract for supply suddenly had to scramble to obtain even a fraction
of their needs. With the threat of having to cease production without fresh
newsprint supplies, a midsize printer with a twice-weekly paper in West-
minster, Maryland, fell into the acquisitive hands of Landmark, which
could provide the needed commodity. Over the following 10 years, that
paper was transformed into a very successful daily, growing at least 20-fold
in value. Subsequently, Landmark made similar investments to acquire
and transform other papers, including those in Elizabethtown, Kentucky,
and Inverness, Florida.

By 1980, Landmark had assembled a very attractive and profitable stable of approximately 70 rural and exurban newspapers, stretching from
Florida to California. With a keen focus on producing high-quality localized content, its Landmark Community Newspapers division placed strong
emphasis on controlling costs by centralizing billing, personnel benefits,

payroll, and circulation administration functions in its divisional head-quarters in Shelbyville, Kentucky. Further efficiencies were gained from the consolidation of printing services at regional presses, which could be operated more efficiently while minimizing capital invested in plant and equipment. The regional and centralized administrative and production services not only added to the profitability of the group but also freed the local managers to focus on producing a quality editorial product that would endear itself to its community and retain the loyalty of its advertisers.

However, by the early 1980s, other newspaper groups had begun to discover the opportunity. Thomson Newspapers had become a big factor in community newspapers, along with the New York Times Company, E.W. Scripps Company, Lee Enterprises, and Multimedia, Inc. Other entrepreneurial publishers, such as Boone Newspapers, had bought up such papers to create their own small empires, and other media investors became interested, including Roy Park, who added scores of community newspapers to his broadcast group. That increasingly rabid interest resulted in the bidding up of the prices of community newspapers to levels close to those of larger metropolitan dailies.

Target Media Rollup

Once again, Batten became concerned that prices were exceeding the intrinsic value of the properties, and he directed his divisional leadership to identify alternative investments. While Landmark's metropolitan newspapers began investing in free distribution advertising shoppers, its community newspaper division explored niche publications that would appeal to smaller definable readership and advertising groups. With great hopes of rolling out similar publications nationwide, that division acquired two small groups of nurse recruitment publications and several free distribution papers that appealed to senior citizens and their allied marketers. A separate new division was created to develop and acquire free distribution alternative newsweeklies whose eclectic coverage of contemporary events, arts, and culture appealed to active affluent young adults in larger metropolitan markets. Unfortunately, none promised to produce returns warranting a concerted rollup and development effort.

But then, late one Friday afternoon in 1985, the telephone rang in Conrad Hall's office. Though most of the staff had left for the day, Hall was still busy at his desk because as executive vice president of Landmark, his work never seemed to end. The caller was Jerry Fulp, owner of the Winston–Salem *Trading Post*, a newsprint tabloid devoted primarily to private party classified ads published for a small commission that was levied only if the advertised item sold. A friend of Fulp's had recently sold his free distribution advertising shopper to Landmark's Greensboro, North Carolina, *News & Record*, and Fulp inquired whether Landmark would buy his paid circulation tabloid and its accompanying *Wheels & Deals* photo guide. Having nurtured his publications for almost two decades, Fulp had lost interest and was distracted by a complicated personal life. Rather than concentrate on a business demanding constant attention to address customer complaints and personnel issues, he longed for a pile of cash that would generate a sustainable income if prudently invested: "A million bucks after the tax man takes his slice" was all he needed, and he was highly motivated to sell.

Always alert for a good investment in niche publishing, Hall listened attentively as Fulp related a few of the business's financial details. In minutes, Hall grew interested. Having helped negotiate several of the shopper and alternative newsweekly acquisitions, he quickly concluded that Fulp's publications were highly attractive opportunities and directed Fulp to forward his financial statements and other operational details for review. When the materials arrived, Hall was impressed. In addition to boasting an attractive operating margin, the business owned real estate and a recent-vintage newspaper printing press. Surprisingly, Fulp's price was equal to less than four times its free cash flow, and it appeared that earnings could be doubled by increasing the cover price, which was just a third of that commanded by identical publications in cities such as Norfolk.

From periodic conversations over the previous 10 years, Hall knew that Bill Diederich had advocated the acquisition of similar publications, including Norfolk's *Trading Post*, a tabloid exclusively devoted to private party classified ads for the sale of used cars, appliances, musical instruments, and other consumer goods. With the arrogance typical of newspaper editors, other Landmark executives had turned up their noses at the prospect of investing in such a lowbrow business, and just the year before, the company had rejected the opportunity to acquire a used car photo guide serving the market outside Baltimore. But attitudes had changed as newspaper executives became more attuned to the success of competing free-distribution advertising shopper publications, and Batten's son had just returned from a two-year stint with the Associated Press in London, impressed with the results of its thriving *Auto Trader* photo guide, which had produced an instant buyer for his car.

With Batten's endorsement, Hall quickly negotiated the acquisition of the Winston–Salem papers, and Diederich lobbied earnestly to purchase similar publications. Within months of the acquisition, Diederich directed investment in computerized production and billing systems to increase productivity, and management tweaked the paper's rates to produce impressive growth in the profit margin, demonstrating that the deal had been completed for an astonishing valuation of less than three times the first year's actual pretax cash flow.

Impressed by the profits flowing from the new acquisition, Diederich had the evidence he needed to gain approval for further acquisitions. He compiled a list of similar publications in the top 200 U.S. markets and recruited one of Landmark's enthusiastic community newspaper managers to pursue their acquisition. Within less than a year, Landmark had completed the acquisition of the Atlanta-based Tradin' Times, Inc., the largest multicity publisher of classified papers and used car photo guides, serving markets such as Chicago, Detroit, St. Louis, Philadelphia, Minneapolis, Cleveland, and Columbus. Then, within another four months, Landmark acquired two more companies that published classified ad papers in Charlotte, North Carolina; Columbia, South Carolina; and Buffalo and Rochester, New York.

Diederich perceived that the window of opportunity to roll up those publications would be limited, and he encouraged divisional leadership to proceed aggressively to acquire as many as possible. However, two factors proved to be significant impediments: the integration process and valuation.

The assimilation of those publications taxed the already stretched managerial capabilities of the acquiring division, Landmark Community

Newspapers. The magazines' early founders were motivated to sell because they had tired of their businesses, and so they were quick to depart, leaving a leadership vacuum. Though two had strong lieutenants to assume the management helm, they lacked the breadth of experience needed to orchestrate a seamless integration, and two other magazines had no qualified management at all. Moreover, like any prudent new business investor, Landmark's managers were conscientiously striving to learn as much as possible about existing operations before adopting new processes or modifying strategies.

Because of the assimilation difficulties, divisional management adopted a very conservative valuation approach for other prospects that expressed an interest in selling, and that represented the second (and largest) impediment to its making more acquisitions. Perceiving no alternative buyers, management believed it could patiently wait for sellers to reduce their prices to bargain levels. Whereas *Tradin' Times* was acquired for about six times its forecasted first-year cash flows (less than one time revenues), subsequent transactions were completed for less. In fact, Landmark was beaten at the negotiating table in its attempt to acquire the New Orleans *News on Wheels* in 1988 because it refused to increase its offer to something close to four times cash flow despite the fact Landmark's own classified papers were growing at double-digit levels.

In early 1989, it missed acquiring the *Auto Trader* publication licensee in Detroit and San Antonio because it offered values equivalent to four times cash flow while the original licensor, Stuart Arnold, clinched the deals at close to five times. Arnold's offers had been a surprise because he had always insisted that he would never be interested and had refused to discuss selling his own properties to Landmark. But then, in May, Landmark learned that Arnold's acquisition efforts were being bankrolled by Cox Enterprises, Inc. Owner of the *Atlanta Journal & Constitution* and dozens of other newspapers, Cox was over five times the size of Landmark, and the two had repeatedly competed to acquire broadcast stations and cable television franchises over the years. Now Cox had again entered the competitive acquisition fray by contracting to acquire all of Arnold's *Auto Trader* operations, including his Florida, Texas, Nevada, and California publications; his printing and production plants in Florida and Nevada;

and his assets as the national licensor of the trade name to U.S. affiliates. Moreover, Cox had enlisted Arnold to help reacquire his more than two dozen licensees scattered among the largest U.S. cities.

News of Cox's investment was chilling. Landmark's management knew that Cox was a substantial shrewd competitor for quality acquisitions. In many respects, it was actually a more aggressive practitioner of Landmark's acquisition and development strategy. Founded with Dayton's *Daily News* by three-time Ohio governor and Democratic U.S. presidential candidate James Cox, Cox Enterprises had acquired substantial newspapers in Atlanta, Palm Beach, and Texas; had invested heavily in radio and television broadcast operations since the 1950s; and had bested Landmark by making more substantial investments to develop one of the country's largest cable TV operations in the 1960s and later decades.

Simultaneously, a Montreal entrepreneur, John McBain, had partnered with Torstar Corp., the owner of the *Toronto Star* and other Canadian newspapers, to consolidate the *Auto Trader* business in Canada. Landmark had commenced its rollup with a two-year head start and an almost open field for classified ad and photo guide acquisitions, but it was now confronted by two deep-pocketed, sophisticated competitors for the same properties. Recalling his disappointment in failing to capture more cable outlets, Batten resolved that Landmark would not make the same mistake and opened the corporate treasury to pay aggressive but rationally prudent prices in the competitive feeding frenzy that followed.

Within weeks of the news of Stuart Arnold's sale to Cox, every *Auto Trader* licensee and several publishers of unaffiliated classified ad publications became gleefully aware that the big-money boys were after them, and they celebrated as the bidding war progressed over the following months. With prices tripling to an average of three times revenues, previously indifferent publishers were transformed into eager sellers.

While the accelerated price competition motivated McBain to return his concentration to acquiring the Canadian *Auto Trader* magazines and similar classified papers in Europe and Asia, Landmark and Cox duked it out for supremacy in the United States. Having completed just five such acquisitions during the three years before Cox's entry, Landmark inked 19 deals in the subsequent 20 months while Cox made 14. By October 1989, the two companies had consolidated more than two-thirds of the U.S. classified ad paper and used car photo guide business. Cox's properties were primarily Sunbelt operations, covering almost all of the West Coast plus Arizona, New Mexico, Texas, Alabama, Georgia, and Florida. Landmark's publications included almost all those serving the industrial Midwest (plus Tennessee and Kentucky) and the Mid-Atlantic (from South Carolina to Rhode Island). The remaining independent publications (notably including San Diego and California's Orange County) remained with their founders, who were not then motivated to sell for any price.

By mid–1989, both Landmark and Cox were contentedly operating their portions of the U.S. classified ad publication business. Though their investment had skyrocketed and the assimilation of so many acquisitions had been challenging, they were rewarded with businesses that were growing at an impressive clip, churning out better than expected profits. Those profits grew even faster as the two companies introduced computerized production systems and adopted companywide the best practices discovered among the individual operations.

Their apparent success attracted the attention of another media giant that began to covet their position. Executives of United News & Media, a British newspaper publisher and operator of free distribution apartment and homes real estate guides in the United States, met secretly with Cox to propose the acquisition of its newly assembled *Auto Trader* business. Hearing a price more than double the acquisitions' costs, Cox management was intrigued, but it knew Landmark could potentially bid the price up higher. However, by the time Cox's investment bankers produced the necessary pitch book, the broad media industry began experiencing uncertainty along with the general economy. Though Landmark's Diederich strongly advocated paying the price to acquire the business, Cox's expectations were too steep, and even United News demurred on paying anything close to its original indication.

Trader Publishing Company Partnership

Although it failed to produce a sale, Cox's marketing process for its *Auto Trader* properties facilitated the development of a warmer relationship with

Landmark. Cognizant of the benefits arising from the merger, the two subsequently agreed to contribute their classified publication divisions to a new partnership, owned 50–50, with leadership primarily provided by the Landmark management team, led by Conrad Hall. Consequently, on April 1, 1991, Trader Publishing Company came into being with consolidated revenues of almost $150 million.

With the original 38 acquisitions as its foundation, Trader's management continued to expand operations as it cultivated new launches in cities such as Kansas City, Roanoke, and Hartford. The core products, moreover, were growing dramatically, and spin-offs of supplemental segmented products functioned as accelerants. Whereas the first *Auto Trader* included used vehicles of every description, it would eventually be divided as it gained critical mass into segregated products such as *Truck Trader, Boat Trader, Cycle Trader, RV Trader, Big Truck Trader,* and *Heavy Equipment Trader.* Recognizing the nationwide appeal of certain collectible vehicles, Trader also produced and distributed national publications, including *Old Car Trader, Walneck's Classic Cycle Trader,* and *Yacht Trader.*

Other publishing segments offered comparable opportunities, and Trader had the confidence and skill to expand its prospecting efforts to include new targets that could be exploited. Scanning the competitive marketplace, it discovered a variety of free distribution automotive publications that offered it the opportunity to capture a greater share of the commercial automotive advertising market. Before its merger with Cox, Landmark had acquired two free distribution auto guides, but the operations had not developed much beyond their original base. Then, within a few months after Trader's creation, the new partnership's managers stumbled across the free distribution *Diablo Dealer,* a four-zoned San Francisco auto advertising publication group whose rapid growth had earned it a position on *Inc.* magazine's list of the fastest-growing entrepreneurships. Its acquisition led to several more deals and the eventual launch of the *Auto Mart* brand as Trader's national group of free distribution auto guides featuring local commercial car dealership advertising.

As covered in more detail in Chapters 4 and 11, Trader then proceeded with the rollup and rollout process with employment publications, motel guides, apartment magazines, and a variety of Internet businesses.

Chapter 4

Prospecting for Opportunities

"Where is he?!" sputtered the always punctual Larry Coffey, president of Landmark's community newspaper division.

"You know Bill better than I do," Hoffmann said sheepishly, also a little impatient because the divisional chairman, Bill Diederich, had still not arrived for the scheduled dinner with his six top Kentucky managers. "Like I said, he called three hours ago from Nowhere, Indiana, and said he had a few more stops to make."

"A few more stops!" Coffey said, suddenly smiling, bemused. "He just can't control himself. In the distance, there appears another sad little convenience store, and his car just naturally swerves in. Can't you just see him, looking like some itinerant German shoemaker, ambling in, looking for any new publications, asking the pimpled clerk how many copies the shop sells during his shift?"

"Yeah, I don't know where he gets the patience. It's like he has all the time in the world, and, like Peter Falk's Columbo, always 'there's just one more thing.'"

"You're right about that," concluded Coffey. "But he provides a sterling example of how it should be done. What other billion-dollar company's number-two executive would spend more than a week driving over 2,500 miles along the byways from Norfolk to Wisconsin to Louisville and back to Norfolk, turning into every strip shopping center, gas station, grocery store, and convenience mart looking for publications and grilling the shop staff?

Not only does it demonstrate the level of his interest in identifying prospective targets for acquisition in the classified publication business, it should inspire the rest of us to work just as diligently to remain inquisitive, pay attention to details, understand the intricacies, and devote all our energies to achieving success."

"Understood," Hoffmann said, also impressed. "After Bill's debriefing, I'll be heading out on my own odyssey through America's retailing heartland."

A fundamental problem faced by rollup practitioners is that the vast majority of businesses are not instantly identifiable in an easily accessed database. They too often remain invisible in the marketplace, and substantial effort must be expended to locate desirable prospects.

Following Frank Batten's directive, in 1982 Landmark's community newspaper division embarked on an effort to identify for acquisition "targeted publications"—niche magazines or papers dedicated to a small subset of readers or consumers. The ideal acquisition prospects would have substantial development potential either within their currently defined market or as models for replication in other geographic markets.

As printers of other publishers' products, Landmark's production plants gave management a convenient window to observe and review alternative products, but too many seemed to be struggling concepts or simply comparable versions of its existing newspapers and shoppers.

To accelerate the discovery of different publishing models, Landmark appointed a director of specialty publications to lead the effort, and he proceeded with several initiatives:

- The printing plants' salespersons were instructed to provide examples of every existing and prospective customer's publications for review. They were encouraged to share any insights into concepts they had discovered or heard about from their numerous contacts.
- All the company's field managers were requested to provide samples of all the magazines, papers, direct-mail publications, and other targeted media distributed within their markets.

- Media brokers (people enlisted to help owners sell their businesses) were contacted by phone and letter to request information about all of their publishing clients.
- Ad agency media catalogs (including *Standard Rate & Data*) were reviewed to identify differentiated targeted print products.

During that process, several promising opportunities were considered and pursued, including direct-mail nursing newspapers, senior citizen monthlies, and boating newspapers. However, management was myopically focused on identifying interesting publishing opportunities that incorporated meaningful editorial content to leverage the company's core expertise as a newspaper publisher, and though it had samples of hundreds of "all advertising" media, it dismissed them as uninteresting prospects.

Because the division's operations were confined to more rural markets, its director of specialty publications personally traveled to dozens of metropolitan markets, spending one or two days in each locale visiting scores of convenience stores, grocery stores, malls, and other high-traffic areas to pick up the publications he discovered. He simultaneously asked store clerks and managers which, if any, of the publications sold well or were picked up in substantial quantities, and he asked whether they received any other valuable advertising materials by mail or other means.

During his various city tours, he also visited the phone company to obtain a complete Yellow Pages (during those days there were no accessible Internet databases) and the various community Chambers of Commerce to obtain media lists. In addition, he interviewed the Chamber of Commerce executives and other knowledgeable media authorities to solicit their insights. With that information, he compiled a catalog of the newspapers, publications, shoppers, and other media for consideration.

To evaluate a specific niche, he researched the business segment, including its growth prospects, competition, and operating challenges, and sought to identify several products serving that niche, analyzing their operating models and probable financial performance. To obtain more authoritative information, he met with a variety of industry experts and community development managers, carefully quizzing them to get their insights and forecasts.

In evaluating the nursing and senior publishing segments, Landmark's analyst was particularly gratified when publishers willingly agreed to meet and gladly shared a wealth of information as they related their perspectives. That experience established such meetings as an effective tactic for initiating contact among prospective acquisition targets.

Trading Post and Auto Trader

After the fortuitous discovery and acquisition of the Winston–Salem *Trading Post*, Diederich, the special publications director, and a company staffer conducted a comprehensive search for all similar publications in the United States. They scoured business directories and checked with business contacts to identify all likely prospects, and they called convenience stores and newsstands in the top 150 metropolitan markets to find out whether there were similar products. If one was identified, they requested the name, address, and phone number of the publisher as listed in the publication. They then obtained representative copies of the publications and advertising rate cards, which they analyzed to calculate the average number and size of ads, their average cost, and the publications' probable annual revenue.

As was described earlier in this chapter, Diederich personally drove a 2,500-mile circuit through 10 states, stopping at an estimated 500 locations to check for publications, inspect their marketing tactics, inquire about their apparent acceptance, and assess their competitive position. The specialty publications director completed similar tours in different parts of the country, and within a relatively short period they produced a prospect list of approximately 100 publications.

Once it was compiled, they obtained credit reports from Dun & Bradstreet on each publisher. Available by fax for a nominal fee, the reports provided at least cursory information about the ownership, office location and size, number of employees, and credit status. In some cases the reports contained a definitive statement of revenues, and a handful included summary income statements and balance sheets that the owners had disclosed to the ratings agency.

To contact the prospects, Diederich recruited Barney Oldfield, a recently retired executive who had been instrumental in cultivating relationships to help Landmark with its TeleCable rollup and rollout. Oldfield and the specialty publications director proceeded to contact each business owner to inquire about his or her interest in meeting to discuss industry prospects and "business opportunities." Such opportunities, of course, included a simple willingness to discuss operations and best practices, but inevitably, the conversations led to a discussion about possible interest in selling.

Employment Guide

Several years after the 1991 formation of Trader, its management again began to search for new niche publishing opportunities. It was particularly interested in targeted publications that would capitalize on the rich revenue base represented by the help-wanted classified section of the metropolitan newspapers (notable for extraordinarily high ad rates and profitability).

The process moved slowly until the founders of the Detroit *Employment Guide* contacted Trader, as is described in more detail in Chapter 11. Already prepared to sell, the entrepreneurs struck a responsive chord with Trader's interest in the recruitment segment, and their publications were quickly snapped up.

To identify other existing employment publications like the one it had just acquired, Trader's chief financial officer contacted the *Auto Trader* field office managers, requesting that they and their circulation managers carefully comb their markets to collect samples of recruitment publications. Approximately 20 were discovered, and with information culled from Dun & Bradstreet reports, the CFO contacted the publisher of each one to propose a meeting to discuss "business opportunities of mutual interest."

Dealer Specialties

To familiarize themselves with industry developments and opportunities, Trader's top managers regularly attended significant trade shows as one of their prime means of identifying prospects for consideration. At those meetings, they paid particular attention to meeting the leaders of the industry's ancillary vendors who were pitching their varied products and services.

Among the many discovered was Dealer Specialties, a franchisor whose integrated software and Internet-based system facilitated the collection of vehicle descriptions for the preparation of point-of-purchase promotional window stickers. As discussed in Chapters 11 through 13, its data collection utilities made it highly attractive as an acquisition that would support Trader's Internet development strategies. However, because of its owners' high price expectations, negotiations progressed slowly. Trader therefore contacted the few competing vendors it had identified as part of its customary due diligence and began negotiating to acquire Maronie Information Services, the second largest company serving the segment. Fortunately, Trader succeeded in acquiring both, and after completing the acquisition, it turned its attention to acquiring their principal franchisees. As part of its customary communication process during the integration process, Trader advised the larger franchisees that it would be interested in acquiring them, and it completed deals with those which offered to sell at attractive prices. The pressure to complete deals as quickly as possible was reduced because as franchisors, the two companies retained the right of first refusal, ensuring their preferential purchase rights in case a third party stepped in.

The underperforming franchisees in large markets were of particular interest as acquisition targets. Conscious that pervasive penetration within the major metropolitan markets would be critical to long-term success, Trader's divisional head of new ventures, Mitch Brooks, recognized that lackadaisical performers would stand in the way of progress. Brooks therefore made their acquisition a priority, particularly because they provided a fertile opportunity for more rapid development; and, because they were poor performers, their owners were more motivated to sell and for prices reflective of their diminished historical results.

Travel Media Group

Throughout its development, Trader also cultivated relationships with the myriad business brokers and investment bankers who periodically represented sellers of media properties. Historically, Trader had experienced little success in completing such transactions because the brokers successfully ignited a bidding war among prospective acquirers, and Trader's conservatism usually resulted in its losing out. In 2000, however, Mitch Brooks was contacted by an investment banker who was managing an auction for the sale of Exit Info Guide, a business acquired from its founder a few years earlier by a small private equity group. As the publisher of a network of free distribution motel discount coupon guides available on racks at highway rest stops, the company had substantial appeal.

When told of the opportunity, Trader's CFO was crestfallen. In 1983, he had met with a Kentucky dreamer who had launched a similar, miserably failing version of the motel coupon guide. Shortly afterward, in 1984, he had discovered in Florida a paid version of the publication, and he'd kept a copy as an example of arcane niche media. As a paid guide, it also was failing, but it eventually was converted to a free circulation version and subsequently grew substantially. In the intervening years, the CFO had picked up copies, and he'd actually used a couple of the coupons because they offered much better deals on motel room rentals than those available through the more popular AAA and affinity motel discount programs. If he had contacted the Florida owner a few years earlier, Trader could have acquired the business for less than a tenth of the price the investment banker offered.

As luck would have it, a high-flying Internet company was interested in the business, and the price shot up well beyond the level Trader considered rational. The CFO, however, identified the four other significant publishers in the niche and eventually succeeded in acquiring three of them. But just as Trader was closing on the acquisition of the second largest of the motel coupon guides, the investment banker reconnected with Trader to advise that the Exit Info Guide deal with the Internet company had collapsed, and Trader proceeded with purchasing it as its second acquisition in the segment.

Internet Rollups: Homes.com

The frothy market for the launch of Internet companies in the late 1990s meant that there was an overabundance of entities to evaluate for possible acquisition. However, as history would demonstrate, few were actually viable and almost none were affordable. Even the most questionable prospects were operated by starry-eyed entrepreneurs who were deluded by the apparent riches available from new venture investors and the public stock market.

Trader's approach was to establish friendly relationships with the founders of as many as possible of the Internet businesses closely related to the industry segments served by Trader. With its sales tentacles extending to almost every local market, Trader was blessed with an intelligence network that could identify comparatively small operations that were gaining traction with commercial clients, and by attending trade shows and maintaining an attentive ear to the gossip of industry networks, its managers successfully identified the more nationally prominent players. Trader's acquisitions of the real estate web-hosting companies Advanced Access and Katabat were very much a consequence of its concerted efforts to develop warm associations over time; and there were many other examples, including the watercraft portal Boats.com and the auto dealer web hosts Dealerskins and XIGroup.

In addition, maintaining close contacts with the business brokers and investment bankers was important. Because of the market's focus on "everything Internet," both sellers and brokers knew there was good money to be made by pitching even lukewarm Internet ventures to the salivating big-money investors. Trader therefore routinely contacted as many brokers and investment bankers as it could, reminding them to include Trader among those interested in any prospective client they might offer for sale. Its efforts resulted in the opportunity to acquire 123Movers.com, a lead generator for moving companies, and eNeighborhoods, a real estate web-hosting enterprise that aggregated and distributed community data and demographics for its clients.

However, despite its best efforts, Trader inevitably missed some prime opportunities. There were just too many intermediaries to cultivate effectively, and occasionally it was only the accidental discoveries of its field personnel that enabled it to capture a desirable property. The investment banker–led auction for Homes.com was very near its final stages when one of Trader's managers heard about the opportunity through the industry grapevine, and it was only through its quick footwork that Trader captured the last seat at the table of last-round bidders for that property. Careful to keep its powder dry for one final round, Trader held back on its final bid and was shocked when it was informed that the company would be sold to another buyer. In desperation, it made one more offer with a price 10 percent above its prior bid, but the brokers rejected it, saying it was too late: The sellers had already committed to doing the deal.

Dejected but certain that there would be many more deals to do in the future, Trader's deal makers licked their wounds. But three months later, the brokers of Homes.com called again. It seems the presumed buyer had balked at a few key elements, and Trader would be invited back to the table if its offer still stood. Trader agreed to move forward, and after several months, it completed the acquisition of Homes.com.

Chapter 5

Rollup Valuation

How much to do the deal?

Exhausted operator: "Just make me an offer."

Wild-eyed dreamer: "Enough to make me richer than God."

Small business broker: "Two to four times the sum of EBITDA and the owner's draws."

Investment banker: "Good question, and there's no simple answer. To establish a base expectation, we'll perform exhaustive discounted cash flow analyses, employing Monte Carlo iterations on a multitude of projections supported by your worst-case/best-case/most-probable forecasts. We'll assess those results in juxtaposition with all relevant comparative transactions completed in the last five years, taking into consideration existing market conditions and the inherent desirability and growth prospects of the specific industry segment. We'll then conduct an auction among all potential acquirers, carefully identified within our comprehensive, proprietary database, maintaining a persistent commitment to exploiting our personal relationships and in-depth knowledge of each bidder's strategic imperatives and psychological hot buttons to exact premium valuations. Then we'll aggressively manipulate the auction's conclusion to compel the highest possible transaction level. Our fee, by the way, includes our reasonable expenses plus a percentage of the whole transaction, calculated as 5 percent of the first million, scaling down to 1 percent of every dollar over $4 million, subject to a seven-figure minimum. And of course we'll want our people to have a preferential shot at assembling a suitable level of stapled financing (for the customary additional fee)."

Prudent practitioner: "The lowest possible value acceptable to the seller, ideally substantially less than six times EBITDA but subject to a maximum of eight times EBITDA."

Momentum investor: "Whatever it takes to compel the prospect to sell."

Industry consolidation is the label the media apply to a rollup of the big boy companies, and among the biggest are the auto manufacturers. In the late twentieth century, the world witnessed Ford acquiring an equity position in Mazda in 1979, its outright acquisition of Jaguar and Aston Martin in 1988–1989, and its purchase of Volvo in 1999. Chrysler captured its now signature Jeep brand in 1987 with its purchase of AMC, and of course the biggest transaction in the automotive industry was Daimler-Benz's $37 billion merger with Chrysler in 1998.

That Daimler–Chrysler merger represents one of the best examples of the risks and pitfalls surrounding the valuation of large transactions in industry consolidations. It in fact provides a chilling reminder that even a seemingly compelling deal predicated on sound industry fundamentals and the competitive necessity to achieve manufacturing scale can produce disastrous consequences. Although almost no one foresaw the auto industry's economic devastation a decade later, hindsight demonstrates that deal mania and excess optimism can lead acquirers astray by encouraging them to underestimate risks and overestimate merger benefits to justify prices far in excess of intrinsic values.

Armed with exhaustive analyses and discounted cash flow analyses from at least two of the largest investment banking firms, the boards and shareholders of Chrysler and Daimler were reassured about the fairness of the valuation. Yet less than a decade later, having few positive interim dividends, Daimler hastily *gave* Chrysler to the private equity firm Cerberus Capital. The deal had a purported $7.8 billion price tag, but Cerberus actually contributed $5 billion of that amount to Chrysler's auto operations and another $1 billion to Chrysler's finance arm. After accounting for guarantees to offset $1.6 billion in Chrysler's preclosing losses, Daimler projected a net payout of $650 million on top of the charge of $4 billion to $5.4 billion for transaction-related expenses.[1] Yikes! What happened to the $37 billion valuation of Chrysler in 1998?

The Chrysler example is instructive not only because history confirmed the magnitude of the experts' apparent valuation errors but also because the transaction became the subject of detailed case studies that subsequently were employed by numerous business schools to teach thousands of prospective MBAs the process and propriety of the methods that produced that $37 billion valuation. The case material, in fact, is presented as a sterling example of the scholarly way to perform discounted cash flow analysis (DCF) in the definitive, authoritative graduate school text on acquisition practices, *Applied Mergers and Acquisitions* by Robert Bruner.[2]

In retrospect, we understand that the DCF forecasts vastly overestimated Chrysler's value because of overoptimistic assumptions regarding profit growth, stability of cash flows, and synergistic benefits. Rather than annualized earnings growth of 3 percent, vigorous competition and economic recessions produced debilitating losses, and despite expectations of $3 billion in annualized synergistic savings, the Daimler leadership was forced to admit by 2007 that "it's clear that the synergy potential between Mercedes-Benz and Chrysler is limited,"[3] demonstrating the all too common postmerger conclusion that most synergistic expectations are unrealistic and unachievable, as argued by Mark Sirower in *The Synergy Trap*.[4]

During the last half century, corporate valuations in the frothy world of big-time mergers and acquisitions have been officially predicated on the expected present value of the free cash flow they will generate. In his 1938 classic *The Theory of Investment Value*, John Burr Williams asserted that a company's intrinsic value was best determined by the net present value of its future cash flows: "A cow for her milk, a hen for her eggs, and a stock, by heck, for her dividends."[5] Demonstrating how mathematical formulas could be used to define intrinsic value, Williams's treatise provided the starting point for modern corporate valuation methods, and since that time, libraries have been filled with scholarly works examining his techniques, expanding his analyses to incorporate more abstruse formulas and new levels of sophistication, and demonstrating their application and efficacy. We have, for example, Merton Miller and Franco Modigliani to thank for their careful codification of cash flow analyses, including their principle of capital structure irrelevance[6]; Joel Stern for his work demonstrating the practical implementation of his "free" cash flow method[7];

Steven Kaplan and Richard Ruback for their analysis of free cash flow valuation as a predictor of market value[8]; and Andrew Ang and Jun Liu for their demonstration of how to discount free cash flows with time-varying discount rates.[9]

Today, an astonishingly lucrative industry has grown up around this academic research as investment bankers drool over the multi-million-dollar fees generated while employing those methods to produce "fairness opinions" for the boards of public companies that require confirmation and certification of the "reasonableness" of a proposed acquisition's transaction value.[10] Like Trader, most midtier companies have MBA-degreed managers who have instituted the process for their own merger activities. Even small entities attract valuation experts who employ those DCF analyses as required by divorce settlements, inheritance allocations, tax assessments, loan agreements, and other general applications.

With such wide adoption and with so much research demonstrating its efficacy, the prudence of using DCF valuation techniques is hard to debate, risking persecution of those who question them as flat earth heretics destined to be burned at the stake. But a few salient examples clearly demonstrate how this has led investors astray, supporting the assertion that contemporary DCF valuation in megamergers is used more to justify irrational transaction premiums than to define a firm's intrinsic value. Although they win the plaudits of sellers' boards that are rightfully interested in maximizing short-term shareholder buyouts, the excess valuations prove devastating for the buyers' investors, who, like Daimler, are punished with losses instead of gaining the desired superior long-term investment returns.

In their analysis of all public mergers completed between 1980 and 2007, Bayazitova, Kahl, and Valkanov demonstrate that on average, "value destruction" is the consequence of "megamergers" (those accounting for 43 percent of all merger outlays in absolute transaction value).[11] Because these were huge transactions, we can be confident that both the buyers and the sellers had their highly paid investment banking advisors opine on the reasonableness of the valuations as demonstrated by intricate, carefully crafted DCF analyses. Apparently, the value destroyers were led astray, and we smirk, like Hamlet, "For tis the sport to have the engineer Hoist with his owne petard."

The deficiencies implied by experiences like Daimler's lead many business investors to question the propriety of these scholarly methods, and some have gone so far as to place the blame for recent financial crises on that failure. As the Capco Institute's Shahin Shojai asserts: "This systematic methodological 'deficit' has in my view hampered a serious focus on the construction of models that have a solid link to 'economic reality' and prevented academic economists from communicating to the public, including bankers and policy-makers, the limitations, weaknesses and even dangers of [their] preferred models. ..."[12]

When it comes to valuing businesses, it is clear that Warren Buffett has the magic formula. Repeatedly, his valuation acumen has been demonstrated by his history of completing scores of transactions for compelling prices that deliver superior returns on his investments. He appears to produce valuations instantaneously. As he notes in each edition of Berkshire Hathaway's annual report, he remains eager to receive contacts about potential acquisitions if they stipulate an offering price and meet his published criteria: "We can promise complete confidentiality and a very fast answer—customarily within five minutes."[13] To produce that spontaneous assessment, we can assume that Buffett applies a snap calculation, employing a rule-of-thumb multiple of seller's cash flow tempered by his decades of experience with the probabilities of the future profit performance of the entity within its industry segment during erratic business cycles.

Trader Valuation Rationale

As a critical component of Trader's due diligence evaluation, careful assessment of a company's intrinsic value stood at the forefront, and no deal would be concluded unless management expressed high confidence in achieving a superior return on investment, protected by a comfortable margin of safety.

Over the two decades of its evolution, Trader calculated acquisition bids for hundreds of prospective deals and every one of its 145 completed transactions through voluminous, rigorously manipulated DCF analyses, each carefully evaluated and tweaked through scores of iterations. But inevitably, when management sought board approval to complete a deal, the valuation depended on a simpler criterion: the multiple of the prior year's cash flow relative to prospective long-term profit growth. A high-growth prospect might be valued at eight times EBITDA, whereas a low-growth entity would be valued at six or as little as four times EBITDA. DCF analyses were a required exhibit for every board-evaluated proposal, and they produced tangible benefits. However, the simple cash flow multiples represented leadership's quick reality check on the prudence of the valuation.

The justification for DCF analysis therefore was not that it produced superior valuations compared with those of historic cash flow multiples. Instead, the exercise was valued for its requirement that management carefully evaluate the economic drivers of the business, the opportunities to control costs, the rationality of forecasted growth rates, and the probability of competition and market forces affecting short- and long-term results.

Most significantly, those forecasts established a baseline expectation for the business, an expectation for which management would be held accountable after a deal was concluded and the business was merged into its consolidated operations. Although an outside party may be blamed for overly aggressive appraisals, management could blame only itself if its own forecasts failed to materialize, and those forecasts therefore represented long-term goals that management had an obligation to achieve, knowing it would lose credibility, clout, and deal-making authority if it repeatedly failed to do so within reasonable parameters.

Valuation Methodology

Although forecasts much beyond 1 year are highly suspect, Trader employed 10-year projections to incorporate the influence of recessions, economic recoveries, and random events on cash flows. Cognizant that sustained high growth rates are unrealistic, it was careful to employ conservative, realistic projections. With time, the ability to maintain growth wanes as the barriers of compounding become insurmountable. From 1995 to 2005, only 6 of the 12,000 publicly traded companies in the United States increased profits by at least 20 percent each year,[14] and every one of those businesses declined dramatically during the great recession of 2008–2009. As a respected investor noted, "Because of competition and imitation, most firms tend to regress to the industry norm. Managers quickly adopt successful innovations made by competitors, and competitive advantage tends to be short-lived."[15] Accordingly, in its projections, Trader management attempted to include reasonable growth rates that were consistent with recent past performance and then were reduced to inflationary levels by the end of the decade. It did this even for high-growth Internet businesses because of the risk of technological obsolescence and competitive turbulence as best demonstrated by the declining performance of the 1990s experience with the purportedly indomitable AOL and Yahoo.

Though insistent on conservatism, Trader's management never forecast permanent declines in performance. Seeking businesses with long-term potential and low risk of obsolescence, it considered the prospect of declines sufficient for dismissal of an acquisition opportunity. Inevitably, its optimism proved misguided. Perhaps its biggest mistake was the acquisition of *Auto Trader's* two remaining licensees in 2000 and 2001 for mid-eight-figure prices. With the Internet already clouding print's future, management nonetheless projected a remaining decade of profitable performance, and it attributed value to completing the consolidation of used vehicle data collection to eliminate some minor problems for AutoTrader.com. Unfortunately, the Internet's ascendency consigned the print editions to the 2008 graveyard, and with grim consolation, management licked its wounds with the vain rationalization that those last deals were the equivalent of a final balloon payment on a long-term "virtual" note it had issued in the 1980s when the rollup began.

Because rollups provided the prospect of money-saving efficiencies and best practices, there were reasonable justifications for projecting improved profitability. Often mischaracterized as synergistic savings, such operational cash flow benefits could arise without mergers, but they nonetheless would improve investment returns if they were implemented effectively. Demonstrating caution, Trader's management incorporated only those benefits which it had successfully realized in the past. For example, after success in raising cover prices from $0.25 to $0.75, it comfortably projected similar benefits for future transactions, but it delayed recognition of gains for a minimum of six months to accommodate a cautious implementation process.

In the case of benefits arising from a change of processes, management forecast a much longer realization period. For example, reducing a prospective acquisition's composing costs from $50 a page to $25 a page (versus *Auto Trader*'s $10 a page) was projected to require a three-year implementation period. Because of required planning and training, management projected no savings during the first year and savings of $15 a page in the second year and then capped its savings at just $25 a page in the third year and later years.

One of the most contentious debates about Trader's spreadsheet analyses dealt with the issue of the discount rate to apply to the cash flow projections. Enterprise valuation doctrine emphasizes the use of the weighted average cost of capital.[16] However, management believed that such a discount rate rarely incorporated the true risks associated with realizing those cash flows. Like venture capitalists, Trader management believed that every acquisition implies substantive speculative risk, requiring a promise of a superior return exceeding the risks, cushioned with a large margin of safety. Management therefore established an all-purpose *minimum* hurdle rate of 15 percent as the after-tax rate of return required as a baseline discount rate for almost all acquisitions. That minimum was often increased to as much as 25 percent for particularly speculative high-growth enterprises such as those involving the Internet. On rare occasions, when the investment seemed integral to Trader's core business and promised a risk reduction for its consolidated business, management accepted a discount rate below the minimum. For example, it concluded that the integration of *For Rent Magazine* with Trader's other publications would strengthen its competitiveness, and it begrudgingly accepted a 9 percent after-tax discount rate to justify the winning offer for United Advertising Publications. Fortunately, although its growth projections proved overoptimistic, the $533 million acquisition delivered an attractive leveraged return because borrowing costs dropped below 2 percent when the Federal Reserve slashed rates to lift the economy out of the 2001 recession.

When presented with its first nine-figure prospective transaction in 1992, Trader's analysts developed an impressively intricate, integrated DCF model to produce individualized 10-year forecasts for each of the target's 20-plus component operations. Each one permitted manipulation of its respective economic drivers, and with over 20,000 formulas driven by hundreds of variables, it therefore accommodated a seemingly infinite variety of scenario simulations. However, with so many permutations, the model created more confusion than certainty about intrinsic value. More disturbing, however, is that it fostered delusions about the consolidated organization's realistic prospects. When multiple conservative tweaks to the variables were employed, the valuation accelerated beyond comfort levels, somewhere well over the rainbow into the Land of Oz. As one scholar warned, "Financial forecasts are only as good as their assumptions. The aggregate effect of many small, inadvertent forecasting biases can be huge."[17] Trader ultimately relegated the model to integration planning, subsequently returning to a simplified spreadsheet confined to a dozen economic drivers for the consolidated business. Understanding the difficulties of accomplishing more than a few meaningful objectives, it incorporated only the realistically achievable elements that would produce the most desirable impact on cash flows.

In the 1970s, when media acquisition multiples skyrocketed, Landmark's Frank Batten was struck by the disproportionate contribution of terminal value to Landmark's pricing models. With 70 to 80 percent of the total flowing from terminal values, he argued for increased conservatism, insisting on the substitution of a standard multiple of the last year's EBITDA. He reasoned that if a high-growth company was valued at an eight multiple today, it certainly would not exceed that valuation multiple when sold a decade later, after its business model and competition had matured. In addition, if it was sold, state and federal capital gains taxes would reduce the net realizable multiple. Accordingly, Landmark's terminal value multiple was reduced to just five times EBITDA. Although highly paid investment bankers guffaw at the paltry five times multiple, the broad stock market seems to support terminal value cash flow multiples of five to eight times. Historically, the after-tax PE ratio averages about 15 for the S&P 500 index.[18] Adjusted for taxes, depreciation, amortization, and capital expenditures, the stock market demonstrates an average "price to EBITDA" ratio of eight. However, the market overstates the multiple because it excludes entities that go bankrupt or disappear from the averages. Therefore, because most companies eventually expire, a multiple of free cash flows less than eight times terminal values should be employed for pricing a specific company, and netting out capital gains taxes suggests a multiple of five.

Landmark and Trader Investment Experience

Throughout their eight decades of deal making, Landmark's and Trader's managers experienced a particularly broad spectrum of valuation scenarios. Many of their rollups commenced after they serendipitously stumbled across a bargain transaction: $15,000 for its first radio station, another $15,000 for its first cable franchise, and less than three times the subsequent year's actual EBITDA for the Winston–Salem *Trading Post*.

Of course, they inevitably ran into the opposite experience of discussing acquisition with owners who had unconscionably high expectations. Within a few weeks after a telephone solicitation from Landmark's Barney Oldfield, the delusional owner of a Midwestern photo guide sent a letter to the chairman, Frank Batten, promising the Forbes 400 billionaire that acquisition of his half-million-dollar-revenue publication would generate for Landmark "more money than you have ever dreamed of."

They participated in frustrating investment banker–led auctions that generally ensured that they would depart without a deal. In one notable transaction, there were 27 initial bidders, and Trader was subsequently informed that its bid came in at number two—the second lowest valuation offered. In fact, Trader never posted the highest bid in any auction led by one of the "name brand" investment banking firms. Although it actually won three such contests, one was completed because the seller feared the highest bidder would not receive the government approvals required by Hart–Scott–Rodino legislation and two others were completed when the high bidders became intransigent about various terms and withdrew before closing.

Fortunately, Trader was offered a handful of deals in which the sellers had enlisted small business brokers to orchestrate the process. With their predilection to complete deals at four times EBITDA multiples, these business brokers proved particularly helpful in persuading their clients to complete the transactions on terms that were particularly favorable for Trader.

Because of their subsequent integration into multilayered operations, the individual investment returns arising from specific Landmark and Trader acquisitions are difficult to track. However, the overall results are apparent. From 1964 to 1996, Landmark acquired dozens of cable TV properties for a total investment of less than $100 million, and after receiving nine-figure dividends over its history, it sold its TeleCable progeny to Tele-Communications for $1.4 billion in 1995.[19]

Composed of 145 acquisitions with an aggregate self-funded purchase price of about $1 billion, Trader distributed over $1 billion in additional cash dividends to its partners during its 1991–2006 history, plus the assets and operations of AutoTraderOnline.com in 1999. In 2006, the investment bankers at Lehman Brothers and Morgan Stanley estimated that the residual company would fetch $4 billion to $6 billion (10 to 15 times cash flow) if sold in auction. Although it was subsequently dissolved with a tax-efficient distribution of the highly valued assets to Cox and Landmark, the average return on investment implied by the cash flows earned by the Trader partners would have easily satisfied Benjamin Graham.

Chapter 6

Striking the Deal

"This is an Internet business, son. You can't buy it for peanuts," said the grizzled investor who had used some of his profits from commercial real estate to buy into the burgeoning New Age business just a couple of years earlier.

"I understand. You've got a great enterprise," said Jim Shumadine, Trader's new ventures director. "It would be a tremendous acquisition for us. But you've been losing money for years, and your revenues are still percolating at about $2 million. I'd be misleading you if I suggested we'd value it for anything north of $5 million."

"Five million! Are you nuts? I've probably invested $8.5 million, and I expect to make my money back. It's worth at least $10 million—probably a lot more!"

"I understand. I wish I could be more encouraging."

"And to think I thought I was doing you a favor by calling. You're a friggin' idiot. You don't know what you're doing. I know people at your company, and you'll be lucky to keep your job when your bosses hear about this. But it doesn't matter now. I would rather sell it to the Chinese for a nickel than sell it to you for $5 million."[1]

Many business owners have unrealistic, if not outright delusional, ideas about the value of their businesses. From their perspective, their entrepreneurial enterprise is the most beautiful baby in the pantheon, and its prospects are incalculable. Therefore, when it comes time to sell, they demand a king's ransom, and the acquirer should be ready to accommodate them with buckets of gold.

In addition to steep price expectations, a rollup practitioner must grapple with the reality that the vast majority of business owners are not listing their companies for sale. Either they are happily managing the enterprise or they recognize that their lifestyle is dependent on the generation of cash flow, which is possible only if they continue operating an attractive business. For example, if they are making $250,000 annually from the business, they could not sell it and comfortably invest $1 million (four times their cash flow) to reproduce that income. Because any sale price is usually diminished by capital gains taxes, the prospects for replicating an entrepreneur's familiar cash flow are hampered further, particularly if one looks at U.S. Treasury yields as the most realistic expectation.

The acquirer of multiple small businesses therefore must be prepared to pay up to motivate the majority of operators to sell. However, she cannot pay too much without dramatically increasing the risks and undermining the potential for success. She must therefore be opportunistic and strategic in the process, focusing on acquiring the most value-priced prospects first and waiting patiently for the more expensive companies to lower their price demands. During the process, she will find it critical to devote substantial efforts to cultivating friendly, cooperative relationships with the remaining prospects so that when the time comes, she will be the buyer a business owner turns to when selling becomes attractive.

First Contact

The majority of Trader's deals were initiated by its own employees, who quietly contacted the owners and employed their powers of persuasion to entice otherwise complacent operators to consider selling.

Desirous of completing attractive deals with the promise of a superior return, Trader contacted every desirable prospect, made sure each one understood its interest, cultivated a warm relationship, and waited patiently for the time when an owner became disenchanted with managing the business. That would be the time when Trader could negotiate a more favorable deal.

Cognizant that owners are more prone to welcome entreaties from people who are apparent decision makers, the first contact was almost always made by a senior executive who tried to reflect the genuine interest of an admiring peer. Attempting to inspire an affable exchange to form the foundation of a cooperative association of mutual interests and trust, Trader's representative would provide a succinct upbeat introduction to Trader, followed by a sincere expression of admiration for the apparent success of the prospect's business and the impressive quality of its products. To establish credibility, the executive took care to compliment a specific operational detail as an example of an especially astute component of the business. By comparing it with Trader's own approach, the executive would demonstrate Trader's willingness to share insights, encouraging the prospect to do the same thing. Very quickly, the conversation would turn to a request for an invitation to visit the business to discuss opportunities of mutual interest.

The mission, of course, was to establish a positive rapport and reduce concerns about initiating discussions with a large, perceivably threatening entity, and Trader's entreaties generally produced highly positive results. With friends probably betraying indifference toward his mundane business, the small business owner typically found himself enthralled by someone showing obvious interest in talking about the business. More significantly, Trader exploited the owner's inherent curiosity about the possibilities. Even if not remotely interested in selling, owners understood that circumstances can change and that there is value in developing an understanding of what might be involved in selling a business. Curiosity alone dictates an interest in learning what a company may be worth. At worst, a savvy operator may conclude that he will amass firsthand information about a potential competitor and establish some rapport with its principals. Moreover, those interactions may provide valuable insights and guidance that would help the independent operator enhance his business.

Overcoming Prospects' Suspicion

On rare occasions, a few prospects demonstrated strong paranoia about Trader's executives snooping around their backyard, and a handful proved elusive, refusing to return phone calls. Persistence usually won out, with a dozen weekly calls generally leading to the breakthrough. Occasionally, a "Personal and Confidential" letter addressed to the owner's home provided a brief introduction, followed by a polite request for an appointment to discuss "matters of mutual interest." Alternatively, Trader sought an introduction through a mutual acquaintance or arranged to "stumble" into a meeting at a safe venue such as an industry conference.

Despite such dogged determination, more than one operator remained paranoid about meeting face-to-face. Over four years, Trader's chief financial officer continuously sought an appointment with one photo guide owner, but because Trader had previously acquired her competitor, she was certain the mission was to provide her nemesis with some competitive advantage. Eventually, the polite, persuasive appeals wore down her resistance. Trader ultimately struck a chord by suggesting that like a parent's beloved child, the business would reach the point where marriage to an admiring, well-respected, and prosperous suitor would make sense. Only by cutting the apron strings would the child be likely to achieve its potential, and it would therefore be best to consider merging with a company, such as Trader, that had such promising prospects itself.

For many entrepreneurs, the business is like a child and evokes the same protective instincts. Like a devoted mother, the owners have slaved over its development, almost certainly spending more time with it than they have with their flesh-and-blood children. They have given birth to the new enterprise, nurtured it through infancy, protected and guided it during its troubled years, and brought it to its current maturity. It is therefore natural for owners to be concerned about relinquishing management responsibility. Accordingly, the acquirer should be as tactful to curry favor as any suitor seeking the hand of the king's beloved princess.

Failure to understand these parental dynamics causes some acquirers to err by assuming a threatening stance to compel an owner to sell: "If you don't sell to us on our terms, we'll move into your market anyway, leaving you in the dust with nothing." Even if it is not stated in such reprehensible terms, an acquirer's bluster can easily be interpreted by the operator as implying that sentiment, and the operator's instinctive response will prove inimical to the cultivation and negotiation process. Although a very few weak or disillusioned operators may be bullied into accepting a deal, most will become defensive and some will terminate the discussions entirely. At a minimum, a condescending or insulting harangue will impede the development of the trust and cooperation necessary to facilitate the free exchange of desirable evaluation materials and create a barrier to affable compromises during negotiation.

As the familiar adage advises, "You can attract more flies with honey than with vinegar." Therefore, Trader's emissaries tried to cultivate friendly, supportive relationships to encourage prospects not only to contact Trader first when the time was ripe for a sale but also to sell directly to Trader without soliciting competing bidders. Friends call friends for advice, and they usually earn a preferential seat at any bargaining table.

But befriending prospects is not always possible. As described in Chapter 3, Stuart Arnold, the founder of *Auto Trader*, proved difficult to cultivate, and despite conscientious efforts, Trader's leadership failed to develop a meaningful relationship with him. Although this was mostly due to Arnold's ingrained independent streak, he felt somewhat threatened by the larger company treading on his turf. In early 1987, Barney Oldfield first attempted to contact Arnold, but his periodic calls were uniformly ignored until a year later. Calling Oldfield's home late one night, Arnold rejected the congenial appeal to meet, asserting his strong suspicion of Oldfield's true intentions and expressing disdain for Landmark's incursions into the markets of his licensees. While reassuring Arnold that there were only benefits to be gained from confidential discussions, Arnold remained aloof, and Oldfield concluded that it would take time to modify his opinion. The same conclusion was expressed by several *Auto Trader* licensees with whom Landmark leadership had close relationships, and Landmark, with fervent hope, enlisted those licensees to encourage Arnold at least to consider a personal meeting to initiate a friendship.

It was Cox Enterprises' Bob Musselman, however, who eventually succeeded in breaking through to Arnold. A consummate deal maker, Musselman was then a top executive of Cox's newspaper division, and like Oldfield, he left countless unreturned messages at Arnold's Clearwater office, pleading for a call back. When the secretary eventually told Musselman that Arnold would not return the call unless he knew the specific purpose, Musselman relented, and she dutifully wrote down "He wants to buy your business" on the pink message pad. Involved at the time in distracting litigation over a domestic matter, Arnold found the prospect of selling to "anyone except Landmark" to be of potential interest, and Musselman was the perfect ambassador to cultivate that interest. Though he had risen from the accounting ranks to his more entrepreneurial role at Cox, Musselman displayed much of the verve and risk-taking character that appealed to Arnold. Like Arnold, Musselman enjoyed nights in Las Vegas casinos, and after an evening of drinks and good food, he willingly joined Arnold and his cronies for a late night to continue the discussions. After months of negotiations, Arnold finally agreed to join with Cox to acquire a handful of his licensees as a prelude to selling his own operations. For six months, Cox and Arnold worked together behind the scenes to purchase the operations from eager sellers in San Antonio, Detroit, and Atlanta, in addition to the 50 percent of the Los Angeles business that Arnold did not already own. Throughout that period, Landmark remained clueless that Cox was behind Arnold's rollup.

Handling a Selling Torrent

When Arnold announced the sale of his company to Cox Enterprises, Landmark executives were astounded and crestfallen. While carefully cultivating a handful of small acquisitions in the classified advertising industry, Cox had captured the prize by buying the founder and licensor of the *Auto Trader* brand, along with several of its largest operations. They knew it was time to scramble to accelerate their acquisition efforts before Cox won even more attractive targets.

Immediately after the announcement, several licensees invited Arnold to meet in Las Vegas to discuss similar opportunities for themselves. After receiving Arnold's acceptance, they extended the same invitation to Landmark's deal maker, who finagled a tour of the Phoenix licensee's operations two days beforehand. After discreet meetings with prospective sellers from Pittsburgh and Cincinnati, he joined those sellers on their flight to Las Vegas, where he met privately with the owners of operations in San Diego and Seattle—all before Arnold even arrived in gambling's Glitter Gulch.

Of course, his invitation to and participation in preliminary meetings were orchestrated by the licensees, who were conniving to develop a bidding war for their operations. They had, in fact, also invited John and Louise McBane, who had begun their own rollup of *Auto Trader* publications in Canada with the financial assistance of Torstar Corporation, one of that country's largest media companies.

Upon arriving in Las Vegas, Arnold immediately joined the assembled licensees for an open forum conducted in a comfortable salon at the Desert Inn. Smiling broadly, he glad-handed everyone, and after a few introductory remarks, he proudly announced that Cox would welcome the acquisition of all their publications. But when he projected offers of "about one times revenues," the group became derisive. They had already been promised higher valuations from Landmark, and the licensees waited greedily to hear from the McBanes, who were arriving by stretch limousine from the airport with their own entreaties.

The next afternoon, Landmark hosted a luncheon for the licensees at Howard Hughes's bungalow. Acquired from the Hughes estate by Landmark as a part of the adjoining KLAS-TV broadcast operations, the surprisingly modest two-bedroom cottage included a screening room that had been converted for dining, and the venue represented a compelling attraction to assure attendance (as if the smell of big money wasn't alone sufficient).

It was big money that generated the flood of transactions that followed over the next year. Until that Las Vegas meeting, Landmark and Cox had anticipated that diligent cultivation of prospects would produce transactions at levels equal to approximately one times revenues — 1.5 times at most — representing multiples ranging from four to six times EBITDA. But both companies had already divined the upside potential of those businesses, and within a month prices quickly accelerated to two times revenues, causing the McBanes to return to Canada to focus their efforts on the rest of the world. But that multiple didn't hold for the more patient licensees who let the bidding continue. When the level reached three times revenues, almost every licensee interested in selling quickly came into the fold of either Cox or Landmark.

As a Virginia-based company with a divisional headquarters in Kentucky, Landmark concluded that with rapid consolidation hyping valuations, it made sense to concentrate on solidifying its position in the Midwest, Mid-Atlantic, and Northeast. Its deal makers instantly sprang into action to acquire the *Auto Trader* affiliates in Washington, D.C., Richmond, and Norfolk, and to contribute his clout and authority to the effort, Landmark's president, Dick Barry, flew to Cincinnati to help his divisional manager clinch a deal with that city's publishers before Cox and Arnold could get organized.

Then, a few days later, Conrad Hall, having succeeded the recently retired Bill Diederich, met Landmark's divisional CFO in Washington. During an all-day session, they remained glued to the owner, fearful that he would otherwise return one of the numerous phone messages being left by Arnold throughout the day. Capitalizing on the owner's perception that Arnold had previously snubbed him, the Landmark team worked diligently to persuade him that this was the time to capture the biggest premium for his business, and by six-thirty that evening they found themselves sighing in relief as they executed a letter of intent to acquire the Washington *Auto Trader*. Though there was much to be accomplished before the actual closing, the letter succinctly itemized all the financial details, terms, and conditions and stipulated that the agreement was binding, obligating the two parties to complete the transaction.

To accelerate a quick decision, they employed a clever ploy that achieved 100 percent success in enticing immediate execution of their binding letter of intent. After carefully discussing the boilerplate terms and conditions of the transaction in painstaking detail, they would quickly handwrite the key financial terms on a notepad and then present the full letter along with a $100,000 certificate of deposit to bind the deal. Four times the amount of Cox's rumored binder check, that certificate was an obvious psychological gimmick, but it delivered the crystal-clear message that Landmark was serious. More important, the amount caused the sellers to salivate, and they hungrily signed Landmark's letter of intent that day, committing themselves to selling to Landmark and simultaneously forestalling any discussions with an alternative buyer.

Notably, though specified as the binding payment, the certificate actually required both the buyer's and the seller's signature to be cashed at the time of closing, and Landmark was therefore protected from loss if the deal cratered. Always producing the desired signature, the device was subsequently dubbed Landmark's "lucky CD."

Divide and Conquer

With such intensive interest, Landmark very quickly came to the disappointing conclusion that it could not prevent Cox from making its own deals with the majority of licensees. Arnold's long associations as a licensor provided Cox with the inside track with most, and Cox quickly demonstrated that it was similarly prepared to pay premium prices to meet or beat other offers. To ensure that Cox remained distracted while Landmark acquired nonaffiliates, Landmark's team implemented diversionary tactics by collecting evaluation materials from every licensee, phoning those sellers regularly to express continued interest and coaching them to extract the best price by having both Cox and Landmark compete. Although it never planned to present each prospect with its lucky CD, it maintained the appearance that it was prepared to do so. It not only wanted Cox to remain diverted, it also wanted Cox to consume as much of its acquisition capital as possible on those deals with *Auto Trader* licensees.

With Cox focused on consolidating the remaining *Auto Trader* licensees, Landmark turned its attention to all the other prospects. For three years, Landmark had cultivated relationships with similar classified advertising publishers throughout the country, and some remained unaware that there were potentially three acquirers for their businesses. While continuing its diversionary campaign among most of the other *Auto Trader* licensees, Landmark began an all-out push to conclude deals for those unaffiliated publications in another dozen cities.

Of course, the speed with which those deals were concluded was very much a result of the willingness of both Cox and Landmark to pay premium prices. Values actually had tripled in the year or so since the publishers were first approached, and with so many affiliates selling, there was a bandwagon effect that inspired every publisher to give serious consideration to selling. Most had been in the business for at least 10 years, and few had received any expression of interest from another buyer. Postponing a sale therefore created the risk of losing out on collecting the apparent premium, and with two substantive players having joined the operating fray, there was a clear implication that the competitive operating environment was destined to intensify, potentially placing increasing market risk on the future of an entrepreneur's business.

This rapid consolidation also benefited both Cox and Landmark. Although they both regretted the price escalation, they perceived these publications as substantially undeveloped gems that warranted the high premium. Scale and integration promised to deliver enhanced profits, and adoption of best practices seemed to assure that superior returns would arise from these stepped-up investments. Therefore, consolidation now simply accelerated the achievement of the long-term benefits.

This willingness to pay fat prices was a marked departure from Landmark's more conservative valuation practices. Despite encouragement from Frank Batten to make any reasonable deal while the window of opportunity was wide open, there seemed no particular urgency before Cox's entry, and patience seemed to promise the delivery of better and better deals. The particularly attractive *Tradin' Times* acquisition included relatively underdeveloped publications in seven major metropolitan markets, including Chicago, Philadelphia, Detroit, and Atlanta, and that transaction was completed for less than seven times trailing EBITDA and a much, much lower multiple of the projected first year's cash flow. Subsequent deals were completed for five and then four times cash flows.

Instead of gaining points for striking a lot of deals, the goal had become skewed by the mission of demonstrating prowess at negotiating increasingly attractive bargains. Striving to impress upper management with his particularly astute negotiating acumen, Landmark's divisional deal maker had found himself months earlier scheming to complete the acquisition of the New Orleans *News on Wheels* automotive photo guide for little more than two times EBITDA, and the consequences were predictable. Upon receipt of Landmark's miserly offer, the seller was both insulted and disheartened. He discontinued talking directly to any of Landmark's representatives, referring all contacts to his accounting manager, and quickly negotiated an alternative transaction with another company, which paid approximately four times EBITDA.

The loss of the New Orleans transaction proved highly instructive because it slammed home the fact that when a particularly good deal is achievable, there is far too much risk of losing out by striving to get an attractive bargain, particularly when there are competing buyers on the sidelines.

With that riveting lesson, Landmark's leadership thought that the opportunity to create a national network would slip away unless it dramatically loosened its purse strings. Resolving not to allow its conservative bent impede capture of a generous share of the auto photo guide business, Frank Batten urged aggressive pursuit and repeatedly authorized increasing price multiples to win attractive deals.

Deal without Due Diligence

So determined was Landmark to conclude a few enticing deals that its negotiators began violating its customary rigid rules on completing a rigorous due diligence review before closing. Customarily, before even making an offer, Landmark's analysts would carefully review the prospect's last three years' tax returns, interim financial statements, summary circulation and distribution reports, and a variety of operational statistics, contracts, and other documents. Only then would it make an offer, and if successful in negotiating a deal, its team would then complete a meticulous due diligence review to solidify its understanding of the target. However, to acquire the Chicago *Auto Mart*, Landmark agreed to close without inspecting any of the customary materials.

Upon its acquisition of the *Tradin' Times* group of publications in 1986, Landmark concluded that its previously thriving Chicago classified ad magazine was losing a disturbing amount of market share to that city's *Auto Mart* photo guide. Inspired by Arnold's *Auto Trader*, *Auto Mart* had been founded less than 10 years earlier by Todd Hoffman. However, after its launch, Todd's Florida business demanded more attention, and he returned south, essentially giving the magazine to his twentysomething entrepreneurial son, Mark Hoffman.

Under Mark's direction, the guide developed impressive traction. Running his organization like the club football team he proudly sponsored,

Mark was an extraordinarily competitive operator who drove his staff relentlessly to win. Like a football coach, he pushed every member to perform at peak, providing drills to hone skills and measuring performance by daily results. To capture new business, he worked side by side with his sales team to develop a playbook of winning tactics that were rigorously implemented to achieve their goals. With that attitude, Hoffman represented a fearsome competitor who had the best prospects of dominating the Chicago photo guide market; that attitude made him loath to sell to his unworthy competitor. Accordingly, he had no interest in sharing proprietary financial and operational materials that could give his opponent a potential advantage. Despite repeated generally friendly phone conversations, Mark continuously refused to discuss any operating details, rejecting Landmark's repeated appeals to allow its entry into any of his offices.

Landmark was nevertheless desperate to acquire his business, and its research revealed that the business, though Mark's baby, was actually deemed a Hoffman family asset. To clinch the deal, Landmark's president, Dick Barry, took the lead and arranged a personal meeting with Mark's father, Todd. Over a convivial lunch in Chicago with Todd, Barry waxed eloquently about how impressed he was with Mark's success and management acumen. When another Landmark visitor joined the chorus by saying its managers clearly had much to learn from Mark, Barry deftly opined that Mark could probably learn valuable lessons from working in a senior position at Landmark. A stint inside a large company would give the now 30-plus-year-old Mark something like a graduate degree in organizational management, coupled with more mundane but critically valuable experience with budgeting, long-range planning, and institutional strategy. Perhaps, Barry suggested, this was the time for Mark to take a new tack to gain exposure in a larger professional organization while permitting the family investment to be redeployed into something less risky. Todd nodded approvingly, quickly noting that if it was sold, almost every penny would go to Mark. Still, there was merit in capturing the premium now while giving Mark the insider's tour within a large corporation. Smiling with satisfaction, Todd agreed to discuss the matter with Mark, but he asserted that he couldn't advise Mark to disclose a lot of proprietary information. Barry nodded appreciatively, agreeing that Landmark would do its best to compose a compelling offer with whatever information the family felt comfortable sharing.

Although it was clear that Mark was unprepared to relinquish his business, he did meet with Barry, who flew to Chicago to nurture that personal relationship and apply his persuasive skills, and Mark eventually bowed to the pressures applied by his family, agreeing to sell. In the final negotiation session in the office of his attorney, Mark indicated general acceptance of the terms but then asked about his company-owned Corvette. As Dick Barry explained, "I told Mark we'd give him the car, and that clinched the deal. ... Afterwards our corporate counsel, Becky Powhatan, expressed her outrage. We're giving him all that money, how could we give him a Corvette? And I explained by noting that, first, at Landmark we don't provide company cars; and, second, don't sweat the details to get the deal done."[2]

Despite having sweetened the deal with a cherry Corvette on top, Mark steadfastly refused to provide any insider materials about his company, requiring Landmark to develop its own assessment from public sources and personal market observations. The only financial disclosure Mark made was that his annual sales for the prior nine months exceeded $2.2 million, and on the basis of its understanding of its own operating margins, Landmark eventually agreed on a price, structured as an asset sale, excluding assumption of any liability existing before the sale, with the majority of the cash paid at closing. Before executing the definitive agreement and minutes before Landmark wired the money to complete the deal, Hoffman provided Landmark with an unaudited financial statement to verify his earlier verbal representation.

After the closing, Landmark's team confirmed its estimates and remained content with its deal. Though Mark participated as a full-time consultant during the following year, he quickly demonstrated his interest in pursuing alternative opportunities, and Landmark proceeded accordingly, nonetheless gratified that the business's revenues and earnings continued to grow at impressive rates.

If Landmark had not possessed such a thorough understanding of the operational costs of similar businesses, it probably would have been unable to develop the requisite comfort level to conclude that deal, and it would not have proceeded without its high confidence in the future performance of that still underdeveloped publishing business. Its leaders nonetheless breathed a long sigh of relief after closing, pleased they would not have to worry about Cox subsequently acquiring Hoffman's fast-growing magazine, which could easily have undermined Landmark's established position in Chicago.

Divorce as a Catalyst

Although warm family dynamics made the acquisition of the Chicago *Auto Mart* possible, sometimes the opposite factor motivates a sale, and divorce represents one of the prime catalysts for many transactions. A husband and wife often work as a team to found successful companies, but their respective commitments wane dramatically during periods of marital distress. When the marriage disintegrates, they often find it difficult to manage the business effectively, and as a principal financial asset, the business value becomes subject to division to satisfy the requirements of the divorce decree. Because spouses are unlikely to agree on valuation much less have the free cash required to fund the buyout of the partner's interest, the obvious alternative is to sell to a third party. This occurred on several occasions during Landmark's and Trader's various rollups.

Unfortunately, although the impending divorce might trigger negotiations, it rarely facilitated a quick closing. Inevitably, the marital squabbles spilled into the acquisition process and produced a wide variety of complications that created barriers to a smooth transaction. On two occasions, Landmark had to schedule the transactions to coincide with the completion of the divorce decree, and that led to several contentious standoffs during which one spouse tried to use the sale as a way to gain negotiating leverage on the marriage's division of assets. The worst example occurred when one of the spouses refused to sign any of the sale documents until the other relented on key components of the divorce settlement.

In another case, the husband held 100 percent of the company stock and apparently succeeded in keeping the potential for a sale secret from his spouse. Accordingly, he refused to finalize the terms of a sale until the divorce settlement was concluded, and that meant a delay of several months.

Negotiating Team

As indicated by the examples discussed earlier, Landmark and Trader did not rely on a single person to orchestrate negotiations. The involvement of several senior executives facilitated broader coverage of the prospect universe and dramatically accelerated the rollup process. Although its divisional CFO's efforts were devoted virtually full-time to cultivating relationships and nurturing acquisitions in 1988, it was impossible for one person to initiate all the desirable contacts, cultivate developing relationships, and juggle the prudent interactions necessary to succeed with the dozens of prospects.

Although the periodic inclusion of Dick Barry provided the irresistibly persuasive clout of the company's president to the process, there were others who provided similarly instrumental support. Conrad Hall, of course, was a regular presence in almost every one of the early transactions. In addition, Barney Oldfield shouldered important responsibility for building rapport with a dozen targets, allowing Landmark to leverage his remarkable talents with impressive results. Though mostly retired, Oldfield had polished his negotiating skills and tactful charm during the era when Landmark's TeleCable sought the award of government-authorized cable TV franchises. For the first several years after the Winston–Salem acquisition, Oldfield initiated contact with scores of prospects, visiting several particularly attractive targets to develop friendly relationships, which subsequently were maintained through periodic contact in person, by phone, and by letter. So endearing was his demeanor and magnetism that during the drawn-out cultivation process, one of the owners became so attached that she invited him to sit at the family table during her daughter's wedding reception a year or so before offering the business for sale.

Contributing a handful of personalities to the relationship-building process also addressed the need to accommodate the varied personalities of the myriad owners. Although Oldfield's persona as the favorite uncle earned privileged entrée among some, it may have repelled a few. Clearly, the meeting of Dick Barry and Todd Hoffman proved fortuitous as the two fathers could discuss what might be best for the adult children and the family, and Barry's treatment of Todd Hoffman as a peer certainly led to a closer affiliation as a trustworthy associate.

As a comparatively youthful-looking thirtysomething, Landmark's divisional CFO was usually much younger than the majority of the owners, and the baggage of his MBA education presented the risk that he would be deemed an egghead whippersnapper by the hardscrabble entrepreneurs who had received their education from the school of hard knocks. However, having been well tutored by Diederich and others, he demonstrated an exuberance founded on a genuine appreciation for the owners' accomplishments. His early years of commercial client work in the insurance industry had given him keen insight into the difficulties of small business operations, and he openly expressed his admiration of these owners, their entrepreneurial spirit, and the management acumen underlying their success in a turbulent business environment. A few thought of him as the son they wished they had to bequeath the business to. Otherwise, he was content if they simply understood that he had a genuine interest in the business, shared Landmark's high hopes for the business's continued success, and was a trustworthy professional.

Inevitably, some owners became irritated by or simply dismissive of one of Landmark's emissaries, and it was therefore good to have another player assume the lead. One negotiator failed to make the desired progress with the owner of five publications serving several Midwest cities, and it was clearly a matter of a lack of personal rapport. Having built several prosperous businesses through dogged determination after a brief military stint, the older gentleman dismissed Landmark's divisional representative as "too corporate," too focused on budgets and annual performance plans. His Porsche and airplane were badges of his success and adventurous spirit, and he disdained someone who had found it necessary to attend graduate school to learn a few business lessons.

Landmark's Conrad Hall therefore stepped in, and his charm won immediate attention and acceptance. An engineering graduate of Virginia Military Institute, Hall was instantly perceived as honorable and trustworthy. Both had built printing plants, and that served as the source for animated conversation; the two quickly became affable colleagues who shared a passion for history, exchanging stories and books about Robert E. Lee. In conversations with Hall, the transformation of the owner was astonishing. Previously, he had always been curt and uncommunicative, making it difficult to maintain a dialogue, but Hall had sparked the man's interest. That newfound affinity proved invaluable during the discussions that followed. Although the owner's business valuation was eventually accommodated, significant complications arose from marital issues and environmental problems with the real estate. Those complications required the patient attention of amiable associates who respected each other and demonstrated mutual consideration of the other party's issues.

When Deals Become Difficult to Close

Despite the best efforts of the varied personalities, there were some deals that just could not get done, and that usually resulted from their overly high prices. Several of Cox's deals to acquire Arnold's licensees rose to prices beyond Landmark's comfort level, and it abandoned serious efforts to compete, urging the sellers to get as much as possible from Cox and hoping there would be less available to Cox to compete for the deals Landmark believed were essential. But some were priced too high for any buyer demanding a reasonable return on investment, and some of the sellers simply found it unbearable to sign on the dotted line, the most notable of which was in San Diego.

More successful than any other of Arnold's licensees, the San Diego *Auto Trader* was deemed by both Cox and Landmark to be the best of breed, a true gem to acquire. Its founder, Dave Altomare, had taken Arnold's relatively underdeveloped concept and transformed it over its first decade into the largest-revenue, highest-profit example of the concept in the United States. Within that market, there was no question about the best medium to buy or sell a used car: It was Altomare's *Auto Trader*. Also, its level of customer service was without peer in the industry.

With its focus on acquisitions in the Midwest and the East, Landmark disappointingly deferred to Cox to bid that property in, and Cox's Bob Musselman expended every effort to do just that. Eventually agreeing to a rich premium, Cox proceeded efficiently to complete its due diligence and finalize the acquisition contracts. The day came to close and the eight-figure purchase price was scheduled to be wired, but Altomare refused to sign the closing documents. He had experienced anguished weeks since agreeing to the deal and had tossed endlessly in bed the night before. The prospect of signing made him physically ill, and he could not be persuaded to proceed by friends, family, staff, or advisors. In fact, it took the passage of another 10 years and the threatening strength of Internet classifieds to bring Altomare back to the table to conclude a deal.

Landmark had a similar experience with its Lexington, Kentucky, acquisition. Though a small market, Lexington boasted an extraordinarily impressive example of the auto photo guide. The founder, Maurice Huber, had studied Arnold's concept and concluded that it could be applied to provide advertising coverage over a broad geography of comparatively rural markets served by an abundance of competing weekly newspapers. To get the best deal for a vehicle, consumers would travel 40 miles to neighboring counties if they had an economical medium to facilitate the buying or selling process, and Huber satisfied that need with his *Metro Piston* photo guide, a publication serving all the small towns and counties within 80 miles of his Lexington base.

Having printed his magazine at one of Landmark's printing plants almost since its inception, Huber had a close relationship with several Landmark executives, and once acquisition prices increased to attractive levels, he agreed to sell and signed Landmark's "binding" letter of intent. Before the definitive agreement could be produced, however, he changed his mind. With Conrad Hall assuming the role of conciliatory friend striving to define what might close the deal, Landmark's divisional CFO took the role of the bad cop by stressing that Huber had a moral, if not legal, obligation to complete the deal. Huber bristled at the thought and walked away. Months passed, and through Hall's personal efforts, Huber eventually agreed to a sweetened price. When the day came to close, Hall and another Landmark executive converged on the offices of Huber's attorney to sign the closing documents. However, there were problems, the attorney said, and for eight hours the Landmark team waited to bring the deal to resolution while Huber and his brother remained behind closed doors. Having demonstrated reasonable patience all day, Hall finally notified the lawyers that it was time to go. Claiming that the company's pilots could wait no longer, Hall said that the deal was off if Huber didn't sign in the next few minutes. The lawyers began to scurry, and as Hall entered the law firm's elevator, he executed the last of the documents on the back of his briefcase, closing the deal.

Chapter 7

Structuring the Deal

"I can't believe it!" exclaimed the jovial uncle. "A $3 million football contract!"

"Uh huh! It's awesome, isn't it?" said his exuberant hulking nephew, demonstrating the somewhat dulled speech of a defensive tackle who'd taken a few too many hits.

"Yes, boy, it is. I must admit, when you stopped coming off the bench this season, I figured that was pretty much the death of your hopes for the NFL. So tell me, how'd it happen?"

"Dude, I thought I was heading down the tubes too. But then this agent comes up to me at the Hofbräu last week and says he seen something in me. He says he thinks he can get me a contract if I let him represent me. When he says he'd want 15 percent, I tell him, 'I'm down with that. Whatta I have to lose—have at it.' Then, just two days later, this agent guy calls me up, all hyper. He said it was a piece of cake. I thought I'd bust a gut when he told me it was for three mil! He said it was so easy, he felt guilty about taking the 15 percent. Instead, he says, 'Give me $10,000 up front and we'll be free and clear.' I get the money from my parents, hand him the cash, sign on the dotted line, and here it is: my football contract for three million smackeroos! Yee-hah!!!!"

"Wow!" cried the uncle, studying the contract. "Look at that. Sure enough. It says $3 million—$3 a year for a million years."[1]

In the realm of striking deals, it is sometimes tempting to agree to pay the seller's asking price, especially when you retain the right to set the terms like the scurrilous agent in our parable. As its sadly deluded jock almost certainly concluded later, value is not just how much is paid but also how it is paid, particularly how quickly. In truth, if you could find a $60 perpetual bond yielding just 5 percent, it would produce the $3 interest necessary to fund the football contract's payments, and we suspect that the agent, with the $10,000 already in his hands, will never care whether the nephew ever plays a day, assuming the agent even sticks around to ensure the $3 annual disbursements.

Particularly in the realm of small transactions, it is critical to understand the human elements that affect the ability to clinch a sweetheart deal. Unlike the megadeals trumpeted in the media, the majority are dependent on the individual perspective of a single owner who may be easily swayed by an astute negotiator.

Although nobody will ever be as foolish as that football player, very few people have much experience negotiating these kinds of transactions, and it is rare for small entrepreneurs to seek professional guidance and inconceivable that they will solicit the far more sophisticated advice offered by Wall Street investment bankers. Self-confident and proud of their success, they are comfortable making decisions without professional assistance. In fact, Trader found that they may not even consult an accountant or attorney until after they have signed a letter of intent. Regardless, because those advisors are unlikely to have any familiarity with business valuation in the seller's industry segment, they seldom have any meaningful guidance to offer. Like the business owners, Trader discovered, the advisors were typically harried hands-on professionals, and they usually perceived their key role to be a facilitator of their clients' plans, conscious that those self-made people disliked criticism and tended to express irritation about excess billable hours.

Employ a Skilled Negotiator

When developing deals with those owners, Trader concluded that there was much to be gained by leveraging the talents of a skilled negotiator who was sensitive to the quirks of human nature and employed the best tactics to capture tangible benefits and preferential pricing for the businesses that were acquired.

Even a novice understands that sellers are almost never firm on price, but it is the experienced negotiator who is comfortable with the required give-and-take of haggling to produce the most advantageous deal. In the early days of acquiring cable franchises, one of TeleCable's executives quickly developed a reputation for simply offering the amount previously approved by Frank Batten. When the prospect responded with a counteroffer, the executive found it necessary to request an increased authorization, shattering his credibility as an astute deal maker.

However, one of Bill Diederich's regular admonitions was to "beware of what you offer, for they may accept." Although acceptance of a first offer may be a desirable outcome, it suggests that the buyer could have gotten a better deal, and he'll kick himself for having left too much on the table.

Although many buyers may not be guilty of making compelling first offers or be too quick to accede to sellers' demands, few conduct negotiations in a manner that retains the respectful and cooperative spirit that best facilitates an advantageous deal.

Early on, one of Landmark's managers regularly made the mistake of striving to persuade the owner that her business was not worth the asking price: "I'd like to pay what you ask, but your business just isn't worth it for these reasons." The supporting analyses might have been rationally compelling, but they led to unproductive debates, with the seller arguing that Landmark's representative either didn't understand or was sadly mistaken. In essence, the seller interpreted the comments as suspicious objections, denigrating her business, operating results, and prospects. Instead of producing a deal, this tactic therefore tended to make the seller defensive, creating another barrier to agreement and evoking a desire for an alternative buyer who wasn't so critical and insistent on a discount for a variety of specious reasons.

A more successful tactic was demonstrated by the shrewd Conrad Hall. Hall would focus on demonstrating how much Landmark had struggled already to justify its offer. When the seller presented reasons to increase the price, Hall would quickly agree that those justifications were already incorporated in the valuation. Displaying genuine interest and sincerity, Hall would have the seller provide painstaking details and then confirm that he had considered each item and agreed unequivocally with the seller's assessment. The discussion would then return to the financial terms instead of being diverted by divisive, counterproductive, and usually irrelevant arguments about the differing values.

Part of Hall's enviable skill was that he remained acutely attuned to the seller's body language and verbal tics, which provided clues about how much accommodation was needed. Intuitively, he would capitalize on the various "tells" while displaying a consistent attitude of interest and charm, increasing the seller's trust and willingness to complete a deal with Hall's honorable organization.

Many owners start out with an irrationally high expectation about the worth of their businesses, and they must be handled tactfully. During Trader's efforts to acquire a variety of Internet business, it was routinely dismayed by absurd price expectations. Although it was purposeless to pursue most of those deals, some were so attractive that Trader's management made special efforts to cultivate a deal over an extended period. One seller group suggested that its business was worth $20 million. While expressing admiration and complimenting their success, Trader's representative suggested there was no need to waste the sellers' time because Trader's value was "south of $5 million." Though it popped their balloon, the "ballpark" estimation did not undermine continued friendly communications, and a year later, when valuations had collapsed, Trader recommenced the process, ultimately agreeing to a $4 million transaction.

A skilled practitioner also knows that sellers often negotiate against themselves. Subject to the compulsions of "deal psych," an inexperienced seller becomes impatient, reveals too much, and ultimately relents too quickly. After receiving a seller's higher counteroffer, Trader's representative took an arbitrary recess but returned to the negotiating table 30 minutes later, prepared to split the difference. However, he first urged acceptance of the earlier terms. The seller, instead of reiterating his counteroffer, surprisingly accepted Trader's terms, saving Trader the 5 percent it had almost offered to sweeten the deal.

Asset Purchase Versus Stock Sale

In the vast majority of acquisitions, the principal payment is made for either the assets or the stock of the company. A stock purchase is literally a purchase of the shares of the company, inclusive of everything included on the balance sheet as well as all the known and unknown liabilities and assets associated with the legal entity. An asset purchase is the more selective acquisition of just the components specified by the purchase agreement, and the purchase price is paid directly into the company, whose stock remains in the hands of the original owners.

For the uninitiated, characterizing a transaction as an asset or stock deal may seem inconsequential, but there are both risk management and tax considerations that strongly argue in favor of asset deals.

From the perspective of risk management, an asset deal can protect the buyer from liabilities arising from the business's past operations. In contrast, when stock is purchased, the buyer assumes all the acquired company's known and unknown liabilities (generally characterized as contingent liabilities). If, for example, the company dumped toxins onto its property five years earlier, the acquirer of the company's stock would have to pay all the subsequent penalties and costs of remediation. Rarely identified before closing, the costs of such contingent liabilities can prove devastating, as Bank of America discovered after its $4 billion takeover of Countrywide Financial. At just one-sixth of its prior value, Countrywide appeared to be a screaming bargain, but since the 2008 acquisition, its contingent liabilities arising from soured home loans have generated huge costs for mandated loan repurchases, court judgments, and penalties. In the first half of 2011 alone, Bank of America paid out $12.7 billion to settle Countrywide-related claims, and in September 2011, the Federal Housing Finance Agency filed suit for restitution of another $26.6 billion in Countrywide loans sold to Fannie Mae and Freddie Mac.[2]

When a buyer acquires assets from a company, the selling company remains in existence, and the selling shareholders retain the legal obligation for the remaining liabilities it incurred during its past operating history. Thus insulated, the buyer has legal protection from exposure to past liabilities, providing reasonable assurance that he or she will not have to absorb legacy costs relating to the company.

Although few stock deals expose acquirers to significant undisclosed legacy costs like those of the Countrywide deal, the cost of every acquisition will be affected by the buyer's choice between an asset or stock deal, particularly as a result of tax considerations. With enactment of the Tax Reform Act of 1987, acquiring assets instead of stock provides the acquirer with a direct government subsidy in the form of tax deductions, effectively permitting most deals to be completed at a significant discount from their nominal face value.

Under current tax regulations, the buyer is permitted to amortize the full cost of an asset acquisition as a tax-deductible expense. Alternatively, if he buys stock, he can deduct only those values remaining on the company's books at the time of acquisition, and among small business operators that could be almost nothing. For example, by structuring a $10 million acquisition as an asset deal, the buyer can deduct the $10 million over time as an expense, sheltering $10 million of future profits from taxes and producing approximately $4 million in tax savings accrued over the maximum 15-year amortization period, assuming a combined state and federal tax rate of 40 percent. Assuming a discount rate of 5 percent to adjust for the time value of money, the resulting $2.5 million in "net present value" savings implies that the $10 million deal actually cost only $7.5 million, an effective discount of over 25 percent. A $10 million stock deal, however, will most likely cost the full $10 million payment because the book value of the company's assets may already be close to zero, providing no tax shelters. The true cost of the stock deal can therefore be 33 percent more ($10 million versus the after-tax net of $7.5 million), effectively giving the buyer the ability to pay 33 percent more in an asset sale instead of a stock sale.

Fortunately, most small owners have little reason to prefer a stock deal to an asset deal. Because their enterprises typically are organized as proprietorships, partnerships, Subchapter S corporations, or limited liability companies, the proceeds from an asset sale are subject to the same tax impacts applicable to a stock sale.

Unfortunately, for companies that have been legally organized as C corporations (C-corps), there are onerous double tax consequences that penalize their shareholders in an asset sale. First, the corporation has to pay approximately 40 percent state and federal tax on its capital gains from the asset sale, and then, on their receipt of the residual cash, the shareholders have to pay tax on their gains (a combined state and federal total of about 20 percent). Assuming the owner's investment in the C-corp had a $0 basis, an asset sale with a $10 million capital gain would net just $4.8 million after the double tax impact, whereas a stock sale would net $8 million—67 percent more! Shareholders of C-corps are therefore loath to agree to an asset sale.

The tax on asset sales for a C-corp represents a compelling justification for entrepreneurs to elect an alternative form of legal organization for their enterprises. If the company was established as a C-corp, its owners should consider reorganization under another form if a future sale is contemplated. Regrettably, the reorganization cannot be performed contemporaneously with a sale because regulations dictate that it will be treated as a C-corp transaction for tax purposes regardless of an interim change. According to Internal Revenue Service rules, the entity will usually need to have completed its reorganization at least 10 years previously to escape the double tax penalty.

A prior reorganization, however, may present the opportunity for an alternative structure to capitalize on the benefits of an asset sale versus a stock sale. While assessing a free photo guide operation in the South, Trader discovered that although currently a limited liability company, the organization had been a C-corp during the first 8 years of its 10-year existence. Fearing that the asset sale would not qualify for preferential tax treatment, the seller's tax advisors suggested an installment sale with the majority of the purchase price payable sometime after the tenth anniversary of the company's conversion to LLC status. The implied payout after eight years, of course, represented an advantageous deferred payment, providing financing benefits if the seller accepted a rate lower than Trader's alternative long-term bank borrowing costs. Although the seller argued that the deferred payment should earn interest several points above the applicable Treasury bill, Trader ultimately persuaded the seller to accept the 30-day LIBOR as the rate because the seller was saving so much in taxes.

Except for this installment sale strategy, the only other tactic Trader employed to mitigate some of the cost of stock deals was to persuade the seller to apportion as much of the total payments as possible to nonstock payments such as noncompetes, employment agreements, and earnouts. The total amount of those alternative payments could be deducted, sheltering profits from taxation and producing a net present value discount of about 25 percent of every dollar so allocated. However, because those payments incurred higher ordinary income tax rates (approximately 40 percent combined state and federal), sellers negotiated aggressively to maximize the proportion allocated to the stock price, which incurred a combined tax cost of about 20 percent.

Mitigating C-Corp Exposure

Regrettably, most large, long-established companies are organized as C-corps, and the purchase of stock is the only practical option. The loss of the opportunity to amortize the purchase price increases the net cost of the deal and reduces the potential return on investment, and the risk of exposure to contingent liabilities further complicates the transaction. To mitigate this exposure, Trader tried to obtain some protection in stock transactions by negotiating indemnity provisions in the acquisition agreement. When the original stock was closely held by just a few sellers, Trader persuaded many to remain individually liable for contingent liabilities (ideally in perpetuity but occasionally for a period limited to five years). Although this in practice provided the needed protection, Trader nonetheless remained exposed to the risk of loss from the potential of the sellers subsequently losing the wherewithal to pay.

In the case of stock deals involving numerous owners, there was less opportunity to obtain such warranties because it was impractical to obtain agreements from all of them to share the exposure. In 2004, Trader's management was ecstatic when it discovered that Homes.com could be acquired to help leverage Trader's *Harmon Homes* real estate guides and Internet services. However, because Homes.com was a publicly traded C-corp with scores of shareholders, structuring the acquisition as an asset deal was impossible. Fortunately, its exposure to liabilities was minimized because it had recently emerged from bankruptcy and its responsibility for those earlier debts had been wiped out. Although Trader's exposure related only to liabilities arising since Homes.com's emergence from bankruptcy, Trader nevertheless sought to place the majority of its purchase price in escrow for a period of five years. When this was rejected by the owners as unacceptable, the two parties agreed to place 10 percent of the price in escrow to compensate for any previously undisclosed liabilities discovered during the first year after closing. At the end of that year, the residual balance would be paid out to the shareholders. With only a one-year insurance policy, it then became incumbent on Trader's staff to do its best to identify all potential liabilities during that period.

Cheap Financing: Surrogate Escrow

Although success is unlikely to be achieved with any offer including a million-year payout like that in the football player parable, conscientious attention to a transaction's financial structure can dramatically improve the return on investment. An advantageous structure not only will reduce the net present value cost of a transaction but can produce impressive tax shields, risk management benefits, and operational advantages.

The most obvious benefit of structuring a payout over a long period arises from the time value of money. Any postponed payment remains with the buyer to be leveraged through supplemental investments until it is paid out. As long as the effective interest payment on the deferral is less than the cost of capital, the buyer saves money and increases the return on investment.

The second, less obvious but often more valuable benefit is that deferred payouts can provide a surrogate escrow account to provide a source of funds to compensate the buyer for any indemnities subsequently owed by the seller. In almost every transaction, the seller makes a broad variety of representations and warranties about the business, and the definitive agreement specifies the obligations he or she owes if the buyer suffers losses arising from a fraudulent representation or violated warranty. To collect such payments, it is advantageous to have funds conveniently escrowed to be tapped when due. Having the ability to offset deferred payments represents an ideal escrow because it permits the buyer simply to transfer funds from the one pocket of money previously owed to the seller back into the buyer's other pocket of funds due from the seller.

Of course, both the seller and his counsel will advocate 100 percent payment at closing to ensure collection and mitigate the risk of disputed offsets. However, in the real world of small transactions, deferred payments are more often the rule than the exception. Small business brokers customarily prepare their clients for deferred payments because they know that Small Business Administration (SBA) lenders favor funding transactions that include seller financing. Valuing the added measure of implied security, SBA lenders understand that such a structure ensures that both buyers and sellers will retain a stake in the success of the business after the closing. Accordingly, on transactions valued at four times the owner's cash flow, it is reasonable to expect the SBA to lend half the funds, with the buyer contributing a quarter as the equity investment and the seller committing to accept the buyer's note for the remainder. To sustain collectability of the deferred payment, the seller will retain a vested interest in assisting the business after the closing, perhaps motivating him to supply direct assistance while discouraging activities that might negatively affect the business's ability to pay amounts still due.

During the rapid rollup of *Auto Trader* licensees and similar publications, Landmark capitalized on the benefits of deferred payment structures by persuading sellers that they were customary. From 1985 through 1989, it paid just over 70 percent of the aggregate purchase price at closing, with the remainder paid over the subsequent six years. Moreover, by characterizing most deferrals as noncompete payments, it incurred no interest costs, representing an interest-free loan for the period, effectively reducing the purchase price and increasing the return on investment.

Less devoted to this approach, Cox Enterprises paid over 97 percent of its acquisition costs for its *Auto Trader* licensees at closing, with less than 3 percent payable over seven years. Arguably, Cox may have reduced some of its up-front acquisition costs by paying so much at closing, effectively capturing a "prompt payment discount"; that is, some sellers may have accepted a lower purchase price because they received their full payment at closing.

From Trader's experience, its management concluded that smaller business owners are far more focused on the total dollars than on the payout schedule. Repeatedly, a seller drew a line in the sand, insisting that she would not accept anything less than a specified dollar figure. Then, after the customary wrangling, the seller agreed to sell for that figure, but with half payable at closing and the other half payable in five equal installments over the next five years with no interest.

As Trader began completing larger transactions, it found itself in competition for properties whose sellers were guided by more sophisticated professionals. Relative price multiples increased, and the sellers became less willing to defer payments and far more conscious of the tax implications. Trader therefore was compelled to be more accommodating, so much so that for the period after 1994, only about 6 percent of the payments were deferred for acquisitions under $500 million and none of the payments were deferred on its single deal over $500 million. However, this low share was very much skewed by the approximately 30 largest acquisitions. For the over 80 transactions valued at $5 million or less, Trader persuaded sellers to accept deferrals of 31 percent of the total payments over five years.

Including All the Cash Receivable

To impress on the sellers the total financial rewards arising from a sale, Trader's negotiators habitually summarized all the cash payments they would receive in writing: the larger the perceived number, the more compelling the motivation to sell. In making its offers, it therefore carefully itemized the proceeds, including the following:

- *Working capital:* In purchases structured as asset deals, the seller retained cash and accounts receivable, offset by the accounts payable. Although the sellers already owned this cash, it remained locked in the business if ownership continued, but it would be liquidated into free cash after the sale.
- *Employment agreements/consulting payments:* All contractual obligations contributed to the owners' proceeds.
- *Noncompete payments:* Usually paid proportionally in five annual installments, the total represented a non-interest-bearing deferred payment.
- *Interest payments on seller financing:* On the rare occasions when deferred payments were characterized as a loan, Trader included the associated interest payments as part of the total proceeds.

- *Asset (or stock) purchase price*: Constituting the majority of the transaction total, this was highlighted.
- *Contingent payments*: On the rare occasions when the seller could earn additional amounts based on the postclosing performance of the business, the maximum potential was added to the total.

Landmark's Winston–Salem *Trading Post* acquisition underscored the benefits of this approach. Knowing that the seller wanted $1 million after taxes, Hall demonstrated that the substantial surplus working capital would offset capital gains taxes, and the five subsequent noncompete payments would be taxed at lower rates because the seller's projected income would place him in lower brackets.

Repeatedly, while negotiating transactions, Trader found that sellers had a final acquisition price in mind, and the inclusion of every payment helped it bridge the divide between the two parties' numbers. Periodically, when the seller sought one more dollop of cash, Trader characterized the profits earned in the weeks before closing as the last contribution to achieve the seller's goals. Essentially, Trader's negotiators helped persuade the seller by spotlighting all the cash and benefits the seller would receive.

Structural Components

As was implied above, most of Trader's transactions included components in addition to the asset or stock purchase price. Among the most important were those paid directly to the owners for their personal services and commitments under consulting, employment, noncompete, and earn-out agreements. Though primarily designed to ensure access to the critical skills and clout of the owners to support the business, they also provided substantial tax and risk management benefits.

Consulting and Employment Agreements

Most entrepreneurs understand that they make lousy employees, and the prospect of working for a larger company does not interest them. They relish their independence and bristle at having to consult with superiors about decisions they make. Moreover, many are motivated to sell because the business has lost its rewarding challenge and has been transformed into something that is more boring and frustrating than energizing and psychologically fulfilling.

Accordingly, the seller is likely to find distasteful any requirement that she remain employed beyond a relatively short transition period. In Trader's experience, among the 145 transactions completed between 1985 and 2005, only 13 of the principal owners remained as employees and only 3 extended their stay beyond one year. So intent on leaving was the owner of the Buffalo, New York, *Show & Sell* that he accepted a compromise with the proviso that the deal would close quickly to facilitate his escape to Florida before the snows commenced. To satisfy the seller's needs, therefore, the acquirer should anticipate the owner's departure after closing.

Clearly, the owner's exit could present a nettlesome problem. The owner may possess that special pixie dust which makes the business thrive, or the owner's departure may create a leadership vacuum, leaving the staff without a guiding force. These concerns may cause acquirers to have qualms about completing a transaction, particularly if the acquirer has no alternative promotable management talent to lead the organization.

As a practical matter, however, retention of the owner is rarely a positive. His decision to sell usually demonstrates his desire to disengage from the responsibilities of management, and his motivation will predictably decline further after a sale. He is also likely to be a barrier to change, preferring to continue operating according to his well-established routines instead of the needs and dictates of the new owner. His presence therefore may undermine the effectiveness of integration plans, hamper the adoption of best practices, and forestall the achievement of development goals.

Fortunately, most businesses already have on board an acceptable replacement manager who has developed a reasonably thorough understanding of operations while serving in a secondary capacity. Most owners, having become discontent with the daily grind, will have already begun the passing of leadership responsibilities to one or more capable staffers, and those individuals are usually excited by the opportunity to assume greater authority. Moreover, accustomed to adjusting to the whims of a sometimes capricious owner, these employees are more likely to accommodate change and support the new initiatives of the acquirer.

The primary need therefore is to obtain the commitment of the seller to provide transitional assistance, and this can be accomplished with a consulting agreement or occasionally with an employment agreement.

A consulting agreement establishes a specific obligation for the seller to provide assistance during the transition of ownership. No matter how thorough its due diligence, Trader's management never believed it could obtain a truly comprehensive understanding of the business operations, and continued access to the owner's knowledge and expertise was therefore valued. Similarly, the owner often had special relationships that Trader needed to leverage. For example, one advertiser insisted that it had a preferential rate schedule, and Trader had the former owner resolve the matter amicably. With the consulting services, Trader remained confident that it could tap the owner's expertise and capitalize on the owner's clout when needed during the transitional period. Although there was some risk that the owner would not be particularly cooperative, in most cases the owner's devotion and loyalty to the business provided the necessary motivation to respond positively and perform in the company's best interests.

Theoretically, employment agreements served the same purpose as consulting agreements. Arguably, they provided much more owner access and implied a stronger overall commitment to serve the company. Trader's experience, however, was that in practice, they accomplished little more than a consulting agreement. Very quickly, most owners who sold the business became disillusioned as an employee of the larger company. Accustomed to calling all the shots, they soon became annoyed by supervisory oversight. Budgeting, writing annual plans, submitting capital expenditure requests, and following the dictates of human resource directives were just a few of the vexing responsibilities that tended to erode the former owner's willingness to continue "working for the man."

Similarly, the owner often became uncomfortable with his or her staff's changed perceptions. Before selling, the founder of one Midwest photo guide perceived that his continued leadership would facilitate his enterprise's development, and he was adamant about staying involved. Impressed with his skills, Landmark leadership encouraged him enthusiastically, suggesting the potential for expanded involvement with other operations, and when he insisted on a two-year employment term, Landmark accepted and proceeded accordingly. However, within weeks after the closing, the seller discovered he had been mistaken. Although he remained comfortable with his duties, he thought his dedicated, handpicked staff now looked at him as if he were just another employee, and he admitted feeling awkward and almost embarrassed when he came to work.

As Landmark's president, Dick Barry, subsequently observed, "We took on former owners as managers with the sincere goal of working productively to achieve the best results for the enterprise, but we were mindful of the fact that most soon check out. Psychologically, they often have difficulty with how their baby is treated within the organization, or they begin to chafe from the structure."[3] Although other former owners used different terms, almost all who became employees expressed some displeasure with their emotions as an employee after the closing.

With the observable disengagement and rapid departure of owners, Landmark's and Trader's leadership concluded that the employment agreement was designed more to protect the employee than to protect the employer. The seller insisted on language protecting her from early termination and negative work conditions, but there was no terminology that could compel the employee to put forth her best efforts, much less produce superior results for the business. Realistically, the employment contract only ensured that the employee would show up for work.

With less to gain from an employee who simply went through the motions to collect compensation, Trader found it desirable to include a provision permitting the employee to trigger early termination with the residual salary obligations converting to consulting fees. However, such conversion rights encouraged the seller to terminate quickly because they implied that the seller had little to gain from remaining. Therefore, Trader subsequently modified the employment agreements to stipulate a discounted payment of 50 to 70 percent of the residual salary as the termination consulting fee. Nevertheless, while negotiating the acquisition deal, Trader included the full salary in its summary of all the payments constituting the purchase price.

Although some argue that consulting and employment payments are operating expenses rather than part of the purchase price, Trader's management believed they were unequivocally part of the deal's total cost. To realize the anticipated value, Trader needed the services of the seller for the transitional period, and the consulting and employment payments were integral parts of the offer package, contributing to its acceptance by the seller. By segregating them from the asset purchase price, Trader established in the owner's mind the discrete values to compensate for performance, creating a stronger commitment to perform more responsibly during the transition.

Segregating the payments also provided incremental tax benefits. Under current tax law, consulting payments and employee salaries are deductible when paid, providing a tax shield of approximately 40 percent (combined state and federal). In essence, the tax benefit represents a $0.40 government subsidy on every dollar allocated, effectively reducing the net cost of a deal. Unfortunately, though the full subsidy is realized on consulting payments, it is partially offset under employment contracts whose payments are subject to added fringe benefit costs and payroll taxes.

Noncompete Payments

Obtaining protection from future competition from the owner, usually one of the most formidable adversaries in the operating environment, is critically necessary for almost every acquisition. Having created the enterprise, the owner has already demonstrated the business acumen and understanding of the market and industry segment and has an abundance of contacts and relationships that can be leveraged to begin operating an identical enterprise. Notably, the owner built the existing business without those resources and particularly without the impressive cash wired into her bank account to conclude the deal. Unless prevented, she could quickly direct her energies and funds toward recruiting former staff to walk across the street to begin soliciting all her familiar clients. Though most owners have no interest in starting over, a buyer can never be certain that his seller won't. Therefore, it is important to obtain a noncompetition agreement to function as a contractual barrier to such activity.

Designed to restrict the seller from involvement in a competitive enterprise, a noncompete agreement is a formal contract that defines both the duration and the restricted markets and activities. Thus, it represents an insurance policy providing protection against damages that could be inflicted by the seller, and if the seller causes the business damage, the customary noncompete agreement specifies penalties, including a compensatory indemnity payment.

Although it is desirable to restrict the seller from competing in perpetuity, public policy prescribes that only a five-year prohibition is enforceable in court. Hence, Landmark and Trader insisted on the five-year ban in each negotiation, ultimately obtaining agreement to that period in every deal except three.

Ideally, a buyer would like to prohibit the seller's competitive activities worldwide, ensuring that the buyer will not face opposition from the seller as it rolls out the business model to new geographic markets. However, public policy limits the enforceability of a noncompete to markets in which the business actually operated. Landmark and Trader therefore carefully described the established market area, specifying the restricted geography in each agreement by itemizing the counties of a business's current operation.

For the most part, Landmark and Trader experienced little debate during negotiation of noncompetes with sellers. Sellers readily understood the acquirer's desire to restrict their subsequent activities and generally had little interest in becoming involved in competitive businesses. If they expressed a need for unlimited flexibility to do anything competitive, the acquirer inevitably became suspicious and stiffened its resolve to obtain a noncompetition agreement.

The buyers were, however, willing to make reasonable accommodations to facilitate the owner's desire to begin involvement with a specific enterprise that could be construed as being "slightly" competitive. For example, a seller of an employment guide had plans to launch a gardening/home improvement magazine and did not want to run afoul of his obligations by running recruitment ads in his new publication's classified ad section. To accommodate that possibility, Trader specified that it would not be a violation to include those ads in the new publication to the extent that their revenues never accounted for more than 5 percent of the publication's total.

Because it placed such a strong emphasis on its prohibitions, Trader tried to allocate as much of the purchase price as possible to the noncompete agreement. Trader insisted that this was reasonable because the barriers to entry are so low with publications and other media. In fact, many of the founders had launched with almost no capital, relying on their credit cards and the printer's willingness to defer payment for 60 days. To capture the goodwill of the business, the negotiators argued, the buyers had to be certain that the sellers did not launch a competitor.

Efforts to ascribe large values to noncompetes produced impressive success. During the competitive rollup of general classified publications and auto guides between 1985 and 1989, noncompete payments represented 49 percent of the total consideration paid on Landmark's 24 acquisitions and 42 percent on Cox's 14 acquisitions.

The success is perhaps surprising considering that noncompete payments are subject to higher tax rates. During that era, the asset purchase price was subject to a 20 percent capital gains tax (increased to 28 percent in 1986), whereas noncompetes were considered ordinary income that was taxable at a much higher rate of up to 50 percent (reduced to 38.5 percent in 1987 and then 28 percent from 1988 to 1990). Their success was due in large part to the sellers' focus on the gross amount and inattention to the tax impact of such allocations.

The ability to allocate so much to noncompetes was very much predicated on the size of the transaction. With the larger deals came more sophisticated sellers who were prone to seek professional guidance that warned them of the tax implications of excess assignments to noncompete payments. Consequently, in the period after 1994, only about 10 percent of the total consideration for all transactions was allocated to noncompetes. However, excluding the almost 30 largest transactions, fully 50 percent of the total consideration was allocated to noncompete payments among the over 80 acquisitions with a total price of $5 million or less.

Unfortunately, the buyer's willingness to accommodate large sellers by agreeing to minimal allocations to noncompete payments threatened to undermine the strength of its protections. Typically, huge outstanding payments represent the strongest disincentives to a noncompete's violation. Although subject to court injunctions, expensive legal battles, and an indemnity for proven damages, the seller can easily assume that her risk of ever facing substantial penalties will be mitigated by the reality of the dictum that he who holds the money holds the power. When all payments are collected at closing, the seller perceives that the buyer would have to conduct a battle lasting years to reclaim any of the funds. Alternatively, when the buyer holds the money, the seller understands that she probably will forfeit future payments while remaining liable for additional damages. By paying all funds at closing, the buyer unequivocally loses power, but its agreement to do so may be a distasteful necessity to complete many transactions.

The acquirers did, however, obtain some added protection by incorporating a liquidated damages provision in the noncompete. Without that addition, the buyer may be able to reclaim only an amount equal to the actual extent of the proven damages caused by the competitive activity, and its reclamation can be highly problematic. If required, proving the amount of damage is nearly impossible to do with any degree of accuracy; obtaining a judgment may take a decade of litigation; and collection may be hampered if the seller has diverted the funds into bad investments or hidden bank accounts. In contrast, the liquidated damages provision stipulates the specific amount due in the event of a demonstrated violation, reducing the litigation risks and delays and thereby enhancing collectability.

To produce the maximum noncompete deterrent, Landmark and Trader routinely tried to stipulate that the seller would remain liable for paying damages equal to the purchase price paid for his company. They insisted that if the seller went into competition, the full business value was subject to loss and he should therefore refund the buyer's investment. Most sellers accepted this requirement, confident that they had no prospect of violating the agreement. But many bristled at the potential loss for some minor infraction. To reach a mutual accommodation, the buyers regularly agreed to provide notice so that the seller could cease the activity before becoming liable, and they accepted a lesser (but still intimidating) amount for the liquidated damages. For one $20 million deal, Trader grudgingly agreed to allocate none of the purchase price to the noncompete, but it stipulated that the seller would be subject to paying $10 million in liquidated damages if he violated the noncompete's terms.

In practice, the effectiveness of the noncompete agreements proved indisputable in Trader's experience. Obviously, it received substantial tax benefits, exceeding a net present value of $50 million over the 20-year acquisition period, and the buyers forestalled competitive activity among every one of the sellers. During the five-year prohibition period, the company and its predecessors never experienced a single substantive example of a seller violating the agreements' provisions. On the rare occasion when rumors surfaced that a seller was considering a competitive move, one of the buyer's leaders reminded the seller of her obligations, and the problem evaporated.

Although it is certainly true that almost all the sellers never had any intention of competing, it was clearly not the case with every one of them. A little more than five years after Trader's acquisition of his publications, the founding owner of the San Diego *Auto Trader* joined with a group of friends and relatives to launch a competing product, something he almost certainly would have done earlier if it had not been precluded by his five-year noncompete agreement with Trader. In several other circumstances, the owners relocated to launch products in areas not restricted by their noncompete's provisions. The seller of a Detroit employment publication, in fact, used much of Trader's payments to fund the launch of magazines to compete with Trader's similar publications in Atlanta and several other cities.

Earn-Outs

During most of their acquisition history, Landmark and Trader avoided including earn-outs as a component of the deal payments. As employed by many other acquirers, earn-outs promise supplemental payments after a sale, usually contingent on the achievement of arbitrary performance targets. For example, a buyer may agree to pay the seller 5 percent of her company's profits exceeding $10 million during the first two years after closing. By doing this, the seller effectively increases her sale price, but only if the buyer achieves added benefits, presumably above the minimum threshold justifying the deal.

Trader in particular was hesitant to offer earn-outs, suspicious that they could be the source of destructive arguments and possible litigation after closing. If the business failed to generate the seller's anticipated earn-out, it feared that he might claim that the failure was due to some arbitrary action of Trader's that was perpetrated intentionally to deny him his earn-out rewards. The movie industry in particular has a reputation for virulent debates and acrimonious litigation over the propriety of the profit participation calculations, and Trader wanted to avoid similar experiences.

However, during the rise of Internet mania, Trader concluded that inclusion of earn-outs could prove advantageous to complete some deals. Among developing businesses, particularly within the Internet segment, owners often have delusional expectations regarding the probable growth and value of their companies. Debating those perceptions rarely produces a mutual agreement, and the seller can be discouraged from continuing to negotiate with any buyer who fails to share her vision. Rather than participate in such unfruitful discussions, Trader's deal makers concluded that it could be more productive simply to adopt the seller's vision but tailor the price to be contingent on the fulfillment of that vision.

The ownership group of one particularly attractive Internet business originally demanded $10 million for an enterprise with slightly more than $1 million in revenue. Two years after the dot-com collapse, the business had doubled its revenues to $2 million and its owners had reduced their expectations but still demanded $5 million, insisting that their $100,000 EBITDA company would generate over $1 million in profits the next year. Though confident it could increase earnings to $300,000, Trader's management believed that prospects for $1 million were remote. But it had no intention of dampening the sellers' enthusiasm with its more pessimistic expectations, acknowledging instead the possibility of the forecast. Trader, however, based its valuation on its more conservative projections, and its proposed best offer was summarily rejected. After several weeks, Trader begrudgingly agreed to add an earn-out tailored to pay the owners a bonus of $500,000 if the first year's EBITDA exceeded $400,000, another $250,000 if EBITDA exceeded $450,000, and another $250,000 if

EBITDA exceeded $500,000. Accordingly, if the company earned $500,000 EBITDA the next year, Trader would pay a maximum $1 million earn-out.

From Trader's perspective, there was little chance that any earn-out bonuses would become payable, and its leadership questioned whether the sellers actually believed they could achieve their projections. However, it really didn't matter. Their confidence or willingness to hope for the best persuaded the sellers to assume the risk of generating the profits necessary to bridge the difference between the two parties' respective prices. Moreover, Trader would have been ecstatic if earnings had jumped to the projected levels. Although it would be compelled to pay an extra million, Trader's receipt of almost double its projected cash flow would easily justify the payment while dramatically improving the projected long-term return on investment.

The earn-out also served the critical purpose of solidifying the commitment of the owners to remain with the business during the transition period. With such a substantial bonus contingent on success, they had a compelling incentive to take all appropriate steps to implement their plan promptly and efficiently. Simultaneously, Trader found the sellers amenable to adopting recommendations to reduce costs and enhance efficiency because those steps would stimulate EBITDA growth. However, within four months, it became clear that none of the earn-out hurdles would be met. Once disillusionment set in, signs of discouragement and disengagement began to appear. Although they produced the desired motivational stimulus during the initial transition, the impact of the earn-out was the opposite during the later months, particularly after six months, when all hope had been lost. Overall, Trader's leadership concluded that the net effect of the earn-out on operations was positive, and it indisputably had served as an integral component necessary to obtain acceptance of the deal. Most significantly, the earn-out had cost Trader nothing, perhaps saving $1 million it might have otherwise felt compelled to pay to clinch the deal.

On the one occasion when Trader's earn-out provisions produced supplemental payments, the company was compensated by the focused dedication of the retained founders, who devoted impressive efforts to deliver substantially improved growth and profits. Trader also was rewarded by those sellers' later commitment to help enhance performance within other segments of Trader's organization. By agreeing to contribute a share of the ancillary operations' improved results to the earn-out calculation formula, Trader ignited the sellers' commitment and enthusiasm to share their talents, and that produced impressive operating gains among other Trader operations.

Trader's positive experience with earn-outs was very much based on the way it incorporated them in the deal. Because they were exclusively tied to achieving lofty profit goals, Trader never found it necessary to contend with postclosing arguments to invest exorbitant funds and energy to pursue unprofitable revenue growth. When this was suggested, management simply asked how expenditures might affect the short-term profits underlying the earn-out formula, and the advocate's support quickly evaporated upon realizing that it would cost her personally. Such short-term thinking could prove detrimental if maximum revenue growth was important, but among Trader's acquisitions, the more critical need was restraining the acquisition's costs. Accordingly, incorporating earn-outs tied to EBITDA targets worked exceedingly well.

Nonfinancial Deal Components

An experienced negotiator understands that money is not the only factor motivating acceptance of an offer. Most small business owners harbor a genuine affection for their organizations and very much want a new owner to share that affection while accelerating their baby's future development. In one notable example, a previously intransigent founder eventually agreed to sell because she was persuaded that it was time her business moved beyond her own abilities and Trader represented an ideal suitor to hasten the expansion of the enterprise. By selling to Trader, she could enjoy the enhanced success vicariously while beaming with pride over her original contributions and wise decision to endorse the marriage.

However, other psychological needs sometimes take precedence over a deal's financial considerations. For years, Trader had maintained friendly relationships with the four owners of publications serving Indianapolis and

Nashville, and after a prolonged courtship over innumerable dinners and conferences, Trader's top management had developed confidence that it would remain the owner's preferred buyer. Long after all their friends in the industry had sold to Trader, those owners eventually did decide to follow suit, and Trader stood ready to make the best deal. But while it waited, the Canadian rollup engineer John McBane slipped in and inked the deal for his organization. What Trader's leaders had not realized was that those owners' earlier hesitancy was symbolic of their inherent need to act independently, and their decision to sell to McBane was their final demonstration that they were unlike all the other operators. As one executive observed, "I imagined them, heads held high, snickering that they had delivered a stunning defeat to the affable Trader boys, who had been overly confident in their pursuit of conquest. In retrospect, we assuaged our loss by concluding that McBane overpaid and we were fortunate we had not been given the opportunity to beat his deal." (Several years later, McBane offered to sell Trader the same properties, and Trader made what it believed to be an attractive offer. McBane, however, wanted even more, and with the Internet's impact already taking its toll on the publications, Trader's management eventually concluded it was fortunate it didn't win the bid the second time around.)

For Trader, a more rewarding example of the importance of nonfinancial components involved the fulfillment of a seller's desire for power and position. By appealing to one man's desire to assume leadership of one of its brands, Trader completed a particularly attractive deal while simultaneously recruiting a key manager to reverse the sagging fortunes of that publishing group.

As part of its $533 million purchase of United Advertising Publications (UAP) from the United Kingdom's United News and Media, PLC, Trader acquired a group of over 180 *Harmon Homes* publications, free distribution real estate magazines that produced almost a sixth of UAP's revenues while operating at a debilitating loss. Originally consolidated a decade earlier in a massive rollup orchestrated by Hartz Mountain's publishing group, the guides had been acquired several years earlier by UAP, which had repeatedly failed to generate the anticipated return on its investment. Trader, having sold its own real estate guides to Hartz many years earlier, had little interest in the consolidated group, and while evaluating UAP, it ascribed no value to the guides, assuming they could be closed to eradicate their losses. However, once Trader owned *Harmon Homes*, it decided to tinker with the business instead, hoping to resuscitate the publications and reposition their significant revenues into the profit-generating column.

Trader's efforts with *Harmon Homes* were experiencing limited results when its CFO received a call from Ernie Blood, the owner of Carmel Publishing Company, operator of a much smaller group of over a dozen real estate guides. Blood had actually been a founding member of one of the groups acquired by Hartz, and despite his devotion to the business, he had been summarily dismissed by Hartz's management, which wanted to take the publications in a different direction under the newly created *Harmon Homes* brand. Disappointed, Blood turned his attention to a variety of successful commercial real estate investments, and once his noncompete restrictions expired, he began to launch another group of *Homes* guides. He now proposed that Trader buy his publications and appoint him to manage all the *Harmon Homes*.

Despite Trader's long disillusionment with real estate guides, his suggestion had merit. Clearly, Trader was not interested in adding to its underperforming group, but perhaps Blood could orchestrate its turnaround. The risk was that Blood would prove reckless, exacerbating Trader's problems with increasing losses. But *Harmon Homes* did not have much of a reputation, and it would probably benefit from the ministrations of a seasoned executive respected by the industry. Still, Trader had experienced little success maintaining the allegiance of entrepreneurs as part of its management team, and it would have to invest in publications it really did not want.

Blood understood the hesitancy, and with passion comparable to Cupid's unrequited devotion to Psyche, he courted Trader's leadership persistently and diplomatically over several months, deftly persuading them that he had a viable plan and the skills needed to transform the Harmon publishing group into a respectable profit generator. Finally convinced of Blood's sincerity, abilities, and commitment, Trader agreed to proceed, and by offering Blood leadership of Harmon, Trader negotiated especially attractive financial terms to acquire Carmel.

The June 2001 investment in Carmel and the management talents of Ernie Blood did prove fortuitous. Within the first year of his arrival, Blood reversed the losses of Harmon and moved its operating margin into double digits. By 2005, Harmon boasted a 20 percent EBITDA margin, representing a 500 percent return on Trader's cash investment in Carmel. Although it is possible that Harmon's performance could have been duplicated by others, most Trader managers agree that Blood, his operating tactics, and the management team he assembled made all the difference.

Unfortunately, just as the banking industry fell with the mortgage debacle and collapse of housing prices in the great recession of 2008, so too did *Harmon Homes*. The devastation experienced by the real estate industry was mirrored in Harmon's dependence on housing sales and the prosperity of its real estate agents. Its profit margin evaporated, and to protect the group from liquidation, Blood negotiated his own management buyout of the brand and its magazines in 2009.

Chapter 8

Rollup Pitfalls

"Good game!" said Bennie Schmidt, nodding toward the Cincinnati Reds playing down on the field.

"Sure is," replied Britt Reid, but he was thinking of a different game. Less than two years earlier, his company's owner had sold out to Landmark, and here he sat in Riverfront Stadium with one of the real characters in the industry just a couple of days after Schmidt and his partner, Dick Dean, had closed on the sale of their *Wheeler Dealer* auto guides to Landmark.

"What are you smiling about?" Reid asked, suddenly noticing Schmidt's huge grin. "Thinking about that big pile of money in your bank?"

"Heh, heh, that too!" Schmidt chuckled. "No, I was thinking about a month ago when your Landmark honchos flew in to do the deal. Yeah, here they come, flying in on their corporate jet—Dick Barry, Conrad Hall—and Norman driving in from Shelbyville. We took them upstairs to our conference room and handed out *Wheeler Dealer* ball caps. Barry looked real good with one of those on his head, heh, heh."

"Yeah, I saw the photo." Reid smiled.

"They're all ready to do the deal, they yap their gums some, and then they make their offer. They think it's a big number, but nope! Not for us! So, 'course, we had to put old Barry on the elevator to get the deal done! Heh, heh. But he took the ride up, and we broke out our bottle of Dom Perignon."

"Yes, he did. You took him all the way up to the penthouse!"

"More like its roof! But we let Norman keep the plastic champagne flute."[1]

Being put on the elevator, of course, is one of the biggest pitfalls of orchestrating a rollup. Caught up in deal psych and eager to do a deal, an acquirer falls prey to the temptations of raising the price for each successive acquisition to sky-high levels—levels so high that it may be difficult to earn an appealing return on investment.

There are, however, many other dangers. The acquirers of publicly traded rollups have their own set of pitfalls as the incentives of momentum investing compel deals at any price; competition drives prices well beyond reasonable levels; aggregators may move so slowly that others may intercede; and they may insult sellers during the courting process or fail to protect their acquisition from competitive spin-outs. They may overestimate synergies and development opportunities, buy up competitors imprudently, and continue to invest after market peaks and industry changes.

Publicly Traded Rollups Inflated Collapse

The compelling stock market valuations awarded to high-growth companies produce the compelling incentive to create an appealing enterprise to capitalize on the rewards promised by Wall Street after an initial public offering. The opportunity for astronomical short-term gains, however, may be overshadowed by the probable collapse of sky-high valuations when disillusionment eventually returns expectations to earth. As demonstrated by the 1990s flurry of IPOs, the prospect of huge gains was a substantial catalyst for the creation of a dizzying array of rollup niche enterprises, and the subsequent disintegration of most contributed to its denigration as a development strategy.

Replicating the practices of the conglomerators of the 1950s and 1960s, the financiers engineering most of the publicly traded rollups leveraged the public market's overblown expectations and frailties by employing the tactics of momentum investing. As described by one Motley Fool blogger,

> its founder/promoter finds about 5 to 15 companies willing to join
> forces with him in exchange for cash and stock. This cash and stock
> may not materialize until the company goes public (which it

quickly does), enticing investors with its rosy projections and plans. In a sense, the rollup acquires companies on credit! This process likely continues, with the company issuing more stock as it acquires more companies. Let's say that an acquiree's stock price is valued by the market at about 10 times earnings. If it generates $5 million in annual earnings, the rollup might buy it for about $50 million in cash and stock. Meanwhile, the rollup itself might be enjoying a valuation on the stock market of about 20 or 30 times earnings. In this way, the rollup is immediately recognizing a higher value for its purchase than it paid.[2]

This was precisely the practice pursued by John Y. Brown's Kentucky Fried Chicken in the late 1960s: "We had been buying franchisees' stores back for five times earnings, but at one point, the stock was trading at 70 times earnings," Brown said, recalling how his rollup had converted dozens of ordinary folks into millionaires early on.[3]

This was the practice employed repeatedly by Jonathan Ledecky. Completing over 200 acquisitions after his U.S. Office Products 1995 public offering, Ledecky went on to duplicate the strategy in a variety of industry niches, including the floral industry with U.S.A. Floral Products.[4]

In a frothy environment in which the acquirer's stock experiences exuberant pricing, it makes rational sense to make as many acquisitions as possible, assuming each transaction is completed through a stock exchange and the targets have stable or growing earnings that will contribute to the bottom line after the closing. As long as the acquisition's valuation multiple of earnings is lower than the consolidator's, any such stock-for-stock deal will be accretive to the consolidator's earnings: I'll agree to your overvalued price if you accept my even more overvalued stock as the currency to complete the deal.

Will such transactions create value? The answer to that, of course, is dependent on how well the integration process progresses and whether synergistic and innovative development opportunities will be realized.

Buying earnings for a low multiple and then having the stock market value the acquisition at a factor several times greater doesn't continue forever. Even if the consolidator has good success in preserving the earnings power of its acquisitions, experience demonstrates that the company's earnings multiple will decline. For most public entities of the 1990s, reality set in within a year after their IPOs, and continued preferential transactions became difficult. As several Booz Allen analysts concluded,

> many rollups were rewarded handsomely by the stock market during their high-growth, early stages of development—until they reached roughly $500 million in revenues. At this level, investors began to probe deeper, ask tougher questions, and demand better performance.[5]

Accordingly, the early price appreciation rewards are typically followed by the real probability of a burst bubble. As Howard Schilit, president of the Center for Financial Research & Analysis, warned, "these stocks spike up and then, often with very little warning, the stock starts to collapse." Purportedly one-time charges begin repeating, the core company's revenues decline, and the continued acquisition binge fails to mask the growth of serious problems.[6]

With the evaporating opportunity to buy earnings on a favorable basis, a growth stock with skyrocketing earnings driven by acquisitions eventually transforms at best into a value stock with acceptable earnings growth of 5 to 15 percent. Once it becomes a value stock, the earnings multiple falls to market averages, causing the stock price to plummet, disappointing investors and management.

Clearly, the history of consolidators is littered with examples of earnings declines after the absorption of new acquisitions. "On paper, you think that combining some operations can cut overhead and juice earnings," says Comfort Systems USA's Gordon Beittenmiller, but "in the majority of situations where we have done that, companies have underperformed."[7] The earnings disappointments lead to a collapse in market confidence, driving down the stock valuation. Seeing their shares and stock option values evaporate, the organization's best managers become disillusioned and abandon the organization, and the business falls into a steeper tailspin without effective leadership to address its mounting problems.

From 1995 to 1996, the S&P 500 index posted an impressive 57 percent increase, but the strategic rollups put the index to shame. AutoNation increased 1651 percent, U.S. Office Products gained 137 percent, Stewart Enterprises gained 115 percent, and Service Corp. jumped 96 percent. However, for the period through December 1999, the S&P Index climbed another 98 percent, but those rollups collapsed precipitously, including AutoNation (-70 percent), U.S. Office Products (-89 percent), Service International Corp. (-75 percent), and Stewart Enterprises (-72 percent).[8]

Overvaluation Lures

As demonstrated by the earlier Daimler–Chrysler example, the acquirers of large entities are repeatedly forced to justify offers that exceed practical valuations. The consolidators are driven by their deal psych and ego to win the deal at any cost; sellers demand the very highest price regardless; and brokers, of course, want the elevated fees associated with the highest possible winning bid. Rather than base valuations on starkly realistic expectations, acquirers suppress their pessimism. Despite the probable competitive challenges and recessionary downdrafts undermining earnings growth, they discount their applicability. The buyers lose sight of the imperative to build value by investing at relative bargain prices, subject to the delusion that winning means being the high bidder rather than earning a superior return.

Among the rollup engineers of the 1990s, the decision to overpay was predicated on a broad variety of rationalizations, each of which represents a pitfall to guard against. Primary among them are overoptimistic cash flow projections founded on excessive growth expectations, unrealistic cost savings, illusory synergistic benefits, higher costs, and unrealizable innovations:

- Created to deliver consistency and a higher degree of professionalism to outsourced telemarketing services,

TeleSpectrum Worldwide expected steep growth as it consolidated scores of businesses, but it soon found itself losing major customers and revenues instead of increasing its penetration and market share.[9]

- Collision Auto Repair of America rolled up dozens of small car maintenance businesses, projecting substantial savings in infrastructure, administration, and purchasing, but the complexities of management required the institution of expensive overhead far exceeding the projected savings.[10]

- Originally founded to replicate the one-stop-shopping experience and ambience of the big box retailers in the used car business, AutoNation discovered that its inventory sourcing costs ballooned because it had to compete for cars at auto auctions instead of getting preferential deals with trade-ins.[11]

Auction Frenzies

As private companies, Trader and Landmark avoided the public consolidators' compulsion to support their overinflated stock valuations with increasing deal flow at any price. As was described in Chapter 5, they rigorously applied conservative valuation principles to acquisition assessments, and that kept them out of trouble on most occasions. However, when they participated in an auction for a particularly attractive company, they too fell prey to the coercive inducements to increase bids beyond comfort levels.

The compulsion to increase prices is accelerated when multiple entities begin competing to acquire the same companies. Owners of funeral homes were ecstatic when Service Corporation International, Steward Enterprises, Inc., and Loewen and Laidlaw converged to hike prices to acquire their businesses. Similar bidding frenzies were ignited when U.S. Office Products and Corporate Express began consolidating the office products industry; Quest Diagnostics, Laboratory Corporation of America, and SmithKline Beecham consolidated the medical lab business; and Republic Industries and USA Waste competed with Waste Management to acquire garbage collectors.

This certainly happened when Cox and John McBane joined Landmark in the rollup frenzy in the classified advertising business. Disappointed with its failure to acquire more cable television franchises, Batten and Landmark's top managers understood that they should not hesitate to raise valuations when Cox Enterprises began acquiring *Auto Trader's* entrepreneurs. With early offers of one times revenues, Landmark's patient search for bargains had permitted others to identify the opportunity and commit their own resources to competing rollups. Now Batten unhesitatingly approved stepping up values to three times revenues. However, he did that because earlier success had demonstrated that his team could improve operating margins and revenue growth among businesses blessed with such significant development opportunities.

Although prudent for the most part, that confidence in management's projections and their ability to perform occasionally led to decisions to overpay for some businesses that ultimately disappointed. Absolutely dedicated to consolidating Mid-Atlantic market publications, Landmark feared that Cox would capture a foothold in North Carolina by acquiring the unprofitable *Traffic* automotive photo guide serving Asheville and Hendersonville. Management therefore produced projections for its turnaround and proceeded with the acquisition. Unfortunately, despite conscientious efforts, profits never materialized, and the publication was eventually shuttered.

Seeking Excessive Bargains

Overpaying for acquisitions represents a principal downfall of rollups, but there is the contrary risk that the insistence on bargain deals will thwart the acquirer's success in completing desirable transactions.

Trader had the inside track to acquire the New Orleans *News on Wheels*, but its prior success in completing deals with progressively reduced prices led to overconfidence. For months, Landmark's deal maker had carefully cultivated a warm relationship with the publication owner; that relationship was so warm that after enlisting a broker to assist with the deal, the seller insisted that he would work directly with Landmark. The broker, of course, uncovered another buyer, but Landmark's manager remained so confident that rather than make a compelling offer, he presented the seller with terms that were significantly under three times EBITDA. Not surprisingly, the seller was insulted, perceiving Landmark as a bottom fisher unworthy of further consideration, and proceeded promptly to complete a deal at about four times EBITDA with the competing bidder.

This had clearly been a doable deal that would have produced a highly attractive return on investment at even a valuation of five times cash flow. But it went to another acquirer because the buyer was too insistent on getting a bargain.

Similarly, the insistence on finding bargains delayed several other deals, permitting Cox and John McBane to enter and drive up prices.

Spin-Out Risks

Among businesses with low barriers to entry, there will always be the risk that an acquirer will suddenly find itself competing against unexpected new competition arising shortly after the completion of a deal. Disappointed by the sale or the actions of the buyer, key managers and employees may conclude that their best opportunity is to quit, walk across the street, and open a clone of their old employer. Blessed with in-depth knowledge of the business and intimate relationships with the vendors and clients, the highly experienced mutineers effectively "spin out" the full concept as a new competitor, leaving the original wounded and without its full resources.

Arguably, Wayne Huizenga did this in 1995 when he assumed the helm of Republic Industries, a business originally focused on garbage disposal, like Waste Management, the company Huizenga sold in 1984.[12] Similarly, John Hewitt left his position as regional manager of H&R Block in 1981, acquiring the multilocation offices of Mel Jackson's Tax Service the next year to create Jackson-Hewitt Tax Service. Eventually losing control of that company, which was sold to Cendant in 1997, Hewitt subsequently acquired U&R Tax Depot, a Canadian franchisor that he used to expand in the United States in 1998 in the form of Liberty Tax Service through his JTH Tax, Inc.[13]

In 1995, Trader acquired *Show & Sell*, a group of free distribution automotive photo guides serving south Florida. Founded by the enterprising Neil Van Hoogen with less than $1,000 and the willing 90-day credit terms of a friendly printer, the publication had humble beginnings that inspired a few of its managers to recruit some of the best salespeople to launch a new competitive publication. With few barriers, they leveraged strong personal relationships to persuade an impressive share of advertisers to support the new publication. The impact on revenues and profits was immediate, and Trader's ability to replace the group was hamstrung by the publications' declining fortunes. New recruits lacked both experience and personal relationships, and the publications never recovered from the incident.

To protect itself from similar catastrophes in the future, Trader began to require that the sales employees of all subsequent acquisitions sign a one-year noncompete agreement as a condition of employment. On the basis of state requirements, some were given additional compensation to ensure its enforceability and forestall their participation with a competitive enterprise.

Toxic Assets and Litigation

Along with the desired assets of any acquisition, there is the risk of acquiring previously unidentified problems that incur costly unanticipated losses. Sometimes referred to as toxic assets, the contingent liabilities they represent may lead to devastating consequences, as has been most vividly demonstrated by the catastrophic losses incurred by investors in the financial services industry.

Named by *Fortune* magazine as the mortgage services industry's "Most Admired Company," Golden West Financial was the country's second largest savings and loan when it was acquired for just under $26 billion in 2006 by the then $90 billion market cap Wachovia Bank. Unfortunately, Golden West's assets included $122 billion of option adjustable-rate mortgages that suffered a meltdown with the collapse of housing prices. In July 2008, Wachovia announced an $8 billion loss attributable to the mortgage write-down, but continued erosion and declining confidence placed Wachovia in such danger that the Federal Deposit Insurance Corporation (FDIC) was compelled to conduct hurried merger talks, ultimately leading to Wachovia's takeover by Wells Fargo for just $15 billion.[14]

In the realm of rollups, the risks of toxic assets may not be as great as those in banking industry mergers, but their relative impact may be the same. Sadly, a $10 million judgment against a $50 million consolidator may drive it into bankruptcy.

To mitigate the potential for damages from toxic assets, the most desirable tactic for acquirers is to complete acquisitions as asset deals, as was described in Chapter 7. Alternatively, acquirers of stock, like Wachovia, face the risks of losses from subsequently discovered contingent liabilities, and the protections are minimal. Theoretically, the acquirer can segregate the liabilities by operating the acquisition within its original legal entity. Then, if an overwhelming loss is uncovered, it may have the option of simply having that subsidiary file for bankruptcy. Although this may protect the parent from exposure, the subsidiary may be destroyed, and the parent may find itself liable if zealous litigators persuade the judiciary to pierce the subsidiary's corporate veil to collect damages from the parent.

Because of the risk of contingent liability, a prudent acquirer will require sellers to provide warranties on the business, its assets, and its liabilities, and if unanticipated costs are incurred, those warranties should obligate the seller to compensate the buyer. However, the seller's attorney will attempt to dilute the warranties and cap the seller's exposure to liabilities, and it is therefore incumbent on the buyer to negotiate for as much protection as possible. Unfortunately, those warranties may be of little value. Once a seller collects the payment, he and his money may disappear, leaving the buyer with no way to obtain compensation. Moreover, in the case of public companies, collection may prove impossible when there are hundreds or thousands of stockholders. Accordingly, to ensure funding for warranty claims, a prudent acquirer will insist on establishing an escrow fund.

Because of the lingering risk of contingent liabilities, the preferred protection is to exclude any asset with any potential exposure. The need to do this was discovered by United News and Media after its rollup of classified advertising publications serving the New Jersey and New York markets. One of those acquisitions included real estate and was subsequently discovered to have incurred environmental contamination from printing plant wastes; the unanticipated cleanup costs totaled six figures, increasing that acquisition's costs by a double-digit percentage.

Before Landmark made a similar Ohio acquisition, it completed a comprehensive survey that identified an unused underground fuel storage tank on the printing plant's property. To facilitate the closing, the purchase of the real estate was deferred until the seller removed the tank and remediated the land. Unfortunately, despite the seller's best efforts to cure the problems over several years, the authorities refused to certify that there was no residual liability. The real estate purchase was abandoned, and Trader constructed a new plant at another location that passed its environmental reviews.

Independent Owners, Not Team-Playing Integrators

Much of the attraction of rollups among founding participants lies in the opportunity to capitalize on the valuation transformation from single- to double-digit earnings multiples. Allured by an IPO promising a $30\times$ PE, participants greedily agree to a consolidation, expecting to enjoy a vertical launch into instantaneous wealth, coupled with the pride of being a principal leader of a substantial national organization.

Theoretically, the combination of such talent has attractive advantages. As Philip Courten, a NationsBanc Montgomery deal maker, explained at the time: "You take the strengths of the individual entrepreneurs, their knowledge of their client bases ... put them all together and get them to share their ideas. Company X may do something a certain way, and four others can take advantage of that." However, although it has some theoretical benefits, the involvement of multiple owners represents another potential pitfall that can lead to substantial problems. As Courten warned, "It can be like herding cats."[15]

Enticed to join the rollup for the financial gains of the promised IPO, the consolidating owners also expect to retain their past authority and independence. Each may anticipate assumption of a greater leadership role over the entire organization, and a group of 12 owner-led subsidiaries implies 12 chiefs who believe they should define the organization's direction. Conflicts are almost inevitable, and even those willing to accede to a founding architect's leadership still believe that their operations can be best led according to their personal dictates. Then, if the needs of the consolidator conflict with those of the local owner, she will object vociferously, potentially refusing to participate, insisting on managing her business according to its individual best interests. As the Booz Allen analysts noted, many of the deals included owner earn-outs governed by the acquired entity's specific performance, but such earn-outs necessitated continued measurement of the performance of each discreet entity—thereby discouraging integration and undermining delivery of the promised efficiencies of consolidation.[16]

To mitigate conflicts, the owner's departure is usually the only viable solution, and when coupled with disappointing stock price performance, it is often such conflicts that drive owners to quit. Although often necessary, their departures create a leadership vacuum, and if they are not replaced with a capable manager, the business can falter. The experience of almost all medical practitioner rollups perhaps provides the most compelling examples:

- Created in 1988 by former executives of Hospital Corporation of America, Phycor, Inc., was the pioneering founder of the first physicians practice management company, essentially a rollup of the previously independent practices of medical doctors. By 1996, it owned 43 clinics in 24 states, posting revenues of $766.3 million with purported profits of $36.4 million. But by 1999, the company was saddled with multiple lawsuits from participants who sought to void their agreements, large numbers of doctors resigned from its clinics, and it reoriented its focus to seek service contracts without the risk of acquiring clinics.[17]

- Physicians Resource Group, Inc. represented Steve Harter's rollup of the ophthalmology niche with 1996 sales of $411 million. Critics pointed to its poor integration and weak management while Harter protested: "None of the physician consolidations are doing well. … Is it an industry problem or a Steve Harter problem? But I am not going to tell you that this company had my strongest management team. They were replaced."[18]

Cultural Clash

The consolidation of dozens of entrepreneurial enterprises inevitably implies the merger of purportedly similar businesses that nonetheless have varied operational models. Moreover, with diverse leadership traits, their colorful leaders employ different tactics to perform the tasks of their peers. The most successful remain confident that their approach is best and disdain alternatives, and the titular leadership struggles with the proverbial difficulties of herding cats. As Kentucky Fried Chicken's John Y. Brown told *BusinessWeek*, "At one time, I had 21 millionaires reporting to me at eight o'clock every morning. It could drive you crazy."[19] Such competing leadership interests can therefore lead to nettlesome conflicts that hamper integration and undermine the consolidated enterprise's progress.

Having acquired businesses primarily from owners who were ready to retire or pursue new opportunities, Trader rarely retained founders to manage the acquisitions. Nonetheless, it experienced a comparable variety of cultural and interpersonal issues that undermined integration efforts and operational success.

As was described in Chapter 7, Landmark acquired the Chicago *Auto Mart* from Mark Hoffman, an extraordinarily aggressive competitor who had carefully guarded the secrets of his business until the day of the closing. After the closing, Landmark finally had its first opportunity to meet the staff, and it discovered a dedicated crew infused with a messianic passion to defeat the enemy. In their minds, the enemy had been Landmark's auto guide, and with its owner's encouragement, the staff perceived itself as victor, now eager to hear about the burial of its former nemesis. Rather than closing its original publication and backing *Auto Mart*, however, Landmark was far more interested in leveraging the two publications to capture an even greater share of the classified advertising market from the far more dominant local newspapers and broadcast media. That implied a cooperative and concerted effort by the two staffs to fulfill a broader mission against a more substantial adversary, but the acquired employees had no interest in working cooperatively with their former competitor.

For months, efforts to cultivate supportive working relationships went nowhere, and it became apparent that the aggressive and sometimes antagonistic attitude could not be easily redirected toward helping another publication grow. Arguably, the efforts to instill cooperative attitudes actually reduced the competitiveness of the sales organization, causing erosion of the growth trajectory. That was unfortunate because their approach had been so successful against Landmark's publication, and redirecting their energy toward capturing a healthier share of the market served by other media represented a much greater opportunity.

Trader ran into the same problem repeatedly with subsequent acquisitions that had been competitive with one another. The sales organization of San Francisco's *Diablo Dealer* (a used car photo ad tabloid) had perceived *Auto Trader* as its nemesis, and Trader's acquisition of *Diablo Dealer* was resented by many in the *Diablo Dealer* organization. That resentment led to begrudging acceptance of directives, many of which were effectively ignored. Only after experiencing staff turnover and the installation of new management did the organization start thinking of itself as a part of the company instead of an independent nation suffering from the restrictions and evil ministrations of a foreign power.

As an organization grows through acquisition, the instillation of a uniform culture, though desirable, is very difficult. Old attitudes take time to modify, and some refuse to die. In some cases, the only way to facilitate transformation is to replace those most adamantly oppose d to change. But with their replacement comes the risk that something else will be lost, some critical element that had been fundamental to the acquisition's success. Clearly, the disappearance of Mark Hoffman's aggressive competitiveness eroded the energy driving the impressive sales growth of the Chicago *Auto Mart*, and that kind of loss represents another peril associated with completing a rollup and managing its integration.

Buying Local Competition May Not Work

Despite its diminished growth trajectory, the Chicago *Auto Mart* continued to progress rapidly after acquisition, and its return on investment proved most impressive. However, experience demonstrates that acquisition of competitors often fails to deliver benefits, and a variety of academic studies show that most acquisitions completed to enhance market share do not produce better performance.[20] The acquisition of local competitors can therefore represent another pitfall to avoid in consolidations.

During its rollup of employment publications, Trader acquired competing guides in four different cities, and it continued to operate both simultaneously, theorizing that it could be done profitably while preempting new competitors from filling the void if the publications were merged. In practice, one of the titles succeeded particularly well, whereas the other began to struggle. Efforts to rejuvenate the failing title regularly produced a negative impact on the more successful one. In retrospect, little was gained, and the return on investment from acquiring the competitor was negligible, if not negative.

During the frothy era of Internet launches, Trader was led astray with its acquisition of the Plano, Texas, *Employment News*. Having successfully launched its own Dallas edition of *Employment Guide* in 1997, Trader was enjoying robust profitability in the market, but it became covetous of the simultaneous success of *Employment News*. Despite the competition, relations with its founder and publisher were cordial because both organizations were focusing their energies on siphoning revenues from the dominant *Dallas Morning Herald*. The founder, however, demanded a substantial premium for his business, which normally would have stymied the deal. However, when the owners of Jobs.com expressed interest in the publication, Trader became concerned that if acquired, *Employment News* would become the model for Jobs.com's rollout of publications to drive traffic to its website. With that as an added motivation, Trader proceeded to pay the premium price to acquire *Employment News*. Once it was acquired, however, its results began to deteriorate, and Trader was never able to capture the anticipated return.

Nevertheless, sometimes it makes sense to acquire overlapping entities. When the business opportunity is particularly broad or has limited barriers to entry, it can make sense to acquire and establish different brands within the same market segment. Like Procter & Gamble's two competing Pampers and Luvs brands of diapers, there are cases in which multiple brands are needed to command a leading share of the shelf space.

From this perspective, it made sense for Starbucks to acquire Seattle's Best in 2003 for $72 million. Coffee, of course, is something a majority of adult customers consume, sometimes several times a day, and it therefore became compelling for Starbucks to offer a slightly differentiated product to extend its control over a larger share of the marketing shelf space. As the company's chairman, Howard Schultz, stated at the time, "Both [Seattle's Best and Torrefazione Italia] offer superb specialty coffees that are distinct from Starbucks flavor profiles. These brands will allow us to satisfy the desires of consumers with an affinity for the smooth flavors of SBC coffees and distinctive Italian recipes of Torrefazione Italia coffees, while focusing on expanding the demand for these types of specialty coffees."[21]

The secondary brand also permitted penetration into competing venues that would have been otherwise impossible. To differentiate itself, it was critical for Borders to offer a distinguished national brand in its in-store coffee areas that was distinctive from the Starbucks brand already served in Barnes & Noble, and Seattle's Best provided that alternative.

Deal Makers, Not Operators

The lack of critical operational skills among the consolidating architects represents another impediment to a rollup's success. The radiant allure of doing deals attracts financiers and high-energy marketing types who may not have a realistic understanding of a business's prospects, its optimal operational tactics, or the difficulties of integrating dozens of disparate units. Fundamentally, the talents that create good deal makers are distinctly different from those which create good operators.

Warren Buffett devotes his efforts to identifying good investments and deploying capital while delegating operational duties to talented managers who are passionate about Berkshire Hathaway's constituent businesses. Apple's Steven Jobs devoted his energies to product development and operational matters while delegating most acquisition work to staffers.

Despite displaying an astonishing ability to orchestrate scores of transactions, many of the most notorious serial rollup engineers were less impressive with the postclosing integration process. Jonathon Ledecky and Steve Harter completed over a dozen separate rollups, but very few survived in the long term, as discussed in Chapter 2. More important, they may not have the discipline, time, or ability to perform all the management duties necessary to consolidate a national enterprise and direct its performance over the long term.

Arguably, Landmark's and Trader's success derived from the fact their consolidation of small industry niches was driven not by deal makers but by dedicated business managers who were eager to roll up their sleeves and get their hands dirty in day-to-day operations. They were far more passionate about delivering results in accordance with their vision than they were about doing another deal.

Operators Divert Focus from Deal Making

Although being too enamored with the deal-making process may represent a substantial barrier to success, a focus on operations may undermine optimal consolidation of rollup opportunities. Certainly, postclosing operational emphasis on achieving projected results contributed to Landmark's and Trader's successes, but that partiality meant that efforts to continue acquisitions often took a backseat, reducing their prospects for the greater success promised by a more acquisitive effort.

After completing four deals in the mid–1980s, Landmark's acquisition effort went into dormancy as its management team devoted its efforts to integrating the new businesses. After the purchase of *Tradin' Times* in 1986, its principal deal maker became so captivated by the integration challenges that little progress was made toward completing the dozens of desirable deals that might have been pursued. Repeatedly, Bill Diederich urged a greater focus on chasing those deals, but Landmark's managers focused on managing its new businesses, providing time for Cox Enterprises and John McBane to leap into the fray.

Finally goaded into action, Landmark reorganized. Diederich directed his divisional chief financial officer to relinquish his operational duties and turn his attention almost exclusively to acquisitions, and those rejuvenated efforts led to Landmark's consolidating a third of the country's classified ad and photo guides through the completion of 18 deals in 22 months. But its earlier diversion to integration and operations had regrettably provided the delay, permitting Cox to capture another third of the U.S. properties while McBane consolidated those in Canada, Europe, and Asia.

The subsequent 1991 merger of Cox and Landmark properties to create Trader Publishing Company led to a similar acquisition hiatus. Without the threat of competitors sniping away for comparable deals, management focused on the complex integration efforts required to consolidate two large groups of still relatively fresh acquisitions, and Trader's newly constituted board of directors demonstrated its satisfaction by underscoring its preference for the production of profits. In fact, in 1992, Trader signed a letter of intent to acquire the largest *Auto Trader* group in the United Kingdom for attractive terms in the high eight figures, but concern over the economic climate and the required investment led Trader's board to derail the deal just weeks before closing, insisting it would divert management attention from its U.S. opportunities. That deal's termination proved unfortunate because just six years later, the British group was sold to a private equity group for four times the former price, and in 2003, Guardian Media Group bought 100 percent control for a price that valued the group at £1.14 billion.[22]

Since it completed 38 deals during the four years before its 1991 creation, it is perhaps astonishing that Trader made only two acquisitions in the three years that followed: one in 1992 and another in 1994. Certainly, management had a lot to accomplish in digesting the scores of publications acquired earlier and integrating the culture and organizational philosophies of the Cox and Landmark management teams. However, revenues and earnings among its properties grew at impressive double-digit rates during those early years, and those strong financial results confirmed the desirability of pursuing other rollups.

By 1995, the integration challenges had subsided, and the need to establish new avenues for future growth became paramount. Although it retained its operationally focused management team, Trader reorganized to apply more management talent to the identification and rollup of new segments and the development of the innovative and transformational Internet opportunities bursting onto the scene.

Operators, Not Innovators

In the modern economy, businesses will be at great risk of disintegration if they simply remain focused on managing their enterprises according to established patterns. Longer-term success among rollups therefore is very much predicated on the ability of an organization's leadership and staff to identify the transformative innovations that confront their businesses, adjust their model to adapt to the changing environment, and leverage those innovations to grow their enterprises. After hundreds of years of prosperity, the newspaper industry began facing a dark future of increasing irrelevancy as its preeminent editorial and advertising position disintegrated while its core readers died off, replaced by avid users of smartphone and tablet aps that supply real-time information instantaneously.

After two decades of prosperity, text-based classified advertising magazines such as Trader's *Atlanta Advertiser* found themselves losing out in the 1980s to *Auto Trader*, which featured photographs, a superior and far more descriptive solution displaying the differentiating characteristics between one seller's Toyota Camry and another's Honda Civic. The *Atlanta Advertiser*'s 15-word textual ads communicated little compared with the photo ad, which provided the consumer with the graphic information that the Toyota Camry is the larger car, more similar to the Honda Accord.

And then, of course, the Internet presented the opportunity for a gigantic leap beyond the simple photograph. It could instantaneously transmit to the whole world of buyers an infinite amount of information about a car advertised for sale. If Trader's managers had not latched on to that transformative innovation, their brand would have been at risk of vanishing as surely as Borders has from the book-selling industry. As it was, the aggressive development of its supplemental AutoTrader.com Internet service could not forestall the disappearance of Trader's $400 million revenue magazine business in 2009, but it did ensure its brand's transformation into an over $1 billion Internet enterprise.

Skullduggery and Accounting Issues

Thrilled by skyrocketing stock values, the leaders of publicly traded rollups are compelled to accelerate the acquisition pace to maintain earnings velocity even when the deals fail to make economic sense. More problematic, however, is the fact that their compulsion may encourage the commission of fraud to maintain the appearance of the success necessary to support lofty stock prices; the history of rollups includes its fair share of such scandals.

The early poster child of rollups, Waste Management, found itself following that primrose path to scandal. In 1999, after nasty litigation, the company recorded a $3.5 billion charge to rectify false and misleading accounting statements for the years 1993–1996, and with its accounting firm, Arthur Andersen, it paid $229 million to settle accompanying shareholder lawsuits. Then, in November 2001, it paid another $457 million to settle class action lawsuits relating to its 1999 financial statements and security law violations in connection with its USA Waste Services merger in 1998.[23]

Shortly after the Waste Management scandal, the largest corporate scandal relating to rollups came to a boil.

In 1983, former milkman and basketball coach Bernard Ebbers met with two partners in a Hattiesburg, Mississippi, coffee shop, where they sketched on a napkin a business plan to become a long-distance telephone service reseller. Less than two years later, Ebbers became chief executive officer of the still tiny Long-Distance Discount Service, Inc., and he launched headlong into the rapid expansion of the business through the rollup and rollout strategy. With its acquisition of Advantage Companies in 1989, it became known as Worldcom, and it continued the serial rollup of similar companies, including Resurgens Communications Group, Media Communications, IDB Communications Group, Williams Telecommunications Group, MFS Communications Company, and UUNet Technologies. Ebbers's efforts culminated in 1998 with a $40 billion merger with MCI Communications, the largest in history at that time; that was succeeded by a 2000 attempted merger with Sprint Communications that eventually was aborted because of antitrust considerations.

But all was not well. The slowing telecommunications industry led to declining stock prices, and Ebbers had used his WorldCom stock to collateralize huge loans to finance other business endeavors. The declining stock price led to margin calls, leading Ebbers to persuade his board to give him over $400 million in loans and guarantees, and then it came to light that Ebbers had participated in a massive fraud. Since at least 1999, earnings had been overstated by $11 billion by capitalizing telecommunication interconnection operating charges instead of expensing them and inflating revenues with bogus accounting entries from corporate reserve accounts. Those discoveries soon led to the bankruptcy of the company and a 25-year prison sentence for Ebbers.[24]

Although WorldCom's lenders and common stock investors suffered dearly in that debacle, sometimes it is another corporate acquirer (and its shareholders) that pays the penalty. Started in 1994, The Learning Company was created through the consolidation of more than a dozen software companies serving the children's electronic games and education market (including Softkey and Brøderbund), and with the dawning of the new millennium, Mattel hungrily gobbled it up to capture its prominent product lines. While completing its $3.5 billion deal, Mattel executives discovered disturbing accounting issues, but it wasn't until two months after closing that they concluded that Mattel had acquired a house of cards. Less than a year later, along with the departure of Mattel's chief executive and an agreement to pay off $500 million of the acquisition's debt, The Learning Company was given to Gores Technology Group for future consideration of just $27.3 million. Subsequently, Mattel settled shareholder lawsuits by paying another $122 million.[25]

Buying Late in the Product Life Cycle or in an Ephemeral Industry

Another warning about pursuing rollups is to avoid industries whose products or services face impending obsolescence. Although some investors may find the unwanted and inexpensive cash cows of a declining industry appealing, they may be sorely disappointed when the fall proves more precipitous than expected, with the presumed milkable beasts collapsing in the dust before they can produce any return. Even worse is the prospect of latching on to a bottle rocket that shoots skyward, quickly exploding in an evaporating shower of ephemeral sparks.

For a relatively brief moment in telecommunications history, the paging industry appeared to have the bright prospects of a rocket to the moon. In the 1980s, hundreds of entrepreneurs launched paging services to serve medical providers, emergency respondents, service representatives, and essential executives. Then, toward the end of the decade, several concluded that it would be a boon to consolidate services to provide national coverage: organizations that included Arch Wireless, MobilMedia, Metrocall, and PageNet. Founded originally in 1986 to serve the Boston market, Arch Wireless grew quickly through a series of 30 acquisitions to establish itself as the United States' fifth largest supplier of paging services in the early 1990s. Although the cost and availability of cellular phone services were becoming competitive by that time, Arch remained undeterred despite posting losses of $181.9 million in 1997. To become the country's second largest paging vendor, it acquired MobilMedia out of bankruptcy for $649 million in 1998; then, in 1999, in a pitched battle with the competitor Metrocall, it succeeded in acquiring the nation's largest provider, PageNet, a company that had recently filed an involuntary Chapter 11 petition, having never posted a profit since its 1991 IPO.[26] Arch's own bankruptcy followed little more than a year later, and after it and Metrocall both emerged from bankruptcy in 2002, they concluded that their best chance for survival was to merge to create USA Mobility in 2004.[27] However, the paging industry continued to decline, with U.S. revenues dropping another two-thirds from $6.2 billion in 2003 to $2.1 billion in 2008, but USA Mobility persevered, struggling to adapt by offering mobile voice/data services through third-party providers while keeping its focus on providing numeric and alphanumeric messaging services to the country's healthcare, government, hospitality/restaurant, and emergency response sectors.

Trader itself fell prey to the mistake of completing acquisitions at the tail end of their assets' product life cycle. With the Internet clearly in its ascendancy, it nonetheless acquired its last *Auto Trader* licensees in February 2000 and May 2001, barely eight years before publishing its last paid circulation auto guides. Those magazines fell victim to the instantaneous, ubiquitous, and free availability of online classifieds through services such as Craigslist.com, AutoTrader.com, and Cars.com.

Chapter 9

Components of Rollup Success

"That's fascinating!" said Conrad Hall, sitting in an ancient desk chair in the basement of the entrepreneur's home, where the business was operated. But just as he was about to ask another question, the telephone began ringing.

"Ignore it," said the entrepreneur, waving at the phone dismissively. "It'll stop in a minute."

Sure enough, the ringing stopped, and Hall continued his questioning. But almost immediately the phone interrupted him again.

"Go ahead," said Hall. "Answer the phone. I don't mind. You need to run your business."

"Hhmph!" said the probably 60-year-old entrepreneur. "No, go on. If I answer it, it'll just start ringing again."

A bit surprised, Hall continued, and then the phone started ringing a third time, causing the entrepreneur to scowl in exasperation.

"Mr. Hall, do you mind if I turn off these infernal phones. They're driving me crazy."

"No," Hall said. "Do what you think best. But have you thought about hiring someone to answer your phones? It seems like you're losing business if you don't pick up when it rings."

"Hire employees?" The owner sneered. "I made that mistake once! Before you know it, they're complaining about their pay and wanting health insurance and other fringe benefits. When that happened with my one employee, I waited until she quit. I then told my wife, 'Honey, if we can't get it done, it just won't get done.' Mr. Hall, never hire employees if you can manage. They're nothing but trouble!"[1]

Instead of revealing best practices, the evaluation of an acquisition prospect sometimes produces astonishing insights into how poorly a business can be run. The buyer is thus inspired by how easily the business could be modified to accelerate its trajectory toward success. The owners may have a wonderful concept and a hungry consumer base, but they just don't have the business acumen or energy to perform even the simple tasks necessary to fulfill that promise. Answering the phones, hiring capable staff to absorb the service burden, and generating new sales are just a few of the fundamental requirements of operating a successful business, and all must be performed admirably to achieve optimal success.

With a rollup, the need to perform all those critical tasks remains fundamental to success, but as Trader and others discovered, some acquisitions may not even have the staff, programs, and processes in place. The buyer must then devote precious energy and limited resources to recruit new talent and institute efficient operational procedures. Accordingly, the complexity and breadth of integration of diverse, geographically dispersed entities can be increasingly problematic with each successive deal:

- Founded in 1996 with hopes of an IPO on the horizon, Randy McPherson's Collision Auto Repair of America (CARA) quickly scooped up 26 independent car repair shops in five states, achieving peak revenues of almost $40 million in 1998. But as its director of operations concluded, the company "lacked the internal management structure" to manage its broadly dispersed operations. After recruiting expensive talent to enhance and coordinate operations, it experienced exorbitant costs of shuttling trainers and supervisory talent throughout its expansive territory. After its struggling locations continued to flounder, McPherson replaced the shop managers, exacerbating turnover and performance problems. By 1999, McPherson himself was replaced, and his successor, Jim Hawley, sold all but a dozen shops before filing Chapter 7 liquidation that June with year-to-date losses of $2 million.[2]

- Three years after its 1996 IPO, Integrated Electrical Services topped $1.1 billion in revenue after completing a hectic spate of 60 acquisitions of commercial, industrial, and residential electrical contractors. Though it earned early kudos from *CFO* magazine in 1999,[3] the company had already begun experiencing problems with integration and operations. After suffering through several reorganizations and the 2010 annual loss of $30 million on $461 million revenue, its latest CEO was replaced in June 2011 by the private equity executive Jim Lindstrom. Lindstrom continued the restructuring efforts, incurring as much as $5.5 million in future closure costs on top of the June quarter's $10 million loss on $123 million sales.[4]

As implied by examples such as CARA and Integrated Electrical Services, lack of managerial bench strength and the inefficiency of remote management of often overpriced and ill-managed acquisitions can be daunting. Too often the consequences are collapse from mismanagement, expensive disruptions, and increased supervisory and other costs. Critical to success is the presence of insightful, managerially astute leaders who can deliver superior returns on prudent investments as they integrate the acquisitions to leverage the industry's best practices, capitalize on development strategies, and restrain costs. To optimize success and enhance investment returns, the rollup should also have the following:

- Substantial prospects for its short-term replication through start-ups of the business in additional markets.
- The foundation of a significant innovative development opportunity.

Organizations that reap impressive success are the ones that aggressively pursue such replication and innovative development opportunities.

Acquire Value

To earn a comfortable return on any acquisition, every investor should maintain fervent allegiance to Benjamin Graham's insistence on confining investment to that which "upon thorough analysis, promises safety of principal and a satisfactory return."[5] Because of the unpredictability of future performance and the inevitability of competitive and other market pressures, it is also critical to ladle in a healthy dose of Graham's margin of safety whenever one is projecting anticipated returns.

Although it is difficult for rollup artists to admit to overpaying, the evidence abounds with stories of the collapse of entities such as CARA and the struggles of Integrated Electrical Systems. However, no matter how conscientious the acquisition team is, overpayment will inevitably occur during a rapid rollup process. The overzealous desire to "win" the deal motivates recklessness, and uncertain futures ensure errors in projecting future cash flows. Rollup practitioners should therefore strive to retain practical, realistic perspectives as they project returns cautiously.

As was described in Chapter 5, Landmark's and Trader's management strived to maintain valuation sanity by grounding projected cash flows on demonstrated historical results and reasonable forecasts. They then rigorously evaluated carefully constructed discounted cash flow analyses to confirm their practicality and realism and compared the resulting returns with customary valuation multiples ranging from six times trailing EBITDA (most desirable) to a maximum of eight times (appropriate for highly attractive growth targets).

But inevitably, exceptions were made, and for good reason. Some businesses promised extraordinary growth, and past cash flows failed to account for the acquirer's ability to reduce expenses and raise revenue to enhance profits with more efficient processes and best practices. In those cases, higher valuations appeared rational. However, realizing those benefits is far more difficult than estimating them, and prudent management should remain suspicious about their achievement until they are recorded in the financial statements. Still, sellers often demand premium prices, and competition for desirable companies sometimes dictates paying more than one prefers. To complete those deals, risks must be taken, but the buyer should be prudent.

In the early stages of its rollup of classified ad publications, Landmark became captivated with the opportunity to acquire Tradin' Times, Inc., a publisher operating almost two dozen magazines in nine cities. During the prior few years, the company had been adrift, pursuing a series of product diversification ventures that had increased costs and diverted the staff from its core business. Two of its city operations were actually losing money, and the owner had become less engaged and was disillusioned. Still, though open to acquisition, the owner insisted on a price of over 16 times trailing EBITDA.

A close examination of the operations of Tradin' Times suggested that the losing publications could be closed, the home office could be consolidated with another Landmark facility, and sales efforts could be redirected to the core with impressive results. In fact, even with a reasonably cautious implementation plan, Landmark projected that earnings would increase 130 percent during the first year. After months of patient discussions, the owner eventually reduced his price by 20 percent (still a multiple over 13), and, confident about the anticipated savings, Landmark decided to proceed, perceiving the company's value as equal to less than six times projected first-year earnings. A year later, Landmark was gratified when earnings came in close to projections and revenue growth had accelerated to double-digit rates, promising even better future returns than anticipated.

However, conscientious projections to justify a premium valuation sometimes lead companies astray. In 2000, Trader completed the largest transaction in its history, paying $533 million (including assumed debt) for the United News & Media subsidiary United Advertising Publications (UAP). Representing an almost nine times multiple of trailing cash flow, the price exceeded Trader's comfort level but had been required to win the investment banker–led auction. Having projected early savings from staff reductions and the installation of enhanced production systems, Trader expected to return to a safer valuation multiple during its first year of ownership, but the debilitating 2001 recession had been unanticipated. Revenues were hammered, and earnings dropped by more than half despite cost reductions. Fortunately, as part of the Federal Reserve's efforts to rejuvenate the economy, interest rates plummeted, and Trader's borrowing costs dropped to about 2 percent, permitting a still attractive "leveraged" return on the borrowed $533 million. Moreover, the decline motivated management to accelerate its integration plans, producing substantial cost reductions that positioned the company for the dramatically enhanced cash flows generated in later years.

Restrict Investments to Those Which Can Be Supported

In their rabid efforts to acquire sufficient revenues and scale to satisfy Wall Street's criteria for a public offering, companies such as Collision Auto Repair of America often acquire whatever properties they can without paying particular attention to whether they have the capital necessary to weather any shortfalls experienced by their operations. When several of CARA's units failed to deliver projected profits, its thin reserves were quickly depleted, putting it in a precarious financial position. Its delayed payments created anxiety among its vendors, and potential lenders were discouraged from funding the loans needed to continue the business. The inevitable consequence was financial distress, leading to its eventual liquidation.

CARA was just one of the many rollup enterprises that collapsed into ignominy because they acquired more businesses than they could support during periods of financial reversal. It demonstrates that a prudent acquirer should restrict its investments intelligently.

To protect itself from similar stress, both Trader and Landmark maintained a highly conservative financing discipline, restricting total debt to a level of less than three times EBITDA. Many organizations and investment bankers consider that level too restrictive, arguing that many successful enterprises have flourished with debt levels more than twice that amount. The cable industry is one example in that it has routinely employed leverage of six and seven times EBITDA, but both Landmark and Trader preferred keeping their leverage low to minimize financial stress while preserving their ability to borrow for future acquisitions.

The financial collapse of 2008 quieted advocates of more liberal borrowing. Less than two months after acquiring Landmark's Weather Channel for

$3.5 billion through its NBC subsidiary, General Electric's Jeffrey Imelt found himself running desperately to Warren Buffett, thankful for the investor's willingness to purchase $3 billion of preferred shares, paying a 10 percent preferred dividend (with warrants to buy $3 billion common shares at a strike price of $22.25)[6]; that was quite a stiff yield at a time when the Federal Reserve was pushing down interest rates to historic lows of almost 0 percent. Cognizant that the availability of funds can literally evaporate for even the most respected organizations, few investors should feel comfortable with leverage exceeding four times EBITDA.

Very few companies can command the attention of a Warren Buffett for a bailout, and the precarious state of earnings during a downturn provides further justification for maintaining a conservative balance sheet. Although $100 million of debt may represent a multiple of four times $25 million in EBITDA, it will transform into a 10 multiple if a recession reduces earnings by 60 percent. Assuming that a loan carries covenants requiring debt coverage of six times EBITDA, the borrower will suddenly find himself under the intense scrutiny of his lender, who may call the loan, force liquidation, or worse.

Calamitous market reversals caused Metals USA to file for bankruptcy in November 2001. Founded in 1997 to consolidate numerous businesses that provided value-added processed steel, stainless steel, aluminum, and manufactured metal components, Metals USA had grown from a revenue base of $537.6 million to $2.1 billion in 2000. But it had failed to capture meaningful synergies from its rollup strategy, and it was already under stress when it posted just $71.4 million in operating income to support its $489.9 million in net long-term debt at the end of 2000. Accordingly, it had no cushion when sales dropped 27 percent during the industry collapse the next year, and its $392 million operating loss forced it to rush to the courts for protection in bankruptcy.[7]

Have Dedicated, Talented, Experienced Leadership to Manage the Consolidated Entity

Low-leverage financing and conservative investment practices are part of a prudent investor's disciplined behavior. But it takes careful planning and impressive management skills to achieve projected returns in acquiring multiple operations over a short period, and the implied integration responsibilities can be executed successfully only by having experienced leadership that is fully committed and solely dedicated to the mission of the new consolidated entity.

Because of the complexity and complications associated with integrating multiple acquisitions, a successful consolidation requires the dedicated attention of talented operational leaders who are passionate and knowledgeable about their industry segments. Nonetheless, during the 1990s, some consolidators attempted to roll up several fragmented industries simultaneously despite the fact that they had little experience in the varied segments.

As was noted in Chapter 2, Steven Harter attempted to orchestrate the concurrent rollup of numerous disparate industries with his U.S. Delivery Systems, Incom, HomeUSA, CoachUSA, Metals USA, and TransCom USA, to name the more prominent. Similarly, Jon Ledecky launched several initiatives, including U.S. Office Products, U.S.A. Floral Products, and Building One Services. Although their stock prices experienced meteoric rises after their initial public offerings, it is no wonder that most burned to a crisp as they returned to the earth's atmosphere. Suffering the exponential problems arising from juggling numerous rollups simultaneously, no single engineer had much chance of producing enduring success, and the inability to recruit capable leadership destined those businesses to a rapid visit to hard times on the doorstep of bankruptcy court.

When Landmark began acquiring classified advertising publications in 1985, it had the luxury of doing it at the rate of about two each year. To coordinate the process, it had one of its proven managers fully dedicated to the task, and he had the support of Landmark's infrastructure and staff to provide assistance with administrative matters and the implementation of boilerplate requirements such as human resource compliance programs, accounting procedures, and audit oversight. The breadth of available resources dramatically enhanced integration effectiveness, and the relatively few transactions did not overburden resident talent, which could be allocated at little incremental cost to the organization.

If it is intent on rolling up as many businesses as possible, an independent enterprise will experience a different scenario. Each transaction will require the attention of its best managerial talent, but that talent will find it nearly impossible to provide the necessary supervision in multiple locations. Most likely, the enterprise itself will be in the middle of organizing its headquarters' administrative processes and procedures, leaving little opportunity to direct newly acquired field operations. The result is that the acquisitions are left to operate as they did in the past. Although this has short-term merit (don't fix what isn't broken), there is a critical need to adopt a common reporting platform to ensure coordinated payment of bills, collection of revenues, and fulfillment of service obligations in accordance with the reasonable standards of the industry. Though implying a distasteful level of bureaucracy, its institution provides the means to monitor performance, and it provides the foundation through which overlapping processes can be streamlined and best practices can be instituted.

When Landmark and Cox accelerated their acquisition spree, the demands stressed the limited resources of both organizations, and problems arose as they completed 28 transactions in the 18 months from March 1988 to August 1989. To the chagrin of Frank Batten and Bill Diederich who feared the window of opportunity was closing, Landmark's divisional CEO, Larry Coffey, pleaded for a temporary moratorium on new deal activity. He found that his core newspaper operations were being neglected while his staff was swamped with the demands of organizing and developing new resources to handle the acquisitions' integration.

Quickly realizing that the diversion of Coffey's organization could both undermine its newspaper operations and slow progress on its acquisitions, Landmark's leadership concluded that a new division should be created and appointed Conrad Hall to organize it immediately. Those acquisitions, after all, had a disjointed hodgepodge of production, administration, billing, accounting, and human resource systems, and their efficient consolidation and upgrade promised substantial savings. But the effort would require a dedicated team of capable managers.

As an early champion of Landmark's rollup, Hall was ecstatic about leading the charge, and he promptly assembled from Landmark's management ranks a corps of experienced lieutenants to help. With a decade's experience in advertising sales and management, George Brooks joined Norman Hoffmann, who had managed a small daily newspaper and supervised earlier integrations. Britt Reid, having progressed through the ranks to the position of president of *Tradin' Times*, provided well-grounded insight into the business and industry, coupled with polished talents as a respected and motivational leader. To shoulder the challenges of human resource management, Hall recruited Sunny Sonner, a successful outsider who had an impressive reputation and credentials in that discipline. With this cadre of experienced professionals, Hall directed efforts to consolidate operations by leveraging the resources already employed in the field, insisting that the decentralized approach would leverage the talents of knowledgeable local veterans and mitigate the need to add expensive home office overhead.

Likewise, from the start of its rollup efforts, Cox understood that it needed a dedicated organization to command the consolidated entities, one that would not be diverted by legacy businesses. Having acquired Stuart Arnold's $30 million base of operations in Florida, Cox chose it as the foundation for development and appointed Bob Musselman to consolidate its 14 acquisitions from that headquarters. Having risen from Cox's accounting ranks to assume broad management duties at its large metropolitan dailies, Musselman was well prepared to assume the complex organizational mission required for the integration, and he appointed Lou Tarasi from Arnold's organization to help improve the effectiveness of the field's sales organization and provide seasoned insights into the intricacies of the business. To add more administrative depth, Musselman recruited Mitch Brooks and Bill Dorsey, two rising stars from Cox's newspaper division. With a strong background in accounting and audit, Brooks focused on administrative, production, and distribution systems to improve their efficiency and effectiveness, and Dorsey took over the duties of Arnold's struggling controller to formalize the accounting and administrative systems introduced by Musselman and Brooks. Together, the four devoted full-time effort to bring sanity to the chaos presented by the cascading needs arising from the newly acquired entities.

Remain Devoted to Identifying Best Practices from Each Acquisition

In the world of acquisitions, the leaders of the acquiring entity are prone to perceive themselves as the winner, and as winners, they are likely to believe they have achieved success because of their superior knowledge, ability, and insights. They may therefore proceed to implement changes on the basis of their prior experience without considering alternatives. As *Star Trek's* Borg insist, "You will be assimilated."

In the world of rollups, that perception of superiority can be particularly damaging. Most rollup practitioners are new to the segment they are consolidating and are certainly unfamiliar with the individual operations they are acquiring. Moreover, as one fragment of a broadly diversified group of mom-and-pop independents, each acquisition has a different variety of processes and procedures supporting the similar operations and concepts.

Accordingly, an astute acquirer should proceed as if he were a passionately interested student, fervently committed to identifying the critical success factors underlying each acquired business. His goal should be to compare the operations with others, meticulously evaluating relative benefits to define the elements most capable of delivering optimal results. With that mindset, superior programs can be plucked from the acquisitions and past operational experience, and their prior applications can guide and inspire adoption and implementation throughout affiliated operations.

In Trader's experience with the *Auto Trader* licensees, each operation seemed to achieve its results because of something unique to its specific location. The Phoenix owners had captured the most impressive share of private party advertising, Seattle did the best job in selling advertising among commercial used car dealers, and Lexington had superior success in penetrating small contiguous markets. Even the operations managed by the dimmest owners seemed to be doing something better than their peers: One had created an astonishingly cost-efficient distribution system; one paid retailers just 20 percent of the cover price instead of the more standard 30 percent; one had a successful ad cultivation program; and one had some clever point-of-purchase displays that appeared to boost single copy sales. From those experiences, Trader's management assembled a slate of initiatives that could be implemented among sister operations to accelerate growth and profits.

Even when Landmark and Cox merged their operations, the two teams found that they had learned different lessons, and by conscientiously assessing their different perspectives, they developed more optimal solutions. For example, Landmark had left circulation billing and management to field operations, simply providing better computer systems and tested algorithms to designate the best magazine allotments for each store. In contrast, Cox had developed regional hubs to consolidate its circulation's accounting and administration for the hundreds of magazines among 70,000 distribution outlets. Not only were Cox's impressively efficient regional operations more accurate and reliable, the systemwide transactions supplied a superior database to project ideal store allotments.

Engender Commitment to Adopting Productive Changes and Best Practices

The staffs of most acquisitions are comfortable with the way they have done things in the past, and human nature dictates that people usually resist change. Having learned their jobs under different ownership, the employees have confidence in performing their prior duties and tend to experience anxiety and uncertainty when new processes or procedures are introduced. When a new owner suggests improvements, their anxieties usually cause them to nod approvingly even though they may have grave reservations. Many are more concerned about keeping their jobs and endearing themselves to the new employer, and they will hesitate to express misgivings. On the one hand, their accommodating attitude opens the door to automatic acceptance of changes the acquirer wants to make. When the acquirer is confident that changes are critical, this therefore is the time to fiat them through. Implementation of new employee benefit programs, administrative policies, and accounting procedures represents the kinds of changes that are usually best instituted on day 1 as a fait accompli.

On the other hand, the silent acceptance of change may prevent the buyer from discovering critical facts that override the desirability of promptly introducing changes or could create troublesome problems in the future. Accordingly, an astute acquirer should openly and tactfully solicit staff input before issuing directives to implement more monumental changes. By first soliciting the staff's insights and reactions, the buyer encourages a free exchange of knowledge and establishes an environment where problems and solutions can be identified. Objections can be addressed, and examples can be reviewed to persuade the staff of the desirability of a change or the adoption of best practices. That involvement makes the staff part of the decision-making process, and their participation tends to improve their willingness to support changes as they are implemented. In particular, if they can be persuaded of the personal benefits of adopting a new best practice, they may do so more successfully. For example, Trader's emphasis on selling multipage advertising spreads to car dealers generated higher commissions for the sales team, and those financial rewards increased their enthusiasm and efforts.

Obtaining commitment to change is most important among the local managers who supervise the day-to-day operations because it is they who will be responsible for directing staff adoption and adherence to the changes. This group therefore should be assessed carefully to ensure they are truly committed. If they have a negative attitude toward changes, they could very well undermine the change process and its effectiveness.

Motivate Adherence to Developmental Initiatives

Even if local management and the staff profess willingness to make changes, their predisposition and doubts tend to weaken the success of their efforts. Regardless, changes take time to implement, and development of proficiency requires even more time. The acquirer must therefore monitor their adoption and measure their effectiveness to ensure that necessary progress continues.

Trader ran into these issues repeatedly, and they were difficult to resolve without the dedicated attention of local managers. To engender that attention and motivate progress, performance measures were established and monitored for those instituted programs. For example, Trader understood that superior customer service would help solidify its market position, and with the participation of its field managers, it defined and adopted a set of consistent standards, including measures such as how quickly the phone was answered, the promptness of refunds, and the components of phone etiquette, among a variety of other items. To monitor adherence to those standards, some items were automatically measured by the phone and computer systems, and others were assessed through periodic audits conducted by Trader's home office support group.

Offering incentives often can be a valuable factor in motivating change. At Trader, those incentives were sometimes merely part of a manager's annual bonus plan, or they included recognition within company-distributed materials such as its monthly newsletters, which highlighted top and bottom performers. For particularly significant initiatives, a special short-term bonus was offered.

Emphasize Recruitment and Training of Replacement Management Talent

The departure of the founding owners of an acquisition produces a management void that must be filled, and often the entity has no capable lieutenant to be promoted to perform those duties. Alternatively, the person previously promoted demonstrates that he lacks the skills to deliver reasonable, acceptable results.

To address the management vacuum, transferring talent into a location from the consolidator's own staff is rarely an option. Its talent is usually preoccupied by the needs of the deal-making process, and the rapid-fire transactions would quickly deplete whatever bench strength the organization had available. Accordingly, a consolidation effort must incorporate a substantive recruitment, training, and development programs to satisfy the need for qualified management.

In the early days of Landmark's efforts, ad hoc training and development was the foundation for addressing the need for managerial talent. Whoever was best qualified among the acquired staff was the person appointed to manage the new acquisition. A senior executive then mentored that individual through sometimes daily telephone conversations during the first months after acquisition. As the manager grew in confidence and demonstrated her abilities and competence, the mentoring lessened. However, many new managers continued to struggle, requiring closer supervision and guidance, and in some cases, another manager from a high-performance location would visit to provide counseling and consultative support. When it became obvious the appointed manager could not perform as necessary, Landmark was compelled to make another change, either appointing someone new or transferring a manager from another location.

As the number of properties increased, the training/mentoring process proved inadequate to address management needs. Trader found it necessary to implement an independent nationwide management recruitment effort supplemented by a formal training program that lasted for several months, as described more fully in Chapter 10.

Facilitate Rapid Implementation of Revenue Growth and Productivity Measures

The theoretical benefits of mergers are often illusory. Eager to justify the cost of a transaction, an acquirer may blithely hypothesize that substantial costs will be reduced through the realization of synergies of integration and scale, but they may not be specifically identified or proved through past operating experience. As was noted in Chapter 5, Daimler failed to deliver much, if any, of the projected $3 billion in annual savings promised by its merger with Chrysler. To produce the expected return on investment, however, the synergies must be generated, and it is only through demonstrated performance that synergies and productivity benefits become realistic.

Programs to realize presumed revenue synergies and productivity enhancements must therefore be first tested in a supervised environment to confirm that they are pragmatic, reasonable, and achievable under customary operating conditions. During those tests, problems will arise for which solutions can be developed, and if the benefits prove achievable, the process can be refined for more rapid implementation in other operating units.

After Landmark's acquisition of the Winston–Salem *Trading Post*, it tested an aggressive increase of the magazine's cover price, and the results demonstrated that it could be instituted elsewhere with high confidence of success without deleterious volume declines. The experience also produced a valuable template for best implementing the price increase to minimize negative consequences.

Similarly, productivity improvement programs were tested, and those demonstrating good results were rolled out to other locations. Sometimes the programs simply required measuring and reporting results to encourage a focus on the criteria that produced improvements. For example, the weekly calculation of production labor-hours required to compose the average magazine page focused the local composing manager's attention on modifying processes and adopting techniques to improve weekly results to align with those of peer operations.

In other cases, productivity advances required the purchase of capital equipment. To automate ad collection and streamline composition, Trader installed new computers and software; this required a substantial investment followed by more time-consuming installation and training periods to achieve those productivity benefits.

The speed and effectiveness with which those measures are implemented determines how quickly the benefits will materialize. Although care must be taken to facilitate optimal benefits, efforts should proceed expeditiously to accelerate benefits and maximize their contribution to efficiency and profits.

Retain a Keen Focus on Sales, Customer Service, and Efficient Operations

Maintaining a keen focus on developing profitable sales, superior customer service, and efficient operations is an obvious necessity for every business, but retaining that focus and reaping its benefits can be very difficult. Particularly with the departure of an owner who has performed those duties in the past, a new acquisition may not have the supervisory talent capable of delivering even passable results. The local successors may have neither the leadership skills nor the ability to juggle the multiple tasks of operating the local business. They may focus instead on the more mundane and less fruitful tasks of simply processing paperwork and ensuring that employees show up on time. The staff may simply perform specified duties without demonstrating commitment to achieving the overall mission and performing the critical value-adding tasks that ensure future growth and stability.

To ensure that focus and produce progress toward the growth objectives of the consolidated enterprise, the acquirer must demonstrate a conscientious, highly visible commitment to sales, customer service, and efficient operations. Top-level focus and attention is absolutely necessary to keep field management and personnel attuned to those key areas. To cultivate that top-of-mind consciousness, Trader's leadership expressed its commitment to field management from the earliest stages. As it enthusiastically welcomed the staff into the fold, it underscored the importance of building on the company's prior legacy through increased sales and enhanced customer service while maintaining diligent cost controls.

However, far more than lip service is necessary to engender the commitment and maintain the focus. Within the early weeks after acquisition, Trader worked with local management and staff to understand existing efforts to achieve those objectives, and then it supervised the development of the plans that would be implemented to accelerate progress. From monthly financial and operating reports, results were evaluated to assess a location's effectiveness in implementing promising new programs and achieving objectives, giving answers to the question, "How are we progressing with our critical success factors?"

Ensure Constant Vigilance over Costs

In the race to complete acquisitions, there is often a temptation to reduce the complexity of the transition by permitting the acquired entities to continue managing their own accounting and performance measurement systems: "Don't fix what ain't broken." The problem with this is that the multiple independent systems rarely mesh, preventing timely collection of comparable financial and performance statistics for all operating entities. Moreover, most small companies have comparatively rudimentary accounting and administrative systems and have neither the time nor the ability to develop and report desirable new performance data without new systems.

To have the necessary information to manage numerous acquired entities, it therefore becomes imperative to institute formal, regimented accounting and administrative systems as quickly as possible. On the first day after acquisition, Trader would immediately assume responsibility for paying the acquisition's bills and producing its monthly financial statements. Coupled with collection of weekly revenue and cash collection data, that policy gave Trader the weekly financial information necessary to produce consistent income statements that could be instantly compared with those of every other profit center. In turn, those comparisons provided top management with report cards to identify the areas of each operation that needed specific attention.

Further assisting the effort to red-flag problem areas was centralized access to accounts payable and general ledger data. From a quick review of detailed data files, the leadership could promptly identify the source of variances from expected performance. Then those details could be shared with local managers to spotlight areas of breakdown for future attention and improvement.

Shortly after the institution of centralized accounting functions, Trader implemented supplemental processes to collect nonfinancial performance data, including unit sales statistics, customer counts, and composition productivity, among other items, to provide the information for comparative analysis and variance identification, and that information was used by management to evaluate past performance, identify opportunities for improvement, and direct a location's future focus.

High-Value Future Opportunities

Attractive rewards can be reasonably expected from rational investments that may be managed effectively by astute business operators. However, the best returns will come from those acquisitions which are effectively managed and simultaneously offer replicable models that can be rolled out to new geographic or industry segments. Such acquisitions offer the prospect of innovative opportunities that promise transformation into a more competitive business capable of expanding its offerings to satisfy the transitioning needs of a growing customer base. The relevance and importance of these components are addressed in Chapters 11 through 13.

Chapter 10

Achieving Rollup Efficiencies and Implementing Best Practices

"Oh, I've got a lot of good tricks to operate my business," said the harried owner of a northeastern automotive photo guide.

"Tell me more," said Conrad Hall. "I'm always fascinated by the way savvy operators build such impressive success. I bet a woman like you brings a completely different perspective to managing a business."

"You're right about that," said the owner. "One of the things I did was rip out the mirrors from the women's bathroom. The girls spend too much time primping anyway; those mirrors were just a distraction that made them take longer. In fact, I make them clock out when they go."

"That's the first time I've heard that," said Hall.

"Oh, and you know how expensive unemployment taxes can get? I decided I'd try to do something about that by getting the slackers to quit so I wouldn't have to fire them."

"How did you do that?" Hall asked.

"Easy," she said. "I reassigned them to duties that drive them nuts! A little while ago, I pulled a girl off the ad floor, handed her the telephone book, sat her in the storage room, and told her to alphabetize the listings by first name. At the end of the day, when she handed me her work, I yelled at her for doing it all wrong and told her to do it all over another way. In a couple of days she was gone!"

"How about that!" Hall exclaimed.[1]

Not every idea culled from the operations of rough-and-tumble entrepreneurs is a good one. Because of the infinite variety of personal operating styles, an acquirer of multiple small entities will quickly discover a myriad collection of processes and procedures supporting similar businesses. Some are brilliantly astute, some are astonishingly stupid, some are surprisingly contradictory, and, like the example above, some may lead to costly employment practice suits and legal judgments.

Operating well below the radar, small business owners exercise their freedom to do as they please, but a large organization must employ more enlightened practices to produce superior results and mitigate the costs and distractions of regulators and litigators. An acquirer must therefore devote substantial energy to eradicating unproductive and potentially dangerous operating practices and must identify those brilliantly astute ideas which can be replicated throughout the consolidated organization to achieve superior performance.

It is probably easier for professional managers to identify what small operators do poorly than to identify what they do exceedingly well. Exposed to numerous businesses and possibly educated by premier management schools, rollup practitioners are versed in traditional operating procedures and sensitized to the consequences of poor business practices. Fire alarms instantly blare when they see egregious problems.

Identifying exceptional ideas takes more effort. Biased by his or her confidence and past experience, an acquirer may be both blind to the less obvious good ideas and dismissive of unusual approaches simply because they are unfamiliar. With a thoughtful, inquisitive perspective, a prudent acquirer should evaluate each entrepreneur's individual tactics, processes, and procedures to identify the best mix of ingredients to incorporate into the evolving operational and development model of the consolidated new entity.

Sometimes those ideas help inspire the business to reposition itself to capture very different, more sizable markets. When Dollar Tree acquired the Chicago-based Dollar Bills, the knowledge it gained was truly transformative, according to its founding CEO, Macon Brock. Previously operated as a variety store serving the needs of suburban mall shoppers,

Dollar Tree discovered from Dollar Bills the impressive performance of an inventory more devoted to fast-turn consumables such as food and toiletries. Though they produced lower margins, their appeal stimulated higher store traffic and increased volumes, persuading Dollar Tree to include more of those items in its product mix. That transformation proved critical to success in urban environments whose customers had little need for Dollar Tree's original, more suburban-oriented merchandise such as Halloween lawn decorations.[2]

Prospective Rollup Benefits Versus Added Costs

Peter McKelvey, a principal of the mergers and acquisitions advisor LEK Consulting, has succinctly defined the expected benefits arising from successful rollups as including savings from economies of scale, value-cost leveraging, and enhanced revenue generation through redefined products and services:

- Economies of scale have the potential to produce savings in purchasing, marketing, sales, and administrative costs. In health club rollups, they were realized by eliminating the overlap through a combination of back-office functions; funeral service consolidators leveraged their larger size to negotiate better pricing on caskets, flowers, and other goods.
- Value-cost leveraging benefits were captured by temporary help and veterinary service consolidators whose cost-efficient processes increased the value of their services. Although temp services' centralized data collection and billing increased efficiency, customers lauded the improved résumé capture, review, and hiring simplicity; and the vet service's adoption of uniform operating and pricing policies streamlined operations, standardized procedures, and reduced customers' concerns.
- Golfing range rollups leveraged earnings when they redefined their offerings, doubling capacity with the addition of multilevel grandstands. Other industries did the same thing when their

integrated footprint provided the basis for a national service providing better value and coverage than what was available from independent, distinctly local operators.[3]

However, there are added costs associated with merging numerous disparate operations. Rarely do small businesses offer the breadth of expensive employee benefits deemed necessary in the large company they join, and the consolidator is certain to incur substantial additional costs arising from supervisory oversight, travel, supplemental reporting, and other corporate overhead requirements. Because of the problems of integration and managing the more complex enterprise, those costs can easily outstrip the rollup's projected benefits, which may never materialize because of difficulties of implementation. Accordingly, a prudent consolidation effort must include a coordinated integration process dedicated to the realization of those projected benefits, and although the changes must be implemented quickly and efficiently to accelerate their realization, the process must be done in a manner that engenders broad support among employees, management, and vendors while enhancing the business's image among customers.

Identify Opportunities from the Beginning

A successful integration begins before the deal is completed. From the courtship's commencement, the acquirer's preliminary discussions with the owner and tour of the facilities provide the first opportunities to assess operations, evaluate managerial staff, identify problems and potential barriers, and discover best practices that might be employable throughout the consolidated enterprise. A prudent acquirer will make the most of these opportunities, gaining as much insight and offering as little criticism as possible: "How have you succeeded so well? That's impressive. Tell me more. You seem to have such talented staff. Who are your stars? What are your tricks of the trade?"

However, the owner often prohibits full access, and it is only during the due diligence review that a reasonable opportunity materializes to make more thorough assessments. Because of their benefits, almost all the field visits were conducted by Trader's top leaders. Their broader experience provided the foundation for better assessments, and their stature and congenial approach tended to reduce the owner's reticence so that more could be learned. The knowledge they gained could then be incorporated into all the integration and development plans.

Foremost on the agenda was to assess the staff and get new insights into how best to run the business. Of particular interest was the identification of techniques and tactics that could be replicated throughout Trader's other businesses. However, because the owner usually insisted on strict confidentiality before closing, the tours were normally performed under another guise, and it was therefore not feasible to solicit the staff's involvement with the formulation of integration plans.

Work Closely and Cooperatively with the Acquisition's Managers

On rare occasions, the owner's managers could be incorporated into pre-closing discussions to plan the merger's integration process, and such contributions smoothed the transition. When Trader acquired the $300 million revenue United Advertising Publications, both management teams worked together to plan integration well in advance of the deal's completion. A lot of the nitty-gritty details, such as consolidating employee benefits programs, were addressed more objectively, and substantive matters, such as the expected closure of underperforming properties, were evaluated more thoroughly, permitting the development and implementation of better plans. To obtain a quick start on building a more unified culture, UAP's executives attended Trader's annual managers' meeting a month before the merger, and at that meeting they participated as full-fledged members of the leadership team.

The involvement of more participants also meant there were more eyes to identify opportunities to enhance future performance. To capture those insights, Trader's leadership devoted their lunches to debriefing the staff and probing for their observations.

The involvement of so many, however, could threaten a deal. Each participant risked saying something that could derail the transaction.

Particularly in small transactions, there are volatile issues that an inadvertent comment may expose. Extraordinary tact and thoughtfulness are therefore needed to minimize the possibility of such disruptions. A small minority owner, the president of Boats.com, became irritated by discussions with Trader about his noncompete, and his intransigence created a barrier to finalizing the deal. Fortunately, the majority owners eventually concluded that the deal had to proceed and approved a structure that effectively dictated the president's resignation upon closing. Though Trader had genuinely hoped to retain the president's involvement, he refused to participate, and Trader consoled itself with the old adage that "the graveyards are filled with supposedly irreplaceable people."

Enlist Employee Commitment

To ensure smooth operations and continued productivity, it is highly desirable to have the full staff perceive the merger in a positive light. As the people who actually perform the work and provide the public face among customers, the staff members are the most critical determinant of a company's future success, and their enthusiasm for the merger can produce substantive benefits. Inevitably, vendors and customers will ask the staff about the change, and its upbeat responses can enhance the market's overall reaction, potentially improving the business's prospects measurably.

From their lofty position, an acquirer's leaders often assume that the new staff will instantly perceive the benefits of joining a larger organization. The merged company may offer broader opportunities for advancement, enhanced growth prospects, improved fringe benefits, more enlightened employment practices, and more progressive management. However, employees are more likely to view these purported benefits cynically, adopting a "show me first" attitude and harboring fears about potential job loss, changes in duties, and modifications of benefits.

In the stressful aftermath of the deal's close, the new owner's first step is usually to meet the staff, followed by a review of the fringe benefit programs, employee policies, and procedures. Unfortunately, no matter how tactful the presentation is, employees usually experience high anxiety about the changes. Rather than engender enthusiasm and inspire confidence, the meetings are too often pervaded by the employees' suspicions and worries about layoffs and benefit changes. Discussions of new policies and procedures can cause them to have concerns about the necessity to adjust to the new order.

After each of its acquisitions, Trader conducted such employee meetings, striving to reach every member of the organization. In almost every case, one or more of its top leaders stood before the new employees and expressed great enthusiasm for the prospects of working together to develop the business to its full potential. Emphasis was placed on Trader's belief that the staff members and their abilities represented the core values captured with the merger and that through their conscientious dedication, the goals of the combination would be achieved. In the best circumstances, these approximately 30 minutes of congratulatory and motivational presentations did inspire a little confidence, but there seemed to remain an understandable hesitation to believe.

Sadly, to satisfy the imperatives dictated by progressive human resource departments, the bulk of such meetings was devoted to the more mundane and sometimes prickly discussion of employee benefits, policies, and procedures. In almost every case, Trader's benefits programs represented an improvement over those offered by the former owner, and those improvements were stressed in the presentations. However, some employees tended to focus on losses such as slightly higher health premiums versus the added benefits of disability and 401(K) plans. Similarly, the drawn-out discussion on policies and procedures did little to inspire the staff. As employees of a small company, most had never attended such an extensive review, much less given consideration to issues such as sexual harassment, open door policies, and employment of relatives. Not only did the presentations tend to be tedious, they undercut the original enthusiasm engendered by the opening comments.

In truth, however, very little can be said to mitigate the inherent anxiety arising from a change of ownership. Though enthusiastic welcomes and reassuring words may help, the passage of time is the primary balm to assuage employee concerns. If during the succeeding months the company continues to operate smoothly with few employee cutbacks or demotions, the staff members will gradually lose their anxiety and return their full focus to their assigned responsibilities. In the case of the northeastern photo guide mentioned earlier in this chapter, morale and productivity improved dramatically within days of the dictatorial owner's departure and the installation of Trader's more progressive manager. But more common are operations whose paternalistic owners have been well liked and admired as the enterprise's inspirational leaders, and those staffs typically did not adjust until three to six months had passed.

Enlist and Direct the Acquired Management's Commitment

More important than employees' dedication is the acquired management's commitment to the needs of the merged enterprise. The commitment of a capable local manager will effectively mold the attitude of the staff and facilitate fulfillment of the consolidated company's plans and mission. Without that commitment, progress will be hampered.

An acquirer rarely has the bench strength to appoint its own talent to manage the new entity and must usually rely on an existing manager to step into the more responsible role vacated by the owner. In most cases, this is a positive. The owner's most capable lieutenant usually perceives his appointment as a promotion, signifying the new owner's confidence in his managerial skills. Having previously operated in the owner's shadow, the manager should relish the opportunity to blossom with the new responsibilities, and his appointment should comfort employees, who may interpret the action as a demonstrated commitment to the local staff.

Accustomed to taking direction, the former lieutenant also presents the promise of fulfilling the critical responsibilities as directed by the new owner. Typically, she will aim to please, and like any new manager, she will be eager to demonstrate her dedication to the new boss. During most of its acquisitions, Trader leveraged that attitude to facilitate quick changes that produced relatively instant benefits. For example, owners can be particularly cautious about a price increase, fearing it could hammer volumes and destroy market share. That was precisely the attitude of the owner of Winston–Salem's *Trading Post*, which had a cover price of $0.25. Similar publications in other large markets were priced at $0.75, but the owner insisted that that price would result in a devastating drop in single copy sales. After closing, however, the newly appointed manager agreed to levy the increase, and the results were astonishing: Unit sales increased, revenues leaped, and profits skyrocketed.

The confidence derived from past experience and superior research should provide the basis for taking similar risks to produce comparable benefits. Often, an owner has become complacent with his established practices and becomes risk-averse, fearing that making changes would be akin to killing the goose that lays the golden eggs. He will fight such changes, and his departure presents the opportunity for new blood to take the risks. However, such willingness to take risks may be a detriment. The owner may have superior insights, and a prudent acquirer will insist that without contradictory evidence, caution should be the watchword and careful assessment based on operational evidence should dictate plans and implementation processes. When in doubt, an astute operator will determine how she might test assumptions before making radical, irreversible changes. If a change delivers increased ills, she will reverse course just as "Classic" Coca-Cola replaced "New Coke" after its beleaguered introduction.

Identify Value-Creation Best Practices

The acquiescence of an acquisition's staff and manager may deter the identification of best practices for replication elsewhere. In their hesitation to rock the boat during the early stages and with their desire to please, both staff and managers may blithely focus on whatever the new owners dictate. If the acquirer suggests upsetting a productive practice, the staff may simply do as told, fearing that debates could lead to termination and trusting that the new owners know better. However, without years of familiarity with acquired operations, the buyer does not necessarily know better and should make every effort to encourage forthright communications among the staff.

Dollar Tree's Macon Brock recalled how his company's 2003 acquisition of Salt Lake City's Greenbacks, Inc., provided welcome coverage of the 10-state Rocky Mountain markets, but subsequent modification of the store merchandise mix to conform with the acquirer's models produced a disturbing drop in sales. It seems that Greenbacks' original devotion to featuring a larger candy selection had been a pivotal component, stimulating that market's customer traffic, average sales, and market loyalty.[4]

Instead of blindly dictating rapid changes, therefore, care should be taken to demonstrate curiosity about how and why the staff operates the business, encouraging their candidness while retaining an open mind to identify contradictory but better practices and ideas.

Those best practices can range from the minute to the transformational. After the acquisition of Kentucky Fried Chicken in the 1960s, John Y. Brown and his investment group were persuaded by a franchisee to convert the whole concept from a sit-down restaurant to a primarily take-out vendor of the Colonel's famous recipe. That modification dramatically lowered labor costs while feeding the era's exploding demand for prepared foods that could be taken home to feed the family, and the economic efficiency of the concept fueled the launch of literally thousands of outlets, making millionaires of Brown, his investors, and hundreds of franchisees.[5]

At TeleCable, "usually we didn't like to be pioneers," related its CEO, Dick Roberts. "We liked to see what people were doing in various areas, marketing and so forth—capture the good ideas and improve on them. I had an ancestor who was a Caribbean pirate, so being a pirate was easy to us. It was in the DNA." Through its acquisitions and congenial relationships in the industry, it was able to identify and leverage a broad variety of good ideas relating to technological improvements, telemarketing practices, and subscriber administration.[6]

From the entrepreneurs of its numerous acquisitions, Trader learned countless lessons about providing alternative, more productive methods to manage distribution practices, pricing, private party and commercial ad development, product segmentation, and production processes. To earn preferential placement of his *Auto Trader* start-up magazine adjacent to the convenience store cash register, Stuart Arnold had willingly paid retailers as much as 40 percent of the magazine's cover price, and most of his licensees followed suit. But with the acquisition of *Tradin' Times*, Landmark discovered that the now familiar titles had become an actual customer enticement, helping draw traffic to the stores. That was certainly the case with *Auto Trader*, whose product segmentation strategy had pushed its multiple editions onto their own rack some distance from the checkout. Trader therefore reduced the retailer's share of the cover price over time to 20 percent and generated millions of dollars of incremental profits for its bottom line.

Additionally, the best ideas sometimes provided cross-fertilization results for other segments of Trader's business. Adapting the practices used at its *For Rent Magazine* acquisition, *Auto Mart* magazines began incorporating unique 800 phone numbers for each commercial dealer's ads, producing a verifiable record to demonstrate the volume and quality of calls generated by its advertising.

Implement Best Practices

In some cases, instituting change can be a relatively simple process. If a location's staff and management are indifferent about a small change or if it is mainly administrative, it may require only a quick decision and a few instructions: To process payroll, begin using these forms and complete them in this manner. However, when the change involves confronting new risks or requires modification of more ingrained habits, implementation can prove particularly problematic even when the demonstrated results prove its efficacy.

Raising prices or reducing vendor payments often generates significant fears that such actions will undermine hard-earned goodwill, leading to decreased volumes or reductions in the quality of services. Certainly, the decision to triple the cover price of Winston–Salem's *Trading Post* from $0.25 to $0.75 produced justifiable concerns about its potentially devastating impact on unit volumes and revenues. To counter those concerns, the newly appointed manager was persuaded that the magazine's buyers were episodic buyers: They might purchase the magazine for a couple of weeks while looking for a car, but then they wouldn't buy it again for another year. Customers therefore might not even remember its former price, and if the increase caused severe drops in sales volumes, the price could be reduced to its original level, presumably mitigating any long-term damage.

With that rationale providing some comfort, the risk was accepted, the price was increased, and subsequent volume rose. Perhaps because consumers perceived greater value from the higher-price product, the gains may be attributed to the better record keeping and modified auditing practices that were adopted to ensure prompt feedback about the feared negative results (in essence, those more rigorous administration methods may have eliminated losses previously attributable to theft).

Far more difficult to implement are changes requiring the staff members to transform the way they've performed their jobs. People inevitably become comfortable with their customary routines, and dictating change produces at best begrudging acceptance and at worst outright rebellion, either of which could lead to the failure of the implementation effort. To mitigate that potential, a conscientious effort to manage the process must be used to compensate for anticipated problems and motivate the desired behavior. Despite best efforts, however, it may take years to complete the adoption process, as was the case with the modification of *Auto Mart*'s advertising sales strategy.

Distributed as a free publication from outdoor racks and in grocery stores, *Auto Mart* originally was tailored to attract one or two pages of advertising from a broad assortment of each market's used car dealers. Its sales representatives would return to their clients' dealerships each week, determine which advertised vehicles had sold, and then photograph enough additional cars to substitute in the body of the following week's ad. Rather than selling, they were mostly servicing their established client base, ensuring prompt, reliable, and courteous attention. But then, with the acquisition of the Seattle *Auto Guide,* Trader discovered that it was possible to sell as many as a dozen pages to each of the large franchised car dealers. One of the guide's founders, Corbett McDonald, had been the consummate salesperson, and he knew car dealers routinely spent five figures on weekly newspaper and broadcast advertising. It therefore made little sense for his publication to settle for maybe a $500 weekly advertising commitment, and he aggressively began persuading dealers to publish photo ads and descriptions of their full inventory in the *Auto Guide,* which produced measurable incremental sales directly proportional to the volume of cars advertised.

McDonald's successful pitch meant the larger advertisers could be expected to place a dozen pages of ads, generating 5 to 10 times the weekly revenues received by Trader's free auto guides. The implication was huge. Changing the sales approach at *Auto Mart* to reflect that approach could double or perhaps even triple revenues, with an even more impressive contribution to the bottom line. However, simply telling the sales staff to begin selling six more pages every week to their one-page clients wasn't going to work.

To orchestrate the change, Seattle's Jeff Moore, one of Trader's most capable managers, stepped up to the plate. Having discovered its appeal during his early ad sales career with *Auto Trader*, Moore crystallized the strategy as "advocacy" selling. For a client to be an advocate, he had to perceive *Auto Mart* as a primary contributor to his overall sales results. A single ad page would generate only a couple of sales each week, relegating *Auto Mart* to the role of a marketing afterthought. However, with 6 to 10 pages of advertising, *Auto Mart* would begin producing from 20 to 40 percent of the incremental used car sales, making it a marketing necessity just like McDonald's Seattle *Auto Guide*. With McDonald's help, the strategy was implemented in Denver, and simultaneously Moore coached his sales managers to do the same thing in Portland and Phoenix.

Further motivated by a lucrative incentive plan, the sales representatives were inspired to employ the new approach when they pitched their best customers to employ multipage advertising. Of course, those customers resisted change, and it was only the best salespersons who persisted. Having been coached by Moore and McDonald, those salespersons knew it was critical to persuade the owner to test the concept. Their car lot managers might allocate advertising dollars among varied media, but the owners set the budget, and those owners could be persuaded to direct the ad budget *Auto Mart's* way if convinced it really produced sterling sales results. And when it was tested, *Auto Mart* proved that it did. Once a few key advertisers had been enlisted, more dealers followed when the sales representatives pointed to their competitors' success, and revenues leaped upward.

With his success in several cities, Moore persuaded *Auto Mart's* national management to institutionalize the program as a company initiative for 1999.

Local and regional managers joined Moore to establish goals, provide training, and institute the process to convert their organizations to the sales strategy. Later, after the inspired suggestion of the Raleigh (North Carolina) office's energized staff, the program was rolled out under the rallying cry of "Every car, every week," a slogan emphasizing the value of promoting a dealer's full inventory in every edition of the magazine. In cities with particularly capable salespeople and conscientious managers, implementation proceeded rapidly, and award programs and monthly sales newsletters touted the most successful representatives as "Rainmakers," a designation that earned them national recognition and substantial remuneration and prizes. But for most, adoption was a slow process stalled by the hesitancy of the sales staff to change its tactics and modify weak sales skills and by the pushback from advertisers. Over several years of dedicated attention from the *Auto Mart's* divisional leadership, most of the cities, however, eventually succeeded in converting to the sales strategy.

Focus on Critical Success Factors

The requirements of operating any successful business are countless, and to optimize the potential for success, it is therefore critical to focus efforts on those aspects which generate the greatest benefits while fulfilling the mission of the business.

As part of its industry segment rollups, Trader carefully assessed each consolidated group to identify its critical success factors, honing in on the five deemed to be the most pivotal to the overall development of the operations.

At *Employment Guide,* the division's critical success factors were listed as (1) superior customer service, (2) driven professional sales representatives, (3) compelling circulation reach, (4) superior product quality, and (5) highly skilled management. Those factors were published and discussed continuously through integration and development efforts, and the focus on them gave the full management team a framework to guide directions, decisions, and initiatives for each local publication. If problems arose, the question was asked: Which solution would best support the optimal achievement of the critical success factors? If a new initiative was proposed, would its pursuit complement existing efforts or would it undermine the fulfillment of the dictates of the critical success factors?

Although the communication of such critical success factors helps direct focus, it does not ensure devoted efforts to achieve their realization. For example, it is easy to insist that a firm provide superior customer service, but without a set of criteria to define what that means, the quality will vary broadly with each operator's individual perceptions. One manager's assessment that service is superior may conflict with the standards of another. Accordingly, to ensure consistent standards, Trader developed regimented measurement criteria to quantify the level of service and provide definitive feedback to management.

To minimize collection costs and maximize the objectivity of the data, many of the measurements were automated. Phone systems were programmed to record how many rings customers heard before a call was answered, and customer relation management software was employed to monitor and measure the customer contacts and performance of sales representatives.

Hold Management Accountable

Although identification and communication of critical success factors help bring focus to the direction of a business, holding management accountable for their realization remains the decisive component in motivating a business's development.

Although many of the nation's businesses became preoccupied with the formal introduction of Edward Deming's Total Quality Management initiatives in the 1980s and 1990s, Trader simply adopted the concept of comparative rankings, understanding that when something is measured and ranked, results improve. This was particularly valuable for developing businesses whose operating metrics demonstrated the quality of their performance.

At *Auto Trader*, growth was measured by a variety of criteria, including single copy sales, private party ad counts, and the number of commercial ad pages. By measuring those growth metrics and then publicizing them in the form of comparative rankings, arrayed with the best performers at the top and the worst at the bottom, Trader transformed its efficiency assessment tool into a motivational device. Of course it represented a hot sheet for management, providing it with a "to do" list of which operations to compliment and which ones to give more pressure or resources to instigate improvement.

However, simply sending out a bunch of lists might have diluted effectiveness. Managers of start-ups and growing enterprises are absorbed by the pressures of juggling tasks, and the sheer volume of management reports makes them easily ignorable. To ensure that key metrics remained a focus, therefore, Trader began distributing a single sheet each month called the "Good News/Bad News Report," summarizing the 10 best and worst performers for each of the top five measurements. Coupled with pithy commentary, one report (distributed during the weeks of October's World Series) noted: "The fans roared their approval for Homeruns in single copy sales gains from Cincinnati, Charleston, Lexington, Providence and Kansas City. But, oh no! Say it ain't so, Joe! They're batting zero, with strikeouts galore, in Columbus, Philadelphia, Detroit, Twin Cities and Tampa!"

As a single piece of paper, the Good News/Bad News Report could be quickly reviewed, and its commentary captured the attention of its recipients, providing more memorable assessments and regular focal points of conversation among managers and their superiors. Because the report referenced several measurements, some city managers found themselves both complimented for one result and disparaged for another, but even if they were not listed, the report encouraged all to check the complete rankings to determine their proximity to the top or bottom performers. Trader believed its managers were more encouraged to put forth a little more effort to earn themselves a spot among the top performers and perhaps a lot more motivated to escape falling among the worst.

Authored each month by Trader's chief financial officer, the Good News/Bad News Report signified top management's passionate interest in operations and its attention to the key operating statistics underlying success. Field staff knew that the CFO's concentration on those measurements mirrored that of Trader's other leaders, almost all of whom would regularly comment on the rankings during visits and phone conversations with field managers, who were motivated accordingly. In fact, one regional manager galvanized the staff in one underperforming city by setting the year's mission as escaping mention among the laggards or, as he more vividly put it, "Let's shut up the CFO."

Recruit and Train

Holding management and staff accountable necessarily implies performance reviews, efforts to improve performance, and termination and replacement of nonperformers. Training and recruitment of personnel therefore must become a core component of any fast-growing organization whose efforts are complicated by the need for integration of numerous acquired operations.

With the departure of acquisition founders and the replacement of poor performers, Trader soon found itself without the necessary field management to lead its increasingly disparate operations. Promotion of internal candidates, ad hoc mentoring by well-intentioned superiors, and occasional transfers failed to fill local management voids; though some rising employees demonstrated potential, they lacked the skills and experience necessary for success in a general manager's role. Moreover, senior managers rarely found time to provide sufficient guidance to develop green management talent.

To address similar needs, Ray Kroc's McDonald's achieved early recognition for providing professional development of personnel and franchisees through its Hamburger University.[7] Founded in 1961, the university offered a rigorous curriculum devoted to hamburgerology, and its concept was replicated for other businesses in the years that followed by organizations such as Kentucky Fried Chicken and Dollar Tree.

Under the direction of Sunny Sonner, Trader's vice president of human resources, Lars Svendsen organized Trader's professional development curriculum, subsequently christened the MIT (Managers in Training) program. A former auto guide owner who had sold to Trader, Svendsen had earlier managed training programs in the restaurant business; to address Trader's specific needs, he adapted his knowledge with substantial input from Trader's management. After several weeks of classroom training, participants spent comparable time in field offices to learn sales, telemarketing, composition, production, and distribution management.

Recognizing that it lacked developable managers within its own operations, Trader also commenced recruiting experienced talent from outside through a small cadre of professional recruiters. The prospects were scrutinized through a rigorous schedule of interviews among both the regional manager and top management ranks, including Trader's chief executive officer, Conrad Hall. As Hall often repeated, there wasn't a duty much more important than identifying and attracting the best talent to lead the company's field operations.

After being hired, those talented individuals joined the MIT program, completed its curriculum, experienced field operations, and began filling managerial positions as they became vacant.

Although reasonable success was achieved, experience demonstrated that the best managers were those who had spent several years in the business. Despite their rigorous MIT training, outside recruits made mistakes from lack of operational experience, and their personal preferences often conflicted with the cultural requirements of Trader's operations.

Nonetheless, the recruits provided the desperately needed boost to the management ranks of Trader's fast-growing operations. This was particularly the case when Trader began the rapid rollout of *The Employment Guide*. With the start-up of 44 publications over a few short years, it was absolutely critical to attract new talent to step into the leadership roles, and quality training through organized programs and on-the-job experience dramatically facilitated the development of the required management skills.

Implement the Tough Decisions

In every business there arises a multitude of problems, and the problems associated with consolidating a horde of acquired businesses are exacerbated by the conflicts arising from the integration process. Among the most prevalent impediments are those which are people-related. Managers fail to execute their duties as expected, may destabilize morale and demotivate staff because of their weak interpersonal skills, or may be guilty of skullduggery. Even if this is noticed, the leadership may have no identifiable alternatives and postpones action, reasoning that a weak manager is better than none. However, because they undermine results and negatively affect staff and operational efficiency, those problems are best dealt with immediately, before their consequences metastasize.

Unfortunately, there are no easy solutions. Inevitably, it is incumbent on the new leadership to focus on the most critical operational matters, delegate duties to the best available talent, and hold everyone accountable for performance. The adoption of best practices includes the elimination of ineffective managers and staff, and this creates its own problems because most leaders find it very difficult to terminate employees. They agonize over the necessity and often delay action beyond the optimum time.

As was mentioned in Chapter 9, the acquisition of United Advertising Publications immediately preceded the 2001 recession, and the subsequent erosion of revenues produced a precipitous drop in profits. Whereas Trader had previously anticipated a multiyear attrition process to reduce overhead expenses, the approximately 60 percent profit decline dictated more immediate cuts, and the most obvious place to start was the 400-person corporate staff.

Unlike Trader, which championed the delegation of most management and administrative responsibilities to field personnel, UAP administered its over 200 locally distributed magazines from its Texas headquarters. Except for local advertising sales, its corporate staff orchestrated most functions, including booking field staff travel. Rather than simply absorbing routine responsibilities to help intensify the local sales focus, the large bureaucracy had begun diverting field personnel attention with an increasing volume of directives and unproductive administrative drills. Moreover, UAP's headquarters was inefficient. For example, its four-person lease management group handled one-third of the properties handled by Trader's single part-time staffer.

The recession forced Trader to move more quickly to eliminate the inefficient bureaucracy. Over only six months, Trader's controller, Bill Dorsey, formulated and implemented a plan to integrate back-office and accounting functions, Sunny Sonner merged UAP's human resources functions into Trader's, and others consolidated its data processing, information technologies, and other support groups with those at Trader. After 12 months of yeoman effort, a net of over 300 positions were eliminated, and UAP's expensive headquarters lease was terminated. As for the field staffs, rather than finding themselves overburdened, they expressed improved satisfaction with the increased authority and flexibility provided by the more decentralized approach.

The terminations, of course, took their toll on the hundreds of employees who found themselves seeking new jobs in a tough economic environment. Though cushioned by severance packages more than double those of the past, many no doubt struggled; however, the majority subsequently found new employment at firms that provided better opportunities. As head of Trader's human resource department, Sonner bore the heavy burden during local meetings with most of the affected personnel over the many months of the process. Readily admitting it was the most difficult period of her long professional career, she understood that ultimately it simply accelerated a process necessary to position UAP's business to flourish in the increasingly competitive environment.

Integration is wonderful when it can be accomplished without such loss of jobs, but when necessary, it is usually best to complete it as quickly as possible after conscientious planning and careful implementation. Having coordinated the integration process more than 60 times in the past with smaller transactions, Trader had the experience to complete this larger one with both the confidence and the knowledge to pull it off with minimal adverse impacts.

Chapter 11

Rollout Initiatives

"Roll out the barrel, we'll have a barrel of fun./Roll out the barrel, we've got the blues on the run!" sang Richard Jamin with a wry smile on his face.

"Are you nuts! I'm sweating like a pig," said his companion. "All friggin' night we've been driving through town in this cracker box truck like terrorists, stopping at every strip shopping center to plant one of these monster racks with a bag of sand in its base. We've been out here all friggin' night, and we've got at least two more nights before we've unloaded them all."

"What? You'd rather be doing this in the heat of the day? Then you'd be whining about the traffic, humidity, and scorching sun!"

"True enough. But I really didn't think I was signing up for longshoreman duty when I took this job."

"Relax," said Jamin. "This is the easy part. Wait until you've spent a few weeks telemarketing your heart out. Getting sales is the real trick, and it's not as easy as unloading these plastic giants on the unsuspecting turf of Orlando."

"Well, at least it's in the air-conditioned office."

"You say that now, but we'll see what you say when your manager and I turn the heat up if you don't produce the sales."[1]

Similar dialogues occurred repeatedly as Trader orchestrated the launch of 44 *Employment Guide* magazines in almost every major market in the United States in the four years from 1997 to 2001.

Headed by long-experienced media executives, Trader's top management well understood that newspapers' most profitable advertising appeared in the help-wanted section. With rates two to three times those charged to car dealers and grocery stores, recruitment ads came in over the transom with no marketing pull from a sales floor. Only a service staff was necessary to collect ad copy and process it for publication. Therefore, capturing a profitable share of that business had extraordinary appeal.

In the early 1980s, with hopes of building a national publishing business devoted to nurse recruitment advertising, Landmark acquired two small groups of nursing newspapers. However, the introduction in that decade of Medicare reimbursement caps precipitated hospital retrenchments and reduced recruitment demand, and the publications were closed when the previously profitable revenues evaporated.

Shortly after Trader's formation, its marketing head, George Brooks, devised a magazine concept with hopes of tapping into the enticing recruitment advertising revenue stream. But the effort failed to attract advertisers, and it too was quietly terminated.

Right Concept, Key Leadership, Opportune Timing

Then, in 1996, Trader was contacted by the former owners of the Detroit *Auto Trader*. Canadian nationals, Wayne Moriarity and Paul Houlachan had spent the intervening years since their 1989 sale on a variety of new ventures and had discovered that another *Auto Trader* entrepreneur, Toronto's Bill Francis, had created a free distribution recruitment tabloid many years earlier. Covetous of his apparent success, they launched their clone of the publication in Detroit, where employers were charged $1,280 for a 10-column-inch ad in the Sunday *Detroit News and Free Press*'s help-wanted section. Named the *Employment Guide*, the publication had quickly grown to a $3 million enterprise through the efforts of an aggressive telemarketing staff that pitched ads priced at an almost 80 percent discount from the newspaper competition. Having enjoyed the impressive cash flows from their high-margin business for several years, the founders were ready to sell if Trader would pay a compelling price.

Instantly intrigued, Trader's leadership concluded that the *Employment Guide*'s relatively simple business model could be replicated in almost every major metropolitan market, and after its quick acquisition, Conrad Hall appointed Jack Ross, one of Trader's most successful field managers, to refine the start-up recipe and lead efforts to launch identical publications in large markets.

In selecting Ross, Hall had made a key decision to optimize the probability of success. Originally a newspaper advertising representative for Landmark's Norfolk daily, Ross had been recruited in 1989 to manage the Norfolk *Auto Trader* acquisition. He had then moved to Washington to engineer the successful turnaround of that city's *Auto Trader*, which had struggled during the first year after acquisition. After producing impressive results, Ross assumed executive responsibility for several operations, earning a reputation as the company's best field operations manager.

Too often, companies make mistakes by concluding they cannot afford to reassign their best managers to new projects. The core business remains fundamental to producing profitable cash flow, and it is often perceived to be much too risky to transfer key managerial talent to new ventures. However, Trader's management understood that new ventures required the best, brightest, and most energetic leadership, and that talent should be divorced from prior responsibilities to direct its undivided attention to all the opportunities and problems arising with the new venture. If they retained authority over core operations, they would be inevitably diverted and would have an excuse for failure. With only the new venture as their responsibility, they would have a greater incentive to succeed because they would have nothing else to fall back on.

After six months' experience operating the Detroit publication, Ross was confident that Trader had identified the critical factors necessary for success, and top management projected that Trader could quickly ramp up to produce an over $50 million revenue business with a minimum 25 percent EBITDA margin through the aggressive rollout of the concept. To commence the process, Ross recruited Richard Jamin, another highly accomplished *Auto Trader* field manager, to lead the first start-up in Dallas, Texas. Together, the two weren't just quality managers but experienced field professionals, knowledgeable about the operational details of publication sales management and distribution, and they had an ingrained bias to accomplish their mission promptly and efficiently.

The two worked feverishly planning the Dallas launch, establishing an office, recruiting the necessary staff, and setting up distribution points. Expecting to achieve breakeven within three to six months, Ross and

Jamin distributed the first weekly edition in October 1997, and employers gladly bought ads to test the effectiveness of the new recruitment medium. The recruiters were so pleased with the results that they continued buying ads in such volumes that the publication achieved profitability by the end of the month, and Trader's managers knew they had a winner.

While Trader's CFO commenced negotiations to acquire similar publications from their publishers in a dozen cities, Ross worked with Trader's leadership to schedule a rapid rollout to another 50 cities. A few months later, Houston was launched, and Trader discovered that its new publication concept had even more advertising rate flexibility to increase profits.

To orchestrate accelerated launches, Jamin recruited his own cadre of talented managers to lead the charge in several more cities. However, throughout that period, Jamin and Ross demonstrated another key component underlying their effort to produce success: They remained hands-on field operatives. They personally interviewed and endorsed the hire of each manager for every launch, participated in the recruitment and training of new sales staff and the selection of field offices, and routinely showed up the week before the first publication to assist with the placement of the publication's racks at outdoor locations in strip shopping centers and other high-traffic areas. Coupled with their involvement during the sales launch, that participation provided direct insight into operational issues, customer feedback, and quality control considerations, and they were also present to resolve problems and identify opportunities. Perhaps even more significantly, their presence proved highly motivational to staff members who saw these executives roll up their sleeves with enthusiasm and energy to join in the challenging but exhilarating efforts to establish a new successful enterprise.

Of course, the successful rollout of *Employment Guide* magazines to 44 cities also benefited from the robust economic climate of the period. During the late 1990s, when unemployment rates fell below 5 percent in most major cities, employers struggled to recruit talent, and they were easily persuaded to test alternatives to attract new hires. Striking while the iron was hot, Trader's leadership dedicated all necessary resources to accelerate the rollout while the timing was so propitious.

Although the company invested approximately $45 million to acquire 15 publications that produced a 30 percent EBITDA margin on about $23 million in revenues, *Employment Guide's* rollout effort generated similar margins on more than $80 million of *new* market revenue. Because most of the start-ups became profitable after their first month of publication, the initial capital outlays of less than $200,000 per location constituted the sole investment, producing an astonishingly attractive annual return.

Right Concept, Weak Management, Opportune Timing, Slow Adoption

Of course, not every rollout is as fortuitously timed and well orchestrated as Trader's *Employment Guide*.

Less than a year after the 1985 acquisition of the Winston–Salem *Trading Post* and *Wheels & Deals*, Landmark management approved the launch of similar publications in Raleigh, North Carolina. However, rather than recruit a well-regarded senior executive to lead the effort, it delegated responsibility for the start-up to the recently promoted Winston–Salem general manager. With a decade's experience managing the publications' sales, that manager was deemed to have the best overall knowledge of the concept, and she quickly recruited an outsider with some advertising sales experience to lead the Raleigh operation.

Inevitably, problems arose. Although knowledgeable about managing sales for an established operation, neither the veteran nor the new hire had a background in start-ups. More significantly, the new responsibilities of managing Winston–Salem remained the primary focus of the veteran, and the recruit was inadequately prepared to manage Raleigh's launch without sufficient guidance and supervision. In addition, with no experience with similar start-ups, Landmark's management had no substantive expectations regarding reasonable performance levels, and it lacked the operational and financial benchmarks to assess development progress. In essence, there was little basis to decide whether the start-up's disappointingly weak sales volume and revenues were good or bad, and the accumulating losses were rationalized as the necessary investment to build an attractive new business: "You have to spend money to make money" was the consoling refrain.

This experience was repeated during the succeeding two years with the launch of automotive photo guides in Roanoke, Virginia, and Kansas City.

Relatively inexperienced management was recruited to sink or swim with a modicum of support from overtaxed upper management, which was diverted by the demands of established core operations and an increasingly distracting torrent of new acquisitions.

By the time of the launch of the Hartford, Connecticut, *Auto Trader* several years later, however, a body of knowledge had been developed from the struggling early efforts. From that experience, Trader knew it was best to begin operations with highly capable veteran managers who were not diverted by outside demands.

But focused, experienced personnel failed to generate instant success for any of the *Auto Trader* start-ups. Each new geographic edition required the development of a critical mass of consumer awareness and advertising support among buyers and sellers of used vehicles. Until that was achieved, few car sellers would pay to advertise in a skinny, unfamiliar publication, and only the more diligent car buyers would purchase a magazine featuring a suspiciously slim volume of advertised vehicles likely to appeal to their interests.

As a paid publication requiring the consumer to invest $0.75 to purchase and peruse the used car ads, *Auto Trader* experienced a slow inspection and adoption rate. Although its picture ads might represent a better advertising pitch than the 20-word ads in newspapers' robust classified sections, the comparative dearth of prospective offerings made the medium at best a secondary source for car buyers. During the early stages, therefore, *Auto Trader* start-ups remained relatively invisible, hidden among the clutter of more familiar media while building a reputation through aggressive telemarketing, gorilla marketing, and other affordable promotions and sampling campaigns. Development proceeded so sluggishly in competitive media markets that management eventually concluded that those start-ups should be predicated on a disappointingly patient seven-year maturation process, producing interim operational losses of about $1 million. However, after progressing through a well-executed development process, the publications could generate an attractive 30 percent EBITDA margin on a multi-million-dollar revenue base.

Because of the long, risk-filled development process, management concluded that the acquisition of existing products represented the absolute best route to market coverage if they could be acquired for reasonable prices. In fact, if there was an established paid automotive photo guide already in the market, the prospects of successfully launching a competing title were grim. Once a publisher had established awareness as the most comprehensive compendium of used vehicles, consumers demonstrated little interest in investing in another ad in a clearly smaller publication whose puny size suggested it was *not* the marketplace. If that competing publisher had no interest in selling or demanded an unreasonably stiff price, that market remained outside Trader's coverage area.

Underexploited Market, Enhanced Product, Leveraged Resources, Free

Although auto manufacturers provide car dealers with bountiful budgets to promote the sale of new cars, there are no such subsidies to market used cars. Every dollar spent by dealers on used car advertising therefore represented an expenditure demanding proof that it generated profitable car sales.

The traditional newspaper and radio and television broadcast media, of course, have long histories of delivering acceptable sales results for their advertisers, but they are expensive, and newspapers' editorial departments in particular tend to irritate car dealers, who are particularly sensitive to the negative implications of publicized automotive recalls, consumer protection issues, financing practices, and other downbeat business news stories and commentary.

To capture more of the used car advertising budgets, Trader management had previously considered the concept of a free distribution advertising periodical devoted exclusively to individualized photos of dealers' inventory. In 1989, its Landmark predecessor had acquired two free distribution used car dealer magazines serving the Baltimore and Washington markets, but their relatively weak performance under uninspired sales management failed to generate enthusiasm for their subsequent rollout to additional markets. In 1992, however, a well-respected media broker, John Cribb, encouraged Trader to acquire an impressively successful four-zone free distribution automotive tabloid serving the greater San Francisco market. *Diablo Dealer*'s success provided the proof of concept, and Trader quietly acquired it.

While Trader's leadership planned the launch of a replica of the *Diablo Dealer* concept in Chicago, Robert Berndt, the local manager of the Atlanta *Auto Trader*, suggested the acquisition of one of his city's automotive photo guides, which could be bought for $25,000 from its undercapitalized founder. Perceiving some value in the publication's distribution outlets and the publisher's key contacts with a few substantial car dealers, Berndt met with a Trader executive to formulate the creation of a somewhat modified publication that would leverage the sales relationships of Trader's Atlanta sales force. Consisting of full-page ads featuring photos of 12 to 15 value-priced used cars from a specific dealer, the proposed magazine would also have ads that would permit each dealer to promote the differentiating characteristics of his or her dealership, such as liberal dealer financing, attentive customer service, and other soft-sell benefits. As free publications distributed in high-traffic venues, they would be quickly picked up by consumers actively in the market for a used car. Within months, that plan and his staff had transformed the formerly struggling 24-page publication into the renamed *Auto Mart* with well over 100 pages of highly profitable used car display ads.

Unlike its underperforming Baltimore and Washington free magazines, Trader's Atlanta launch was directed by a talented, highly motivated manager of one of its most successful *Auto Traders*. Berndt demonstrated that his enthusiasm and commitment could transform a customarily rigid sales organization into one that was inspired to employ its existing relationships to create a new and competitive publication. However, though competitive, that new publication was positioned among both sales staff and car dealers as a supplemental medium that would extend the advertiser's reach to a different target audience: car buyers unwilling to purchase an *Auto Trader* or newspaper in convenience stores but easily enticed to pluck free copies of *Auto Mart* from racks in grocery stores, outside Walmart, and in other high-traffic locations.

With the almost instant success of the Atlanta *Auto Mart*, Trader's leadership recognized that it now had its publishing model, and it soon began the rollout of the publication in every *Auto Trader* city, capitalizing on the knowledge gained from the Atlanta experience. Within two years, over 70 *Auto Mart* launches were successfully completed, and almost every edition generated attractive incremental earnings. However, the revenues quickly plateaued, and the lagging growth was attributed primarily to the complacency of a sales staff with loyalties divided between the two competing concepts they represented simultaneously. Having developed their sales skills pitching *Auto Trader*, they understandably devoted less attention to the new *Auto Mart* concept.

To reignite *Auto Mart*'s growth, Trader's leadership concluded that it was necessary to segregate the two business models and have them compete aggressively against each other. To direct the reorganization and creation of the new *Auto Mart* division, Trader appointed Bill Rieth, one of the company's foremost marketing executives. After honing his skills during the original rollout of *Tradin' Times* almost two decades earlier, Rieth had risen to the role of Trader's Midwest regional manager. To support his efforts, Rieth was given free rein to recruit his own cadre of talent from within Trader to lead the new organization, and that group developed and implemented the plans to divide the existing field sales staffs between the *Auto Trader* and *Auto Mart* organizations.

As was discussed in Chapter 10, the 1996 Seattle *Auto Guide* acquisition gave Rieth's team a template for motivating its dedicated sales staff to attract multipage advertising commitments from franchise car dealerships. Operating independently with an aggressive development strategy, the *Auto Mart* organization grew to a family of 110 publications by 2005, distributing over 2.2 million weekly copies in over 100,000 locations, serving 90-plus major U.S. markets. Including less than $23 million revenues from acquired publications, total *Auto Mart* revenues that year exceeded $150 million, with profit margins averaging over 25 percent.

Franchised Rollout, Reacquisition Rollup

When an enterprise has insufficient human or financial resources to orchestrate the rollout of its concept, outsourcing the development to energetic franchisees is an alternative. Then, after the franchisees have invested their sweat equity to achieve success, the franchisor or another larger enterprise can acquire the franchises and merge them into its more streamlined organization.

Coming close to bankruptcy on at least two occasions, Harland Sanders had spent decades in the hospitality industry when, in 1952, he persuaded Salt Lake City's Pete Harmon to become his first franchisee. Three years later, Sanders incorporated as Kentucky Fried Chicken and hit the road full-time in his white suit and colonel's goatee to entice more enterprising entrepreneurs to begin serving his distinct pressure-cooked chicken recipe. By 1963, Sanders had enlisted over 200 franchisees to manage over 600 units throughout the United States and Canada, and the company attracted the attention of 29-year-old attorney John Y. Brown and his well-heeled golfing buddy, Jack Massey. In 1964, they acquired Sanders's franchising business for $2 million, and two years later they led an initial public offering, raising $280 million for the investor group. With the extra capital and freshly minted stock as his currency, Brown reacquired scores of locations, employing the momentum investing strategy of the era, as was noted in Chapter 7.[2]

Similar stories abound about many of the country's most visible restaurant and retail chains, and the chronicle of the rollout and subsequent rollup of *Auto Trader* represents one of the more anonymous examples. Attracted by the balmy climate of Florida, the itinerant insurance salesman Stuart Arnold fled the Northeast and launched his first *Auto Trader* photo guide in 1975 in Clearwater, Florida. Capitalizing on the fact that a picture is better than a thousand words, it achieved rapid success, and Arnold encouraged several of his more energetic employees to relocate to other cities where they could launch their own edition in exchange for a licensing fee of $0.25 per page. Subsequently, he received unsolicited inquiries from a few independent entrepreneurs who saw the advantages of affiliation and struck the same deal with them. By 1989, he personally owned operations covering all of Florida and Las Vegas, owned a 50 percent interest in the publications serving Los Angeles, and had licensees in almost 20 cities (not including the unlicensed, unaffiliated publication groups that had usurped the trademark in Canada and the United Kingdom). As was described in Chapter 3, Cox and Landmark conducted a pitched battle from 1988 to 1990 to acquire 33 related publishers, investing about $160 million to acquire publications with revenues of just under $100 million.

Trader recognized a similar opportunity when it stumbled upon Dealer Specialties in 1996. Founded in 1990 by Mike and Jack Nenni, Dealer Specialties was established to provide car dealers with an outsourced service to produce and install detailed descriptive window stickers on used cars similar to those legally mandated for new cars. Using the firm's proprietary software, its representatives visited car dealership clients to record approximately 90 data points about each car. They then plugged their laptops into a printer and outputted a label that they posted inside the car's window. Paying a negotiated price of $5 to $8 per car, the dealer was ecstatic to have a professionally designed point-of-purchase sticker to help market his used cars. Not only was it an inexpensive service, it gave the dealer a third party to hold accountable if the label included any descriptive errors.

Because of the probable slow development of the low-revenue service business, the Nennis concluded they could not afford funding for the development of proprietary operations in each city and decided to license the software and business practices to individuals who could solicit and service clients themselves. "If we were a wholly owned company, we would have needed managers and other midlevel employees," Nenni related several years later. "We would be constantly looking for replacements, and there would be little, if any, loyalty. By providing a business opportunity to this type of person, we did not need a large infrastructure. We could run and grow the business with as few as five employees. We could expand into major metropolitan areas simply by finding someone to do it for us. They would be financially motivated."[3]

By 1997, the Nennis and their brother George had attracted a group of 175 franchisees, employing about 600 service reps to produce about 2.5 million window stickers for almost 5,000 used car dealerships. Netting more than $0.50 per sticker as a franchising fee, the brothers found themselves in a most fortuitous position when the Internet arose as a promotional medium. Already possessing the most detailed database of used cars for sale, they quickly modified their software to accommodate the collection of photos, and they automated distribution of the full data stream to online advertising services such as AutoTrader.com, Cars.com, and Yahoo! Autos. With all those ingredients in place, they were positioned to charge their dealer clients for the service—all for a nominal incremental fee paid by car dealers, collected by franchisees, and deposited into a Dealer Specialties bank account.

While nurturing the relationship for the distribution of Dealer Specialties' advertising data on AutoTrader.com, Trader executives repeatedly tried to persuade the Nennis to sell. Although the window stickers by themselves represented an important value, the compelling attraction for future exploitation was the collection of data in a digital form for subsequent dissemination to the eventually thousands of promotional websites. Coupled with its addition of complementary digital images of each vehicle, the Dealer Specialties services represented an efficient utility to collect and disseminate promotional data among burgeoning advertising media of the future, and as such, they promised transformation into a pipeline delivering profits akin to those of credit card processors collecting fees on each transaction.

After two years of conscientious negotiations, Trader finally succeeded in acquiring the Nennis' company as the calendar digits rolled to the year 2000, and after integration, Trader began reacquiring its most attractive franchisees. Like most, the company's franchise agreement dictated that Dealer Specialties, as franchisor, held a preferential right of first refusal if a franchisee tried to sell. Permitting Dealer Specialties to intercede to repurchase a franchise for terms proposed by any third party positioned it as the obvious buyer of the large franchisees, particularly since it also retained the right to reject purchase by parties that failed to satisfy reasonable financial and business-related criteria. (Small operations, essentially those capable of supporting only the owner and a couple of employees, would be best operated by a new franchisee.) Accordingly, by the end of 2006, Trader had completed just over 60 transactions, acquiring franchisees with almost $25 million in revenues for an equivalent investment.

Chapter 12

Innovation of Process

"Pump it up!" Jack Ross urged Richard Jamin as he punched in a faster speed on his treadmill in the motel exercise room.

"All right, I'm with you," Jamin replied as he increased the speed of his treadmill alongside Ross. "I can keep up."

"You'd better, girlie man," Ross retorted, mimicking the Austrian accent of *Saturday Night Live*'s Hans and Franz in the bodybuilder skits. "You'll need your stamina to handle everything on our agenda."

"This feels like all the *Employment Guide* launches," Jamin puffed. "The more we do, the faster we have to run."

"You got it, girlie man!"

"I guess it's all uphill from here," Jamin joked, wiping sweat with a towel. But as he did, his foot caught the left edge of the treadmill, causing him to fall face forward on the rotating belt, which instantly shot him off the back of the machine. Jamin looked up, uninjured but embarrassed by his klutziness.

"And you'd better watch your step and keep on your feet!" Ross laughed.[1]

Run faster, watch your step, and keep on your feet are good advice for any operator, and the adoption of innovations can help a businessperson do all three.

- Dollar Tree had missed the early bandwagon for adopting point-of-sale inventory management, which at that time was dependent on mainframe computers linked by costly dedicated telecommunications lines, but in the new millennium it had no legacy systems holding it back as it leapfrogged forward with far less costly and much faster checkout scanning systems communicating via the Internet to improve productivity, increase the timeliness and accuracy of inventory replenishment, delight customers with detailed receipts, and manage purchasing and logistics more efficiently. As its 2002 annual report stated, "By knowing how products sell and where they sell best, we can bring goods to the right distribution centers and ship them more efficiently to the stores where they are needed. This helps us improve sales and margins and is a key piece of our supply chain improvements."[2]

- As a pioneering seller of advertising on all-cable networks such as USA and the Family Channel, TeleCable was quick to develop software and equipment to automate the management and broadcast of locally prepared ads in the correct programs on its multitude of network offerings. As its CEO, Dick Roberts, related, "that had huge manpower implications," saving substantial costs and delivering the lion's share of the proceeds to the bottom line. Additionally, enhanced customer service and accelerated revenue recognition were facilitated by similar automated processes: "The telemarketers had the ability to say here's the offer and, by the way, we can put that on your system as we speak."[3]

At Trader, process innovations were identified and implemented at many levels to enhance profitability by streamlining operations, stimulating new revenue streams, and increasing competitiveness. New automated systems eliminated labor costs and sped production, technological innovations facilitated viable new marketing strategies, and both factors made the company a more agile operator that was capable of outrunning its competition.

Magazine Production Innovations

Back in the 1960s when entrepreneurs created the first classified advertising publications, such as *Trading Post*, the process of composing its pages with their thousands of liner ads was cumbersome and labor-intensive. Without computerized systems and inexpensive composition equipment, individual ads were prepared with ordinary typewriters and then pasted onto waxed pages for delivery to offset printing presses. The founder of *Tradin' Times*, Pete Banner, followed others in the 1970s when he transitioned from typewriter ads to those generated by IBM composers, automated equipment that produced uniform quality with justified type. To maintain his competitive edge, he rigorously guarded the secret to organizing the massive volume of individually typeset ads: a carefully arranged set of dozens of aluminum ice cube trays.

By the time Landmark acquired those publications, most of the ad preparation process had been converted to some form of computerized device, but the cost of hardware and creating sophisticated ad management software precluded almost all from realizing the full potential of computerization. The consolidation of several publishing companies gave Landmark the scale to warrant the development of proprietary software, and by the early 1990s it had converted all its operations from pasting up individual columns of ads to laser printer outputs of complete pages. Though it required a seven-figure capital expenditure on new computers and software development, the returns were instantaneous upon installation. Annual composition costs dropped by more than half, and record keeping, billing, and management information efficiencies contributed to improving the quality of customer service, accounting accuracy, and the monitoring of each operation's performance.

Similar advancements occurred with the production of the *Auto Trader* photo guides. At the time of acquisition, most were produced by a composing staff that matched individual halftone photos with their 20-word typeset car descriptions and then manually arranged them on a waxed page. Because most ads ran consecutively for three or four weeks, care had to be taken to remove old ads on a timely basis while ensuring that current ads remained queued for publication. Leveraging the advances in digital photography to lower costs dramatically, Trader developed software and systems to produce full pages of ads by automating photo and text matching, which simultaneously improved the accuracy and reliability of ad publishing schedules. Over the several years of conversion, composition costs dropped by more than 50 percent to an average of $11 per page, with some locations posting costs as low as $7 per page.

During its evaluation of United Advertising Publications in 2000, Trader discovered that UAP had composition costs of $32.50 per page. To help justify the premium cost of the acquisition, Trader projected that its methods could reasonably reduce costs to less than $25 per page, saving a minimum of $8 million annually after completion of the conversion. Within two years after acquisition, those expectations were exceeded.

Technology Costs and Telecommunications Innovations

The revolutionary advancements in computerized equipment and software represented innovations that facilitated the impressive benefits described above. Rapidly declining equipment costs accelerated their adoption and reduced the capital expenditures necessary to deliver their benefits.

With their early commercial models carrying price tags of $1,000, digital cameras were not immediately an economical alternative for companies such as Trader, which employed hundreds of photographers throughout the country, but as prices plummeted to half that amount, they became compelling innovations screaming for adoption. Not only did digital cameras provide more cost-efficient integration with the computerized composition systems, they also eliminated expensive silver-based film, processing chemicals, and the associated labor and hazardous waste costs.

The computers also dropped precipitously in price, as did the laser printers necessary for outputting paginated editions for delivery to the printer. But soon, with enhanced technology and lowered telecommunications costs, those paginated production copies became obsolete. Previously flown or driven at great expense to distant printing plants, the hard-copy materials were replaced with digital equivalents that were transmitted electronically over phone lines and eventually the Internet. In addition to courier and transportation costs, the new process eliminated the 2- to 12-hour delivery delays, extending deadlines and the time during which customers could submit advertisements.

Circulation Management Innovations

Computerization also facilitated Trader's adoption of innovative circulation management programs that improved single-copy sales at low incremental costs. Historically, magazines were distributed to convenience stores, and on the basis of past sales, the outlet allotments were adjusted to minimize both the next week's sellouts and the return of unsold copies. Previously, most entrepreneurial publishers had relied on subcontracted distributors to monitor that information to administer store replenishment, and their effectiveness was hard to supervise or enhance successfully. That lack of accurate tracking data also opened the door for theft that could easily be hidden by dishonest distributors. Motivated by the scale of their acquisitions, Trader developed more efficient data processing and telecommunications systems to collect and analyze historical data on every outlet's weekly sales of each magazine. Employing those data, predictive algorithms more accurately projected the necessary weekly volume needed to stock each location's racks to produce the optimum sales without incurring excessive costs for unsold copies.

The importance of more accurate computerized replenishment programs grew exponentially as Trader segmented the original *Auto Trader* into its numerous niche titles, such as *Truck Trader, Cycle Trader,* and *RV Trader.* Although an individual may be able to predict a single high-volume magazine's sales, that individual's ability deteriorates rapidly with each additional title, particularly when some titles sell only a few copies each week. With product segmentation, Trader began distributing as many as 16 niche titles to its over 80,000 convenience store and other sales outlets, and replenishment efficiency could be enhanced only through sophisticated algorithms driven by highly detailed historical sales data.

The computerized circulation systems also facilitated more accurate and timely billing and collection, and the ability to audit each distribution route's performance relative to its historical and seasonal trends mitigated some of the potential for distributor malfeasance.

Innovation of Sales Process

As technological advancements reduced costs and enhanced performance, Trader also benefited from the adoption of innovative sales and marketing strategies.

As was discussed in Chapter 10, the Seattle *Auto Guide* program to attract multipage advertising commitments from the largest car dealers motivated Trader to adopt that innovative sales approach for all its *Auto Mart* magazines, dramatically increasing revenues and profits. Similarly, the many acquisitions gave Trader abundant opportunities to evaluate how different entrepreneurs achieved success, and from that assessment, it identified the programs that could produce the most benefits if replicated throughout its other operations.

To build private party ad counts and revenues, some locations employed aggressive telemarketing programs to solicit customers who were placing ads in competing media. Trader's evaluation determined that their effectiveness remained dependent on the quality of supervision and staff training, and the difficulty of orchestrating efforts among the high-turnover staff prevented most local operations from achieving optimal success. However, Trader's Tom Malone-Povolny had engineered impressive results in Minneapolis–St. Paul and remained unwaveringly committed. To replicate his achievement among all its cities, Trader concluded that it could centralize the program in three telemarketing hubs, and with Minneapolis taking the lead, it installed sophisticated autodialing telemarketing equipment, dramatically increasing even that city's efficiency. At its peak (perhaps to the chagrin of the American public), the telemarketing operations were completing over 6 million telephone solicitations each year, generating attractive incremental profits and simultaneously building awareness of Trader's publications and services.

The efficiency and effectiveness of telephone sales to cultivate commercial accounts was driven home with the acquisition of the Detroit *Employment Guide*. The founders, Wayne Moriarity and Paul Houlachan, discovered that soliciting recruitment ads did not require the high face-to-face service component of the automotive publications. Although car dealers required ad representatives to collect descriptions and photographs of advertised vehicles from physical inspections, the personnel departments created most of their own recruitment ads and were comfortable handling everything by phone, fax, or electronic mail. Ad sales for *Employment Guides* therefore could be handled efficiently by telephone. By recapturing lost selling hours previously devoted to driving between client offices, representatives could solicit a larger volume of prospects, a necessity considering the episodic advertising needs of many employers.

Furthermore, telephone sales permitted the assembly of the sales team in a single location, dramatically simplifying supervision and permitting the implementation of group motivational tactics. For example, every time a solicitor made a sale, she rang the office gong in celebration, simultaneously earning public recognition and goading other staffers to generate their own sales. In addition, each office regularly conducted sales contests with incentives prominently displayed to stimulate exemplary performance. During the May promotional period, the Oklahoma City office inspired its telemarketers by setting up a compelling display of the month's prizes on the sales floor, including patio furniture, picnic gear, camping equipment, and outdoor games and novelties.

Product Segmentation Innovation

While selling cars at a Florida dealership, a British citizen discovered a copy of Stuart Arnold's *Auto Trader*. The man was John Madjesky, and on returning to the United Kingdom, he persuaded a partner to join him to launch a similar magazine. Within a few years, the two had achieved extraordinary success, expanding from their base outside London to cover most of that country's cities. To accommodate exploding ad volume, he segmented the content geographically with separate editions for most major cities. However, volumes grew so large that he reduced ad sizes repeatedly, shrinking the photos to the size of a postage stamp and using minute type to squeeze as many as 54 ads per page, as he did in his Thames Valley 452-page edition.

Florida's Arnold, however, pursued an alternative innovation to handle the skyrocketing volume. At the original price of $0.25, the profitability of his single copy sales was very much dependent on restraining production costs, and excessive page counts meant higher printing costs. However, he feared that shrinking ad sizes would irritate both advertisers and magazine buyers. Noticing that a substantial volume of his Florida content consisted of boat ads, Arnold reasoned that he could create a completely separate *Boat Trader*. After all, consumers were interested in buying either a car or a boat, not both at the same time. Hence, they might appreciate a guide with only boat ads or only car ads.

When Arnold launched *Boat Trader*, combined single copy sales for the two magazines leaped. Previously, many boat buyers had never considered buying *Auto Trader* to search for boat ads. Now the *Boat Trader*–emblazoned publication grabbed their attention in convenience stores, and they bought a copy. Moreover, Arnold's profits leaped because the production costs of the two smaller magazines were lower. For example, rather than printing ten thousand 300-page magazines (3 million pages), Arnold printed eight thousand 220-page *Auto Traders* and four thousand 150-page *Boat Traders* (20 percent more magazine copies but only 2.36 million pages, representing a 21 percent reduction in newsprint consumption and costs).

The compelling economic justification for that innovation led to further product segmentation as ad volumes continued to grow. New spin-offs included *Truck Trader, Cycle Trader, RV Trader, Big Truck Trader,* and *Heavy Equipment Trader*. In San Diego and Phoenix, growth compelled even more tightly segmented products. Phoenix divided *Auto Trader* into separate European, Asian, and domestic manufacturer editions and then divided them further by advertised price, including *Truck Trader—Under $5,000* and *Truck Trader—$5,000 and Over*.

After consolidating the majority of U.S. publishers, Trader adopted the segmented approach for some of its underdeveloped markets. Although it lacked the volume for separate publications in each market, Trader reasoned that some segments encouraged buyers to conduct vehicle searches over broader geographic areas, and it therefore produced regional editions covering several markets. For example, the boat ads from the Washington, Baltimore, Norfolk, Richmond, and Roanoke markets were combined in a single magazine that was distributed throughout the Mid-Atlantic region. Now boat sellers could reach the prospective customers in the relevant geographic market instead of a newspaper's more limited coverage area, and boat buyers were delighted to purchase an alternative publication that featured a much larger inventory covering the full market they would consider. The innovation was a success among consumers, helping Trader gain increased market share and higher profits.

Breadth and Depth of Content Innovation

Through most of its early history, Trader and its forebears had devoted their efforts to creating and leveraging an attractive media business founded on the publication of concise descriptions coupled with a single black-and-white photograph. Technological innovations made possible the efficient capture and distribution of a far more definitive descriptive data set, and consumer demand produced profitable new business opportunities such as that exploited by Dealer Specialties.

As a hardworking car salesman in Raleigh, North Carolina, Mike Nenni fully understood the incremental advantages of offering used car buyers a more definitive description of a dealer's inventory. Accustomed to the comprehensive details of a new car window sticker, consumers were disappointed when required to ask for similar information for the used cars that caught their eye. Many suspected that their innocent questions would lead to the hard sell from a high-pressure salesperson, and they were doubtful about the answers supplied by the car lot's often ill-informed staff. Nenni reasoned that used cars required a point-of-purchase descriptive posting as detailed as those on new cars and persuaded his programming wizard brother, Jack, to create software to simplify data collection on a laptop. Beginning with the translation of the car's vehicle identification number, which defined an impressive array of manufacturer-installed components, the software guided the user through a physical inspection of a vehicle to collect supplemental data and confirmation of other components that might have changed. For example, the car might have an upgraded audio system and other modifications that were installed after it left the manufacturer. Once collected, the data were automatically manipulated by the software to produce a professional window sticker that could be instantly produced on a simple printer for application on the car.

The software program and inspection/collection service was the foundation from which the Nennis created Dealer Specialties. As the company developed, the brothers discovered that the provision of the labor and expertise to collect the data and apply the window sticker to the car was integral to the service. Although the software could be easily used by a conscientious employee, the dealers preferred to have their staffs focus on customer sales and service and liked having a third party to blame if there were errors on the sticker. By subcontracting the service to a Dealer Specialties representative, a dealer could hold it liable for damages, and Dealer Specialties would consequently emphasize accuracy to mitigate its exposure.

Once compiled for the window sticker, the Dealer Specialties database produced new opportunities. No dealer routinely collected such detailed information, but the Nennis understood that dealers would value the data for incorporation in their own management information systems. They generated strong dealer enthusiasm when they offered distribution of the data to Internet sites such as AutoTrader.com.

The acquisition of Dealer Specialties gave Trader the opportunity to leverage those innovations in the quickly developing Internet economy. With Internet advertising services proliferating rapidly, it suddenly became economically viable to distribute advertising descriptions that were more comprehensive than the customary 20-word description. In the confines of a small print advertisement, it was feasible to publish only the car's make, model, year, mileage, price, and a few other notable details. With the Internet's insignificant incremental costs, it became equally viable to include the almost 100 descriptive elements from the Dealer Specialties window sticker with the content distributed and hosted on online databases, and *Auto Trader's* single black-and-white photo could be replaced with a dozen color shots and perhaps an individualized video. By 2006, the Dealer Specialties software was interacting with over 2,300 web services, providing dealers with an integrated pipeline to distribute their data for their full vehicle inventories to almost every significant Internet advertising database. Coupled with its original window sticker business, the combination of services permitted Dealer Specialties to serve over 9,300 car dealer customers in over 120 markets throughout the United States in 2006, and each month its staff gathered data, produced window stickers, and distributed descriptions for an average of over 400,000 additional vehicles to thousands of websites.

Organizational Innovation

Part of the anticipated benefits of acquiring dozens of small operations within an industry is the savings achievable through the consolidation of administrative and other back-office functions that can be performed more efficiently by dedicated centralized resources.

In practice, the achievement of such operational savings is elusive within the consolidated group of such small enterprises. Usually run by determined, cost-conscious entrepreneurs, small companies either don't waste effort on many of the unprofitable administrative requirements of a large company or outsource them to an efficient outside contractor. Integrally involved with all daily operations, the entrepreneur dispenses with the necessity of internal audits or human resource initiatives and typically delegates the performance of payroll, accounting, and payables functions to a small accounting firm that provides comprehensive services for scores of clients for a few hundred dollars per month.

A consolidator, familiar with the regulatory and operational pitfalls of a large business, finds itself compelled to superimpose bureaucratic processes on the previously "lean and mean" acquisition, raising instead of streamlining costs. On top of these expenses are the acquirer's supervisory costs of executive salaries, administrative staff, travel, office rents, and other overhead charges that the independent operator never experienced.

The added costs can be devastating. In his analysis of Collision Auto Repair of America, the reporter Ilan Mochari ascribed the death of that rollup to "overhead bloated by hasty acquisitions." According to its former director of operations, Dennis Kennealy, the company "lacked the internal management structure," and it added top-notch executive staff to manage its far-flung operations. The result "was soaring overhead costs and chaos," eventually causing the company to collapse in Chapter 7 bankruptcy in June 1999.[4]

Though not driving United Advertising Publications to bankruptcy, the development of a sprawling headquarters severely diminished its profitability and effectiveness, as was described in Chapter 10. Trader's substitution of its own decentralized administration approach transferred authority to field operations, permitting the elimination of UAP's executive team, its $8.5 million in associated costs, and over 200 bureaucratic positions, along with an unproductive technology group that had failed to launch competitive Internet services. Freed from distractions and with the authority to proceed quickly and aggressively, UAP's field management produced an impressive revenue and earnings turnaround in the increasingly competitive environment. New robust Internet services (ForRent.com and HarmonHomes.com) were launched to produce impressive traffic and revenues, and the work of its 400-person home office staff was distilled to the critical support tasks performed by a group less than one-fourth the size.

Trader's managerial emphasis on addressing a handful of critical success factors represented another form of operational innovation for UAP. Rather than being diverted by mundane reporting dictates and a blizzard of ethereal initiatives, the field managers focused on delivering the results that mattered, and they produced an impressive turnaround founded on the company's critical fundamental initiatives.

Somewhat surprisingly, the increased decentralization of authority produced other benefits normally achievable only through centralization. With their focus on producing bottom-line results for their own operations, field managers responded more promptly to opportunities to reduce costs. They reduced travel, finding lower-cost alternatives through Trader's online systems; negotiated more aggressively on office leases; and focused more conscientiously on squeezing out unnecessary expenditures. No longer diverted by vendor-sponsored boondoggles such as trips to the Masters Golf Tournament that Dallas executives had enjoyed, company negotiators were able to command lower prices from the printers and other vendors.

To facilitate the measurement of the organization's progress, data collection was automated through more computerized management information systems that delivered the feedback promptly with an emphasis on the data most critical and relevant to the achievement of key objectives.

Chapter 13

Transformative Innovation

"You are acquainted with the five stages of new ventures, aren't you?" Landmark's president, Dick Barry, asked Norman Hoffmann, his recently appointed director of specialty publications.

"No, I'm afraid I'm not," Hoffmann said sheepishly, a little embarrassed by his ignorance.

"Well," Barry continued, "you need to know them, considering that you're taking point to find new specialty publications to acquire and develop for our community newspaper division.

"Stage 1 is wild-eyed enthusiasm for the prospects. That's the stage we're in now. The world is our oyster, and everything is possible.

"Stage 2 is dawning disillusionment. That's when we realize that things aren't going to work out quite like we thought. Expenses are higher, revenues are disappointing, and operations aren't running as smoothly as expected.

"Stage 3 is mad panic, the period of terrified fear accompanying the quandary over how the heck we're going to get ourselves out of the mess.

"Stage 4 is the search for the guilty, when the champions of the new venture are terminated.

"And stage 5 is promotion of the nonparticipants. That's when the company naysayers earn their rewards."

"I'm not so sure those give me much confidence about my future, especially stage 4," Hoffmann said, chuckling weakly.

"Oh, don't worry," Barry said with a broad smile. "You know we reward those who take risks even when they lead to failure, because those failures often lead us to better results. Our perhaps overoptimistic acquisition of suburban shoppers resulted in the pivotal acquisition of the Winston–Salem *Trading Post*, and look where we are with The Weather Channel now. We were on the verge of shutting it down, and now its profits position it as one of our smartest new ventures."

"Sounds good.... Just remember that when I'm struggling during stage 3," Hoffmann mumbled.

Accompanying all innovation is the risk—sometimes substantial risk—that the innovations will lead the company down an expensive path to abject failure and the possible death of the organization's core business; preferably, the innovations will lead the company up the sharp curve of the new or rejuvenated product's life cycle toward enviable prosperity. This is particularly true for innovations that are fundamentally transformative. On the one hand, the prospect of such innovations places the investor at risk of acquiring a viable business today that will become obsolete before she or he can earn a satisfactory return. On the other hand, the acquirer's opportunity to leverage those innovations through the investment may produce unanticipated extraordinary returns.

Evolutionary Transformation in the Cable Industry

The evolution of the cable television business is a good example of the exponential returns associated with investments in industries that are experiencing sequential, transformative innovation.

Television had barely been introduced to the largest cities in 1948 when appliance salesman James Y. "Jimmy" Davidson became determined to bring its broadcasts to Tuckerman, Arkansas, a town of only 2,000 people some 90 miles northwest of Memphis. More energetic than other small town tinkerers, Davidson relentlessly pursued its reception with the construction of a 100-foot-high tower atop his two-story appliance store to capture the signals from Memphis's WMCT-TV. Then, to fuel sales to enthralled residents, he began stringing wires from his antenna to the homes of his television buyers. Inspired by Davidson and "the Father of Cable TV" Bill Daniels,[1] hundreds of others followed suit, working feverishly to capitalize on the highly profitable business opportunity of delivering broadcast television to the rural communities of America through a Community Antenna Television (CATV) system.

By the early 1960s, the high profit potential of CATV had attracted a small group of larger established corporations such as Cox and Landmark to begin the industry's rollup/rollout fray. Their television stations had provided insight into broadcast's addictive consumer appeal, they had the financial reserves and cash flow needed to fund the high capital expenditures required to wire communities, and they had the human resources necessary to deal with local government's increasingly convoluted process for awarding franchises.

Until the mid–1980s, however, CATV remained primarily a service for small, distant communities without broadcast television coverage from the three major networks. That changed with the 1972 launch of the innovative Home Box Office and the 1975 microwave and satellite transmissions of superstations such as WTBS and WGN, services that provided compelling supplemental content, transforming cable offerings into a desirable entertainment package that created a voracious demand among the citizens of large cities.

Until that time, companies such as TeleCable had suffered debilitating loses in suburban locales such as Overland Park, Kansas, whose citizens were initially satisfied with the over-the-air broadcasts they received from Kansas City. As TeleCable's president, Dick Roberts, later related: "The bad news is, before the satellite and even before we could microwave signals from independents in St. Louis and Chicago, we bled red, and thank goodness Frank Batten had a long-term point of view. We bled; we did everything we could. We always hesitated to be the first one off the landing craft, but in Overland Park we really had to become forward thinking." But then, with satellite transponder transmissions of compelling programming from new all-cable channels, "Boom! Subscriber growth exploded."[2] Coupled with the revenues generated by marketing increasing tiers of content (such as CNN, ESPN, and The Weather Channel), those highly populated suburban and urban markets fueled the steep climb of the industry's valuation multiples, providing compelling motivation to the small players to sell and thus accelerating the consolidation movement.

Soon, after the launch of so many supplementary cable services in the early 1980s (USA Network, Family Channel, Discovery, etc.), the local cable operations leveraged their distribution monopoly to command carriage fees from some of the less compelling channels among their service offerings to subscribers. However, the high-demand networks, particularly ESPN, were able to charge for their service, and that proved to be the salvation for The Weather Channel, which began collecting $0.02 to $0.06 per subscriber every month from local cable operators. Most important, the majority of all-cable networks had an overabundance of unsold advertising spots, and they gladly allocated a share as a revenue opportunity to induce local cable operators to offer their network to subscribers. "Where we did make money as pioneers was advertising," recalled Roberts. "In the area of advertising, we added a whole new dimension to the company. We were doing proportionally more than the number one company which bought us."[3] In fact, at the time of its 1994 sale to TeleCommunications, Inc., TeleCable's advertising sales represented more than a third of total revenues, a revenue stream that had not existed 10 years earlier.

With the dozens of all-cable networks now a part of the subscriber offering, cable operators found themselves positioned to capture the majority share of a local market's television advertising revenues. Although the local NBC affiliate may have had a commanding viewership, it did not have the advertising spot volume or the combined reach of the perhaps 40 all-cable networks offered by the local cable franchise. Consequently, cable's early rollup/rollout investors were blessed with huge unanticipated rewards, receiving new bounties for having taken the risk of spending large sums on consolidation.

With the advent of Internet services, they were rewarded again. The industry's coaxial cable provided superior throughput compared with the copper wire of telephone services, and cable's offering of Internet connectivity delivered another fresh, highly profitable new revenue stream that became as indispensable to consumers as the original cable service. With the advent of optic cable, the transformative innovation cycle turned another rotation, rewarding acquirers with additional revenue streams, including telephone and other related services.

Evolutionary Transformation in the Cellular Phone

The cellular telephone industry represents a similar example of the transformative power of innovation in the rollup/rollout acquisition strategy. Although it had been dormant for more than a half century, the rapidity of technological change condensed the commercial introduction, rollout, rollup, and innovative development of the cellular phone industry into a period of slightly more than 30 years, leading to almost $200 billion in revenue in 2009.[4]

Although the seed had been planted by Reginald Fessenden's invention of shore-to-ship radio telephony in 1900 and germinated by Bell System's 1946 "mobile" car telephone (weighing 80 pounds), the industry had no practical application until Motorola's Martin Cooper unveiled the first truly portable mobile phone in 1973. In 1977, with authorization from the Federal Communications Commission (FCC), Bell Labs and AT&T demonstrated a prototype of the first cellular system and commenced operations a year later in Chicago with 2,000 trial customers.[5] Demand was impressive, but development was constrained until after 1984, when the FCC began awarding licenses by lottery. With an equal chance of receiving a license, the established communications firms were joined by a swarm of small entrepreneurs and speculators, and sometimes more than 1,000 applicants lined up for a chance at even the smallest markets.[6]

With so many players, the expansion of service accelerated, and the largest operators consolidated their coverage area by buying up hundreds of small speculators who welcomed the opportunity to sell out at huge profits because they lacked the scale to compete. Added spectrum and innovative technologies multiplied the capacity of the systems, increasing the ability of providers to serve more customers and collect their subscriber fees. Then the industry was pushed forward again by innovation as it began selling ancillary products (ring tones, games, music, etc.), introduced new services (voice mail, texting, global positioning, etc.), and leveraged the Internet's expanding universe of services by selling data plans ($41.5 billion in 2009) and a plethora of smartphone applications.[7]

Transformative Innovations in Classified Advertising

In light of the history of the cable and cellular industries, the development of Trader's business opportunities through transformative innovation is a bit mundane. Nonetheless, the classified advertising publishing industry experienced a comparable series of transformative innovations.

"Pay If and When You Sell" Classified Ad Tabloids

Long considered a staple of newspapers' advertising revenue streams, classified advertising originally consisted of succinct word ads placed by private individuals seeking to sell their used cars, homes, appliances, and other high-ticket items. Unfortunately, newspaper ads were relatively expensive, and the risk of failing to sell an item caused many people to hesitate to make the investment. To address those concerns, enterprising entrepreneurs in Boston and Atlanta capitalized on two transformative innovative ideas: (1) create a local niche publication devoted exclusively to private party classified ads and (2) charge advertisers a commission only if the advertised item sold.

After their success, the concept was eventually replicated in Norfolk, Virginia, and several other cities by John DeLeeuw, an energetic economics professor who inspired local Boy Scouts to raise funds for their organization by soliciting ads and selling his publications. Subsequently, while they were based in Norfolk, two navy sailors were impressed by DeLeeuw's concept and returned to the Midwest to start their own versions: Pete Banner started his first in Columbus, Ohio, eventually launching identical publications in another eight cities, and Jim Arbogast established his first tabloid in Dayton, Ohio, and rolled out similar editions in four other cities.

Paid Circulation Photo Guides

While those entrepreneurs were experiencing impressive results, former insurance salesman Stuart Arnold became riveted by the adage that "a picture is worth a thousand words." In fact, he reasoned, when it came to marketing cars, a picture was worth far more than a thousand words, and he therefore championed the next innovative transformation for the classified advertising industry with the introduction of his *Auto Trader* photo guide concept in Clearwater, Florida.

Although uniquely successful, *Auto Trader* was not a panacea for used car marketers. Because its content consisted primarily of private party ads, it appealed chiefly to consumers who were comfortable with independently selling or buying their vehicles through sometimes intense negotiations with unfamiliar respondents to their ads. *Auto Trader* readership was therefore confined to a confident, self-reliant segment of car buyers and sellers. Moreover, some used car dealers found it distasteful to advertise their inventory alongside the typically more "value-priced" offerings of individual consumers. Those dealers needed an advertising vehicle with better reach among average buyers more disposed to working a deal with a commercial enterprise that could offer financing and warranties.

Free Distribution Photo Guides

That underserved demand led Trader to the next innovative transformation. Slightly modifying a concept already exploited by a few entrepreneurs, Trader launched its *Auto Mart*, a product line extension that consisted of only photo ads of autos from the inventories of commercial car dealers. Distributed free, it eliminated the readership barrier of *Auto Trader*'s $1 cover price, and through supplemental distribution outlets such as shopping centers' outdoor racks, its expanded circulation provided new advertising reach to a much broader audience. That enlarged reach and concentrated advertising content generated a strong consumer response for its advertisers, and *Auto Mart*'s quick success in Atlanta encouraged its national rollout to almost every major U.S. market. Although it had no material impact on *Auto Trader*'s development, the *Auto Mart* business quickly grew to over $100 million in revenues in less than a decade.

Electronic Classifieds

Familiar with efforts to develop interactive content for cable television operators, Trader's management perceived that the next innovation might be through some voice-response or teletext service, and it began testing systems to deliver content by telephone and cable wires. But with consumers' increasing acceptance of computer systems in the late 1980s, the launch of online services by CompuServe, Prodigy, and America Online presented the next transformative innovation to the classified advertising industry. However, before Trader could affiliate with any of the proprietary systems, the Internet became a viable mass medium with the release of consumer-friendly browsers and inexpensive connectivity, dramatically transforming what had been little more than an electronic bulletin board service.

Blessed with the largest proprietary database of used vehicles for sale, Trader possessed the most important asset for success in building an online classified ad service: content leadership on a national basis. Unfortunately, the content was dispersed among scores of unconnected field office computer systems, and it consisted of a Brunswick stew of ads randomly composed by millions of private party advertisers. Lacking any uniformity, the various ad databases were loaded with misspellings ("Chevie" and "Chevralet"), abbreviations ("pdl" for "power door locks"), and inconsistent inclusion of descriptive elements. Although usually listing the make and year, the vast majority of ads lacked desirable information such as mileage, color, manufacturer, and factory trim packages (for example, is a Honda Accord a DX, LX, or EX edition?). Sometimes even an asking price was absent, and if the car's overall operating condition was referenced, its characterization might not be reliable.

To create a more viable service, Trader was compelled to consolidate its dispersed ads into a single database; then, to facilitate efficient consumer searches, it had to convert the content into a uniform database format. Although technological advancements and Internet connectivity facilitated their integration within a shared database, the ads' homogenization into a standard format required the development of sophisticated software to interpret, translate, and correct the misspellings and abbrevia-tions. To improve consistency in descriptive content, however, Trader had to institute a more regimented data collection effort by its field personnel, and the modifications required training and added effort, increasing costs and slowing adoption throughout the organization.

From conception to introduction, the process of creating Auto-TraderOnline.com took about a year; the service made its public appear-ance in 1997. Although there were other national services (Autobytel, AutoConnect, CarPoint, Yahoo! Autos, etc.) and although local newspa-pers were quick to publish their ads online, none came close to the breadth of content—particularly private party listings—of Trader's service. Even when a consortium of the nation's newspaper publishers joined to launch Cars.com, they failed to offer as comprehensive a database as Trader's. Furthermore, Trader's core business gave the site a promotional edge. Displayed prominently in most convenience stores and supermarkets, its familiar nationally branded magazines drove consumer traffic to the site during its infancy. Finally, the superiority of AutoTraderOnline.com's search flexibility and content detail was obvious to anyone comparing results with the random content of Craigslist and other services.

Championing the Internet service's development effort was Peter Ill, a highly motivational advocate who brought his Princeton smarts and fighter pilot aggressiveness to build the site's prominence and financial success. By 1999, Trader's online performance was so impressive that its owners prepared the service for an initial public offering by spinning it off and merging the renamed AutoTrader.com with AutoConnect.com, a similar service created by its partner, Cox, and Automatic Data Processing, Inc.[8]

After the AutoTrader.com spin-off, Ill and his staff redirected their atten-tion to the development of other vehicle advertising portals. Trader's broad array of niche titles provided similarly large databases for the launch of sep-arate sites for other vehicle segments. To capture a substantial share of the related Internet advertising opportunity, it leveraged its content superiority through its Traderonline.com umbrella brand with differentiated sites such as BoatTrader.com, CycleTrader.com, RVTrader.com, AeroTrader.com, and CommercialTruckTrader.com.

Cloud Computing and Dealer Web Services

In addition to the vehicle sites, Trader's management began focusing on the identification of the next evolution of classified ad services. From visits to industry trade shows and attentiveness to Internet service developments, Trader's managers concluded that classified advertising portals such as AutoTrader.com were still missing the mark in terms of what car dealers really wanted. Although they drove traffic to client websites, Internet portals displayed the dealer's inventory alongside that of its commercial and private party competitors in an environment that emphasized price comparisons. In contrast, the dealer preferred displaying the inventory in a manner that would promote his differentiated services while enhancing his customer appeal and reputation. Dealers certainly had no interest in promoting visits to national portals. Instead, they preferred investing their advertising dollars to attract traffic directly to their own websites to promote their distinct benefits and their exclusive inventory of new and used vehicles. This was particularly true of dealers with multiple franchises and locations. However, they lacked the sophistication or capital to develop robust platforms by themselves and turned to outside vendors.

Trader's management soon concluded that the cloud computing opportunity of providing hosting services to its vehicle dealers represented the next transformative innovation for exploitation. Faced with roughly similar website needs among the nation's approximate 65,000 new and used car dealers, Trader's Mitch Brooks surmised that there was an opportunity to develop standardized platforms to provide inventory searches, lead generation, maintenance scheduling, and the scores of additional customer relationship management (CRM) components of an online dealer site. Over those common templates, Trader could superimpose the individualized branding and customized graphics to provide each dealer with the site differentiation it desired. As new web service innovations were developed, they could be quickly duplicated and profitably integrated into the sites of a broad subscriber base of clients.

By leveraging its existing dealer relationships and its core competencies in website design and traffic generation, Trader determined that it was well positioned to compete with the scores of small web developers that had sprung up to satisfy the demand. To accelerate its entry into the segment with an experienced group of developers and clients, Trader acquired a few best-of-breed entrepreneurial ventures, including Dealerskins and XIGroup. With that as its base, Trader leveraged its advantages to capture a significant share of the website hosting and services market among auto dealers.

Simultaneously, the establishment of Trader as a provider of hosting services positioned it to take its next evolutionary step of providing innovative, value-added ancillary services to attract traffic to those websites and perform other data processing and customer services on an integrated cloud platform. For example, through its @utoRevenue subsidiary, it began providing a broad array of customer relationship management services, including automated e-mail appointment and maintenance reminders, online service scheduling, e-newsletters, traditional direct mail, and even automated voice messaging of birthday greetings.

Other Vehicles and Real Estate Transformations

In its other vehicle classified advertising segments, Trader pursued the evolutionary development by capitalizing on identical transformative innovations. The liner ads of its *Trading Post* and *Tradin' Times* classified ad papers provided the ingredients to accelerate the development of its *Boat Trader, Cycle Trader, RV Trader,* and other niche photo publication segments. Those publications in turn provided the core content to facilitate development of the Internet advertising portals for their respective segments (BoatTrader.com, CycleTrader.com, RVTrader.com, etc.). Those portals and the knowledge from related auto services led to the creation of Vehicle Web Services, through which it developed an impressive website hosting business for dealers marketing boats, motorcycles, RVs, commercial trucks, and heavy equipment. Combined with its Powersports Network acquisition, Trader's web-hosting revenues grew to exceed those of many of its related vehicle advertising portals, such as CycleTrader.com.

Trader pursued a similar development pattern in its real estate segments. After acquisition of *For Rent Magazine* with the UAP deal, Trader launched ForRent.com, an Internet portal that gave the apartment industry a medium to solicit new tenants by featuring and promoting its varied complexes online. Then, after its acquisition of Resite Information Technology, it used its industry relationships and web development skills to begin providing web-hosting services for apartment management companies.

For real estate agents, Trader's *Harmon Homes* magazine group provided advertising reach among home buyers who eagerly picked up the free publication from grocery store and outdoor racks to investigate market offerings. The individualized listings provided the necessary content for the launch of HarmonHomes.com, and to gain critical mass, Trader acquired Homes.com shortly after that site emerged from bankruptcy after the dot-com bust. With the traffic-building power of Homes.com, Trader was positioned to offer web-hosting services to the industry's over 100,000 real estate agents, and to accelerate its development as a market leader, it acquired several real estate hosting services, including Advanced Access and Katabat Corp. To capitalize on the opportunity to satisfy real estate agents' promotion and ancillary service and content needs, Trader also acquired Best Image Marketing, Inc., and eNeighborhoods, Inc. Coupled with its acquisition of RPIS, Inc., the eNeighborhoods acquisition gave Trader the ability to automate the collection and consolidation of millions of active real estate listings dispersed among the country's hundreds of multiple listing services.

The Innovators' Dilemma

Such transformative innovation can run into barriers from the established old guard of an organization. The preference of field personnel to continue operating in their comfortable rut of publishing customers' ads certainly impeded the development of a robust, high-quality searchable database necessary for the success of AutoTrader.com. More significantly, disruptive transformative innovations often imply advances that threaten to undermine the core business. That risk justifiably causes hesitation if not outright opposition to changing course. Rather than simply addressing the barrier of people unwilling to modify their work habits, those pursuing innovation must confront the legitimate concerns of an organization's leaders who perceive that change could cause substantial deterioration, if not the eventual demise, of the core business.

As Clayton Christensen asserted in *The Innovator's Dilemma*, disruptive technologies negatively affect even the best-run organizations because the slowed acceptance of innovations by a company's core customers causes firms to delay cultivation of new markets, permitting more aggressive entrepreneurial competitors to capture the leadership position. Discouraging progress is the fact that investing in transformative innovation is not perceived to be a rational financial decision:

> First, disruptive products are simpler and cheaper; they generally promise lower margins, not greater profits. Second, disruptive technologies typically are first commercialized in emerging or insignificant markets. And third, leading firms' most profitable customers generally don't want, and initially can't use, products based on disruptive technologies.[9]

Certainly, for traditional media, the initial revenues from Internet advertising represented a minuscule fraction of those produced by their newspaper and television ads, and the cost of technological investments and market development of the initially insignificant emerging markets meant negative near-term (not just lower long-term) margins. Arguably, traditional media's (and Trader's) most profitable core commercial car dealership customers did not originally perceive the value of a new medium that would provide instantaneous access to highly detailed competitive information on both pricing and inventory availability among the full universe of dealers. Having historically promoted a few special value-priced vehicles to entice customers onto their car lots, dealers were accustomed to persuading the buyers to purchase alternative and more profitable vehicles. Dealers therefore had compelling reasons to feel threatened by the prospective arrival of a tool that would provide instantaneous access to a comprehensive database of a market's complete used car inventory along with definitive comparison pricing information.

Accordingly, although motivated to protect their high-margin print and television revenue streams, traditional newspaper and broadcast media were discouraged from pursuing the new Internet opportunities. Their advertising customers were edgy about the new medium, and its revenue potential appeared skimpy and unprotected by meaningful barriers to entry.

Unencumbered by high overhead costs and unimpeded by the customer preferences of the traditional advertising media business, Dealer Specialties arose as one of the nimble entrepreneurial enterprises that could exploit the disruptive innovations of the Internet. Dealer Specialties was founded to satisfy dealers' need to produce and install point-of-purchase marketing materials, and the Internet opened the door for it to create a brand-new "outbound" service that rather than threatening its core promised to leverage its value exponentially. With highly detailed descriptions of a dealer's full inventory already in its database, it found itself in the most advantageous position to provide a service to transmit the information into the promotional databases of new promotional services such as AutoByTel, CarPoint, AutoConnect, and of course AutoTrader.com. By capturing photos and videos with increasingly cheaper digital cameras, it further enhanced its dealer services while transforming itself into an integrated pipeline providing content collection and promotional distribution services to the multiplying high-growth Internet portals and advertising services.

Though dependent on traditional advertisers, Trader was less encumbered by the prejudices and hesitancy of large commercial car dealerships that were wedded to the legacy print advertising business. Its customers were typically the smaller, scrappier dealers who had capitalized on Trader's lower-cost advertising to compete against more dominant players with huge advertising budgets. By virtue of Trader's national branding and content, it perceived a larger opportunity that almost no other traditional media player could capture so easily. Its leaders therefore understood that it made unequivocal rational sense to pursue aggressive development of its AutoTraderOnline.com vehicle advertising service.

By 1999, Trader had successfully weathered the start-up costs of its AutoTraderOnline.com service, and trends promised operating profits by year end. Pleased with the progress, its leadership was confident that the service could eventually transform and replace the printed *Auto Trader*, and they were grateful that its improving traction appeared to ensure a strong position in the competitive marketplace, ensuring the future prospects of Trader as a long-term beneficiary of the used car advertising industry.

But Trader's owners had a different idea. The dot-com IPO pot was still boiling, and the Cox ownership perceived that the business was ripe for merger with its own AutoConnect.com for a subsequent spin-out as a new publicly traded entity. Although intrigued, Landmark's owners initially supported management's preference to continue development within Trader. For months, the owners debated the merits, and Landmark's owners were persuaded that independent development of the Internet service could be a more successful strategy. The merger with AutoConnect would give AutoTrader.com increased market share, providing supplemental scale so that it could better compete against Microsoft's Carpoint.com, the newspaper consortium's Cars.com, and a bevy of other contenders battling for supremacy. Moreover, to ensure its competitive position, the site required continuous substantial investments in product development and promotion to build and maintain "top of mind" awareness. Although the massive promotional costs implied by Super Bowl advertising could be borne by Trader, its management's mindset was more pecuniary, and it might compromise short-term earnings for the long-term benefits of greater awareness and more rapid revenue growth.

Ultimately, with Trader's management feeling betrayed, Cox and Landmark decided in favor of the spin-out of AutoTraderOnline and its simultaneous merger with AutoConnect to create the consolidated AutoTrader.com. To lead the integration, Cox named as president Chip Perry, a marketing talent from the *LA Times* who had helped develop AutoConnect, and it appointed its trusted technology maven, Jim McKnight, to assist as chief operating officer. The two adroitly engineered the consolidation and laid the groundwork for the massive promotional effort that firmly established the site as the nation's most recognizable and comprehensive car sales and evaluation portal.

Though frustrated, Trader's management team did what all professional managers must do. They accepted ownership's decision and refocused their attention on coordinating the spin-out while preparing to redeploy their efforts to new projects. Though disappointed, management understood that the boss may not always be right but is always the boss.

With the passage of time and the cooling of emotions, the spin-out can be viewed more dispassionately. By 2011, it appeared that the owners had made the correct decision because it produced two primary benefits. The first was that the independent service developed more quickly and more effectively and captured more share in the turbulent Internet market. Trader's management would have been inevitably diverted from pursuing pivotal development initiatives because of negative impacts on its print editions, and it would have skimped on promotional and development expenditures because of its more vigilant attention to driving profits. As an independent entity, AutoTrader.com grew rapidly from its 1999 status as a $4 million revenue subsidiary within Trader to a highly profitable, over $1 billion revenue behemoth in 2011.

The second benefit of the spin-out was that Trader's management turned its talents to developing other services and segments. The huge opportunity represented by autos naturally commanded the staff's full attention, and it consumed the bulk of development and marketing resources, relegating other segments to the status of stepchildren. After the transfer of AutoTraderOnline.com, Trader's management redirected its efforts and resources to the development of BoatTrader.com, CycleTrader.com, and several other subsidiary services. Though smaller, those segments grew into substantial businesses exceeding $50 million revenues that otherwise might have been lost to competitors if they had not received more aggressive attention after the spin-out. Similarly, Trader's print publication staff probably did a better job protecting that turf because it devoted undivided attention to selling print's benefits aggressively without concern over the impact on a sister Internet service.

This example underscores a fundamental lesson of organizational development during turbulent times. Innovation leads to nettlesome dilemmas involving how best to allocate resources while remaining conscious of the needs of core customers and operations. Emotionally tied to the competing interests of a legacy business, the management team giving birth to an innovation may have difficulty implementing the optimum strategy for its development. Accordingly, extraordinary steps, although difficult, may be necessary to produce superior results. In ideal circumstances, there will be a dispassionate Machiavellian prince who will intercede to ensure that the best route is taken; arguably, Trader's owners played that role.

Chapter 14

Identifying Rollup
Opportunities

Serendipity. Something interesting catches his eye, and that person suddenly discovers that he has lucked into finding a hot opportunity when he wasn't even looking. That often seems to be the story behind great acquisitions:

- While aggressively developing his Multimixer sales business, Ray Kroc became curious about why a single drive-in restaurant had bought eight of those machines, which made five milkshakes simultaneously. He traveled to San Bernardino to see what kind of operation needed to make 40 shakes at a time and came away enamored with the prospect of replicating the business model. After acquiring a franchise, he bought the business outright and began the process of rolling out locations of McDonald's worldwide.[1]
- Their pickup truck had thrown a rod, and while hitching a ride with Bob Magness, they answered his routine questions to satisfy his curiosity about the big "community antenna system" they'd just built in Paducah, Texas. A business associate later related that the CATV business was "a license to steal," and Magness rushed out to talk with the guys about how he could get the business going in Memphis, Texas. That led to his acquiring franchises and other multisystem operators to lay the foundation for what became Tele-Communications, Inc.[2]

- As the U.S. general manager of Hammarplast, Howard Schultz noticed that a small four-store outfit was selling more of his firm's plastic cone/thermos drip coffeemakers than Macy's was. He flew from New York to visit the Seattle customer and after meeting its owners was consumed by the feeling of destiny. He lobbied hard to persuade the owners to permit him to join the company for an equity stake, and ultimately he bought the business to help him develop Starbucks into its now ubiquitous brand.[3]

A seemingly random lucky event triggers recognition of an opportunity that forms the foundation for a future business fortune. But as the Roman rhetorician Seneca wrote, "Luck is what happens when preparation meets opportunity." In each of the cases above, the lucky individual was a fully engaged successful businessperson whose earlier preparation gave him both the insight to recognize the business's prospects and the experience necessary to succeed in the venture. Although contented in their current professions, all admitted a longing to be involved with something that excited their passion, and while they went about their work, they gave free rein to their curiosity about other businesses, watchful for ones with intriguing prospects and curious about what made them special.

Richard Wiseman, a behavioral scientist and the author of *The Luck Factor*, describes how "lucky" people actively pursue new experiences, noting that "they're prepared to take risks and relaxed enough to see the opportunities in the first place":

We did an experiment. We asked subjects to flip through a newspaper that had photographs in it. All they had to do was count the number of photographs. That's it. Luck wasn't on their minds, just some silly task. They'd go through, and after about three pages, there'd be a massive half-page advert saying, STOP COUNTING. THERE ARE 43 PHOTOGRAPHS IN THIS NEWSPAPER. It was next to a photo, so we knew they were looking at that area. A few pages later, there was another massive advert—I mean, we're talking big—that said, STOP COUNTING. TELL THE EXPERIMENTER YOU'VE SEEN THIS AND WIN 150 POUNDS. For the most part, the unlucky would just flip past these things. Lucky people would flip through and laugh and say, "There are 43 photos. That's what it says. Do you want me to bother counting?" We'd say, "Yeah, carry on." They'd flip some more and say, "Do I get my 150 pounds?" Most of the unlucky people didn't notice.[4]

Being receptive to new ideas and opportunities is important to succeed in acquisitions, but being curious about how businesses work and having the experience to assess their prospects and leverage their opportunities are absolutely critical to separate the wheat from the chaff. Experience in allied but outside disciplines is particularly valuable because it contributes an alternative perspective to that employed by the current business operators. Knowledge of the processes, techniques, and strategies of competing and ancillary enterprises often provides insight into opportunities to enhance or leverage the prospective acquisition.

When Landmark's Conrad Hall received a call about the opportunity to acquire the Winston–Salem *Trading Post*, he was well acquainted with the profitability of the classified ad sections of newspapers, and he knew from his involvement with computer systems that substantial savings could be produced with improved automation if they were adopted by the new business. He was also acquainted with Norfolk's *Trading Post* publication, and he quickly assumed there were similar publications serving most major cities, suggesting a rollup opportunity equivalent to the one Landmark had conducted in the cable TV and community newspaper industries.

Moreover, the luck of the unexpected phone call had been precipitated by Landmark's prior acquisition activities. Its purchase of neighboring community shoppers had generated broader recognition of its reputation for honest, fair, and cooperative deal making, and the *Trading Post's* owner knew from his conversations with another publisher that he'd receive a good price for his publications and that his staff would be treated fairly by Landmark. Obviously, actively closing deals creates awareness of a company's willingness to do more deals, and a positive reputation encourages prospective sellers and their advisors to offer their businesses to add to the future deal flow.

Waiting complacently for good deals to materialize, however, will almost certainly lead to disappointment, and even if an opportunity falls over the transom, the acquirer should suspect that hidden in the bushes there is another involving a similar opportunity that would produce a superior return on investment. Rationally, it makes sense that the best businesses with the most attractive prospects, the best resources, and the greatest talent are rarely the ones seeking to sell. Instead, it is usually the struggling entities with the poorest outlook and the most disillusioned, incompetent management that beg for buyers' attention.

Accordingly, a smart acquirer will invest in creating her own luck by working diligently to ferret out the choice camouflaged opportunities. To do that, it helps to understand the characteristics of the most desirable business, the sources for quality information, and the tactics to turn up prospects. Chapter 4 provided insight into how Trader developed its prospect lists for acquisition after concluding that a particular niche industry held great promise. The following material summarizes much of Trader's philosophy about how to assess businesses to identify those which offer the most compelling development opportunities for investment.

Identifying a good company to acquire should be predicated on the buyer's core interests and resources. The company should have enticing appeal, offer attractive growth prospects, and be acquirable for a value price with expected cash flows capable of producing a superior return on investment with a reasonable margin of safety.

Make It Appealing and Familiar

Life is too short to remain a prisoner in an occupation that doesn't produce pleasure, and the opportunities for success are so varied that there is no need to devote effort to something that fails to stir the acquirer's passion. Inevitably, success will flow more easily from an enterprise that evokes an enthusiastic commitment and inspires the creative juices of its leadership each day. A practical acquirer will therefore carefully assess his own nature and strive to identify those opportunities which will stimulate his interest and entrepreneurial spirit. Only after concluding that the prospective acquisition captivates his interest and inspires his confidence should he expend his energies and capital to cultivate the business's potential.

Unfortunately, businesses sometimes never look better than the day before they are acquired, and it is therefore desirable to obtain as thorough a perspective as possible before committing to an acquisition. Howard Schultz actually worked for Starbucks before he acquired it several years later, and Wayne Huizenga's family had been in the garbage collection business since 1890, providing him with the insider's perspective to facilitate Waste Management's rollup of similar operations. Others prepared themselves by working for similar companies before buying their own operation. For 13 years, John Hewitt worked for the tax preparer H&R Block before acquiring an independent firm as the foundation for his Jackson-Hewitt Tax Service, and he did it again several years later by acquiring another firm to launch Liberty Tax Service. When possible, it is best to gain in-depth knowledge of a business's operational appeal to the acquirer before a deal is struck.

From the corporate perspective, it is too easy to assume that the passionate development of a business can be accomplished by a hired gun: "We'll just recruit a bunch of young Turks to take the industry by storm, and therefore any business will do if it promises an acceptable return on investment and won't distract the CEO from his extracurricular commitments." But that indifference will typically lead to disappointment. If the opportunity fails to incite strong enthusiasm and passion among top executives, it is likely to be treated as a stepchild begging for resources from the B team's management. And without those ingredients (including, particularly, dedicated and astute leadership), the acquisition is almost certainly destined to disappoint, if not fail outright.

An acquisition should also fit within the values and culture of the buyer. Just as it makes no sense for a teetotaler to buy a bar or a minister to buy a porn shop, an acquirer should not buy companies whose products or services fail to generate a personal sense of pride among its owners and staff. Considering the diversity of opportunities, an investor should choose among businesses that provide psychic pleasure and financial rewards.

It Should Have a Bountiful Future

For an individual satisfied with a small manageable business, there are hundreds of thousands of acquisition opportunities whose growth will follow the tide of the general economy. However, if the buyer wants to build a business fortune, it will be vitally important to identify and invest in opportunities that have extraordinary growth prospects.

For a value-conscious acquirer, a cheap price on a low- or no-growth business may appear too attractive to ignore, and there are inevitably a vast number of bargains. However, unless the buyer is prepared to become a serial liquidator (i.e., one who repetitively buys businesses to liquidate for their asset values), those companies are unlikely to produce handsome long-term returns. Warren Buffett's original value-priced acquisition, Berkshire Hathaway, was a textile company that eventually was felled by offshore competition, and he subsequently repeated his mistake in 1993 when he bought Dexter Shoes, a now worthless $433 million transaction he labels his worst investment ever because he exchanged shares equal to 1.6 percent of Berkshire Hathaway.[5] Despite their apparent attractiveness in terms of price relative to their perceived value, those Berkshire Hathaway subsidiaries lacked the necessary ingredients to sustain their original competitive advantage, and the entities disintegrated.

Of course, it is virtually impossible to project with certainty which markets and innovations will produce exponential growth for a specific business. Meteoric growth is dependent on a broad variety of factors, among which management skill and diligence are rarely primary (though absolutely critical). Diligent effort therefore should be dedicated to steering clear of businesses that are on a fixed course toward rocky shores. Why invest in a buggy whip manufacturer or digital pager company when there are so many companies with superior long-term growth and development prospects?

Its Future Should Be Sustainable Without Substantive Risk

Care should be devoted to making sure that the industry has a prosperous future, the promise of long-term growth, and profitability without undue risk from competition. All too often, businesses can be nestled within an apparently comfortable niche that is nevertheless on the cusp of monumental change. Although that change may promise infinitely appealing growth opportunities, it may also represent the abyss in which an unprepared or inept organization may face its unexpected demise. Technological and competitive changes represent the most obvious threats because they may produce such confounding turbulence that even well-respected institutions collapse when they fail to keep up with accelerating product, service, and market developments.

Few today remember Convergent Technologies, which ascended in the 1980s to the mountaintops of networked computing. With its clustered workstations, Convergent produced such a compelling product line that it was able to market its own family of computers while manufacturing private label clones for resale under the proprietary brands of Prime Computer, Motorola, Burroughs, NCR, AT&T, and others. But within a few years, its systems were left in the dust when inexpensive PCs became networkable, and the company was swallowed by Unisys in 1988 after a failed 1986 merger attempt with 3Com.[6]

Likewise, during the brief era in the 1990s when 750-kilobyte 3.25-inch disks represented the customary transportable storage medium, Iomega catapulted to billion-dollar status in 1994 with the introduction of its rewritable 100-megabyte zip drives, but it soon stumbled into obsolescence when the 1997 introduction of inexpensive writable compact disks gained traction, permitting its acquisition by EMC for a pittance.

In the world of entertainment, the Blockbuster rollup zoomed to prominence in the video rental business, attracting a $4.7 billion buyout offer from Viacom in 1994, just nine years after its founding. But by 2010, with the rampant penetration of Coinstar's Redbox and the increasing prevalence of downloadable movies via cable and the Internet, its market cap evaporated when it filed for bankruptcy that September.[7]

Of course, despite centuries of success, the "ink-on-paper" newspaper industry found itself struggling with declining relevancy in the new millennium. Ubiquitous broadband and wireless access propelled almost universal adoption of Internet services as the source for instant information on current events, weather, sports, stock quotes, and entertainment. Simultaneously, the web siphoned off ad revenues from newspapers' most profitable segments, including employment, real estate, and automotive.

Of course, these examples suggest that every business faces the risk of obsolescence, and a prudent investor should therefore capitalize on the opportunity while she can but remain vigilant to identify the most opportune time to sell to someone less prescient.

It Should Have Substantial Opportunity

There is an important distinction between high-growth businesses and those with strong growth opportunities. It may be easy to spot companies that are already growing quickly, and such growth provides vivid evidence of their promising prospects. But that growth usually makes them more difficult and more expensive to acquire. The owners are likely to be enthralled with their flourishing enterprise and interpret that growth as the justification for a high value. All too often, their enthusiasm and perception of worth discourage them from even considering a sale regardless of price. Although such businesses certainly should be considered for acquisition, they may not prove to be acquirable for an appropriate price that is likely to produce a reasonable return on investment.

The better opportunities are usually found among businesses that have not already capitalized on their growth opportunities. In its original form, Starbucks was merely a purveyor of exotic freshly roasted coffee beans to be purchased and ground for home brewing. While on a trip to Milan, Howard Schultz recognized the appeal of selling designer lattés in a convivial environment like that of European cafés, and he subsequently lobbied the founding owners to modify their business model. It was only after he acquired the business that he was able to incorporate fully that innovative change, which of course was fundamental to Starbucks' eventual runaway success.[8]

The best prospective acquisitions should therefore have some of the characteristics that will support dramatic future growth. Specifically, they should include

- Underdeveloped products and services
- A large prospective market
- Geographic expansion opportunities

- Ancillary products and services
- Leverageable brands
- Replicable business models and processes

Underdeveloped Products and Services Are Ideal

Underdeveloped products and services represent the basis from which a business can expand. All too often, business founders are consumed by their personal interests, and their bias may blind them to a larger opportunity. Alternatively, they may be so engrossed in their existing businesses that they fail to pursue better options. An understanding of customer needs and desires coupled with new insight can lead to the identification of products or services that have far greater potential as the foundation for a huge enterprise. Identifying those hybridized seeds for future growth and then aggressively applying the energy and resources to cultivate them can lead to a flourishing business.

Howard Schultz's transformation of Starbucks is a sterling example of employing innovative tactics to exploit an underdeveloped product among a massive consumer market through a national rollout of stores to market his customized, branded coffee concoctions and ancillary products.

Before Starbucks, coffee consumption was a comparatively humdrum affair for the mass of Americans. Although a morning stop at a fast-food drive-through usually included the purchase of a cup, there was very little consumer demand for a "rich, sensual coffee drinking experience." The country was already well populated with coffee shops offering little more than pedestrian brews like those from customer's kitchens and office break rooms, and with soda growing in popularity as a breakfast drink among the young, U.S. coffee consumption was declining at the end of the twentieth century. Passionate devotion to strong coffee carefully brewed from freshly ground, dark-roasted arabica beans was relegated to Europeans, internationals, and a tiny fraction of domestic connoisseurs. Recognition of the addictive appeal of superior strong coffee was something the Starbucks founders were eager to cultivate as they marketed their fresh dark-roasted beans, but it was Howard Schultz who insisted that the critical development opportunity lay in the retailing of the actual drink in a convivial environment with a conscientious barista who would help educate the consumer about the merits of the various concoctions. He discovered he could do that while charging a premium price for what had previously been a low-cost commodity. For the sensual and caffeinated boost provided by Starbucks' customized brew, consumers would rationalize the high price as a well-deserved but still affordable luxury to help them face the workday.

Such revolutionary transformations of commodity products into high-growth businesses are comparatively rare, although bottled water is another startling example. They demonstrate, however, that there are opportunities even in markets that most believe are saturated. Schultz had been astute when he recognized that the founders' passion and messianic zeal for dark-roasted coffee had struck a responsive chord with Seattle's do-it-yourself brewers, and he rightfully concluded that it would resonate just as well with a large segment of Americans if they were offered customized preparation in a convenient location.

Earlier, Perrier had revealed a similar opportunity with water, and after its marketing success in the 1980s along with that of countless regional varieties, PespsiCo launched its own Aquafina brand in 1994, and Coca-Cola followed in 1999 with Dasani.[9] By 2008, bottled water had captured the number two share of all bottled refreshments, commanding a 28.9 percent share with a total of 8.7 billion gallons sold.[10]

Although Schultz succeeded within a saturated commodity market by capitalizing on a premium-quality and premium-priced product, there are innumerable examples of enterprises that have begun to flourish in the fertile soil of hidden markets, and those companies represent the more abundant pools for potentially attractive businesses for early acquisition.

Sometimes the founders have already identified a dynamic growth opportunity but don't have the personal initiative to marshal the resources to develop the business expeditiously. Their businesses may be thriving on a small scale, but their visibility is obscured from the sight of all but the most inquisitive.

With its roots firmly in media, Landmark's management was acutely aware of the profitability of the classified advertising sections of its newspapers, and it had noticed a variety of entrepreneurial ventures seeking to capitalize on that segment. In almost every market, a few individuals had launched free distribution shoppers, paid classified ad papers, and photo guides. But it was almost two decades after the launch of the *Trading Post* in Landmark's flagship city of Norfolk, Virginia, that it acquired the Winston–Salem version of the concept. From that acquisition, it discovered the profitability of that targeted publication segment, and it immediately became interested in identifying others for acquisition.

After acquiring the majority of paid circulation classified ad publications, Trader stumbled across the San Francisco successful free distribution used auto publication called *Diablo Dealer*. With the knowledge gained from two other acquisitions, Trader formulated the *Auto Mart* business model that it replicated in almost every major city.

It repeated the process after its identification and acquisition of the Detroit *Employment Guide*. Providing employers with a lower-cost means to recruit hourly workers than that offered by the help-wanted sections of metropolitan newspapers, the publication opened Trader management's eyes to the existence of similar papers in a dozen other cities, and as Trader acquired them, it rolled out the concept into over 40 more markets that didn't have similar targeted recruitment papers.

A Large Prospective Market Is Desirable

To be large and successful, a business must serve a large customer base that willingly pays a bunch of money for its products and services. Among the most attractive businesses are those which will attract and maintain a broad diversity of customers distributed throughout numerous geographic markets.

Although a single client may generate huge revenues, companies dependent on a small customer base find their futures resting on a much shakier foundation than that of companies serving diversified or mass markets. Government contractors face the anguishing prospect of budget cuts, convoluted bidding and payment processes, political changes and missteps, and arbitrary decisions from lethargic bureaucrats. Commercial enterprises with a handful of clients find their success integrally tied to the economic fortunes of those customers, and the loss of a substantial customer can lead to financial trouble and possible demise.

Businesses with an extensive and varied customer base have less risk and broader opportunities. If one customer segment falters, others may expand their relationship. When there is a large prospective base, there should be more opportunities to cultivate new incremental clients.

A large prospect base does not, however, imply that a business should serve the mass market the way Starbucks does. A business can be even more desirable if it is serving a sizable targeted market of just a few hundred customers within a limited geographic market. As long as its members can be readily identified, the smaller prospect group implies a more efficient cultivation effort, and the tighter focus simplifies the management and servicing of those prospects. Also, a smaller prospect group usually implies an underserviced customer category whose members are likely to respond positively to the attention of a dedicated vendor.

Dealer Specialties was a business created to produce used car window stickers for a potential customer group of fewer than 200 car dealers in North Carolina's Raleigh–Durham marketing area. Though the 20 clients initially served in that market generated measly revenues of about $100,000, the opportunity to solicit the country's 65,000 dealers promised a substantial national enterprise.

Geographic Expansion Opportunities Amplify Appeal

A successful small business in one city implies a substantial national market opportunity. A business model that works well in a single city often can be replicated in most cities throughout the country, and the combination suggests a large nationwide enterprise. Simple math suggests that if Austin, Texas, generates $1 million revenue for a local firm, the 100 largest cities in the United States should be able to produce at least a $100 million business serving the same segment.

That prospect of geographic expansion is what made *Auto Trader* and Dealer Specialties extraordinarily appealing businesses for acquisition and expansion. Every city has scores, if not hundreds, of car dealers, all of which represent likely prospects for display ads or window sticker services.

Some cities, in fact, may already have enterprising vendors performing the work, and those vendors can be acquired. In places where there are none, the business can be launched.

Such national operations should also provide the scale to improve overall efficiency. Supply costs should decrease as buying power increases, and infrastructure costs should decrease as processes and systems are shared over a larger base of operations. In the case of Dealer Specialties, the cost of developing superior software was amortized over hundreds of locations, and the increasing scale produced by its expansion provided continuously improving leverage to negotiate better pricing for its bulk purchases of adhesive paper stocks, reducing supply costs and increasing profits.

Finally, geographic dispersion of the business opportunity mitigates risk. Although some local and regional markets suffer, others may expand, and their growth may counter losses of weak markets. Although business in Chicago may decline during a cyclical or seasonal downturn, that decline may be offset in Florida, where the economy may be much better.

Ancillary Products and Services Should Have Attractive Prospects

In the process of making wine, grapes are crushed for their nectar, and the hulls and stems are left as residue. Rather than just discard the hulls as fermenting garbage, some vintners sell them as feed for animals; other, more enterprising Italians discovered they could make a fragrant 100- to 160-proof premium priced pomace brandy from the residue, and they call it grappa ("grape stalk" in Italian).

The opportunity to take the grape hulls of any business and transform them into a high-margin grappa is particularly attractive.

Colonel Sanders's original chicken recipe was created for a sit-down restaurant environment, but one of his original franchisees, Pete Harman, was inundated by requests from his Salt Lake City patrons for take-out doggy bags. As Harman explained, "A guy in Colorado had bought 500 buckets and didn't know what to do with them, so the Colonel asked us if we wanted to take them off his hands. ... I wanted to get rid of them quickly, so we filled them with 14 pieces of chicken, five rolls and a pint of gravy, and sold it for $3.50." When he sold 300 buckets in two days, he quickly recognized that the expansion opportunity required no further table space, and he proceeded to capitalize on the take-out concept.[11] Then, when John Y. Brown acquired the business from Sanders, he focused on developing franchises that used that take-out formula.

For Dealer Specialties, its grappa proved just as appealing. Trader acquired the business on the basis of its profitability and the expansion opportunity of the core business of producing and posting window stickers on a used car dealer's inventory. However, it particularly valued the digital database of detailed used car descriptions, perceiving the opportunity to leverage Dealer Specialties' electronic grape hulls into a fast-developing new business segment of data distribution to the Internet's mushrooming advertising services. Today, Dealer Specialties generates a far more profitable revenue stream by charging car dealers to transmit their used car data to their choice of over 2,300 Internet marketing services such as AutoTrader.com.

Brands Can Be Leveraged

The latest blockbuster movie gives rise to all sorts of massively profitable licensing deals, from toys to school supplies to soda cups. Leveraging a brand in such a manner is unlikely for typical businesses, but sometimes there is an opportunity. After gaining visibility, Starbucks leveraged its brand by partnering with Pepsi to distribute Frappuccinos and with Dreyer's Grand Ice Cream to launch its own line of ice cream. Trader expanded its photo guide business by launching differentiated titles, including *Truck Trader*, *Cycle Trader*, and *Old Car Trader*. When it expanded into the *Employment Guide* business, it capitalized on that brand when it sponsored highly profitable job fairs in each of its major cities.

In a turbulent industry and market environment, the potential to leverage a company's brands can be critically important because they may provide fertile soil for the evolutionary development of a more vibrant business on an alternative platform. Repeatedly, markets have witnessed disruptive technologies that undermined previously successful businesses in much the same way low-cost airlines destroyed passenger bus services. Although the Internet's threat to retailing's bricks-and-mortar locations was overstated, it has had a profound impact on the newspaper business, whose revenue and readership base are rapidly eroding. That was particularly the case with *Auto Trader* magazine and its offshoots. After all, why would a consumer drive to the local convenience store to pay $1 for a magazine when thousands of cars are advertised on Craigslist and Yahoo! classifieds? Fortunately, the national awareness of the *Auto Trader* brand, its infrastructure to gather data and sell advertising, and the promotional power of its magazines and rack locations provided the basis for launching AutoTrader.com and establishing it as the preeminent site for buying and selling used cars.

Enterprises that fail to exploit their brands can find themselves driven to obsolescence if they don't continue to evolve as demand and consumer expectations change. Astute operators will attend to the opportunities accompanying market and technological changes. Tracing its roots to 1873, Barnes & Noble had developed as a single store with a worldwide reputation for its breadth of books, academic texts, and trade titles, but it had fallen into decline by the 1970s when it was acquired by Leonard Riggio, a former university bookstore clerk who concluded that he could serve students better. He repositioned Barnes & Noble as "the World's Largest Bookstore," offering over 150,000 books and trade titles, and then he expanded aggressively, opening new stores and acquiring BookMasters, Marboro Books, and B. Dalton Bookseller. Subsequently, as Amazon threatened its business by marketing an even more massive inventory through the Internet, Barnes & Noble launched BarnesandNoble.com, which now offers over 1 million in-stock titles, making its standing inventory the largest of any online seller. To defend itself from the risks of electronic publishing, it began selling digital books while putting marketing muscle behind the launch of its proprietary Nook Simple Touch Reader.[12]

An astute investor will remain vigilant for similar brand-leveraging opportunities arising from the products and services of prospective acquisitions. However, she should also remain cautious when ascribing values to them. In the vast majority of cases, such opportunities are far too difficult to exploit, and it is rare that they produce substantive profits. Management should remain devoted to exploiting the potential of the core business, particularly because it often lacks the resources or market entrée to produce desirable returns on brand extensions or licensing deals. It is therefore best to consider such opportunities as a potential cherry to crown the delicious value-priced chocolate sundae of the prospective acquisition's existing product lines.

Replicable Business Models Are Desirable

On occasion, a prospective acquisition's operating model is so versatile that it can be applied to other business opportunities. When this is the case, its acquisition can produce exponential benefits.

Originally founded to facilitate the buying and selling of used cars, *Auto Trader* welcomed advertisers who also sought to sell their trucks, boats, RVs, and other vehicles. As the volume of those advertisements increased, it provided the content to launch differentiated titles, including *Boat Trader*, *Cycle Trader*, and *RV Trader*. Then, when the business added Internet components, the AutoTrader.com model was exploited to guide the development of separate URLs for the other vehicle segments under the TraderOnline.com umbrella, including boattrader.com and rvtrader.com, among several others.

The food services industry has repeatedly tried to replicate various operating models to expand into differentiated dining segments. In 1970, General Foods acquired the three-store Red Lobster from founder Bill Darden, and it gave him rein to expand the concept nationwide. Within just a few years, it encompassed over 400 locations, and Darden and his management team repeatedly tried to duplicate its success with other themes. Though the subsequent York Steak House concept failed, they had impressive success with the launch of Olive Garden in 1982.

The promise of replicating a business model often runs headlong into the reality that it just is not that easy. Although Olive Garden's growth was meteoric, the now independent Darden Restaurants has struggled with several subsequent efforts, including China Host (now closed) and Smokey Bones (sold to a private equity firm). Its Caribbean-themed Bahama Breeze and sophisticated dining concept Season 52 continue to be nurtured as its Red Lobster and Olive Garden restaurants thrive.[13]

Like Darden, Brinker International has pursued a strategy of acquisition and rollout to leverage its operating model. Originally founded by Norman Brinker when he bought the 23-store Chili's Grill & Bar in 1983, the company has invested heavily to extend that chain to over 1,000 locations, primarily in the United States. In 1988, it acquired Romano's Macaroni Grill, seeking to duplicate the success of Darden's Olive Garden, and in 1994 and 1995, it added On the Border Mexican Grill & Cantina and Maggiano's Little Italy. But like Darden, it has had mixed success, leading to its sale of Macaroni Grill and earlier efforts such as Grady's and Spageddies, which it subsequently sold to Quality Dining, Inc.[14]

In addition to substantial growth opportunities, the most desirable acquisition targets feature other characteristics that support their success and protect their future prospects.

The Competition Should Be Diffuse, Lethargic, or Oblivious

"Competition may be hazardous to human wealth," as Fidelity Magellan Fund's investing wizard Peter Lynch is often quoted as saying,[15] and a careful business acquirer should remain attentive to that admonition. Operating a successful business is hard enough without having to battle virulent competitors constantly. In making an acquisition assessment, therefore, it is important to dismiss prospects that remain embroiled in marketing battles that obliterate profits as pricing is driven to commodity levels. Alternatively, if the competition is diffuse, lethargic, or oblivious, the business should be able to develop far more successfully.

Although it is desirable to acquire good businesses without meaningful competition, monopoly status usually implies they are highly regulated like utilities or are the creatures of a bureaucratic government. The cable TV business started out without any substantive competition as its founders rolled out service to rural communities throughout the country, and once they became established, their costly infrastructure made it infeasible for alternative interlopers to attack. Only the deep-pocketed investors in satellite services and the telephone companies with their established networks appear to have any positive competitive prospects.

Other businesses achieve near-monopoly status by creating attractive ancillary products. Cable TV became a viable competitor in metropolitan markets only after it began offering differentiated programming such as Home Box Office and ESPN and superstations such as TBS and WGN. The television industry blossomed during its first three decades, when competition was limited by federal mandate, limiting the number of broadcast licenses within distinct regional markets; nationally, the three networks divided the market, jockeying for market share on the strength of their distinct programming. Locally, individual stations were beneficiaries of their viewership edge if they were aligned with the prime time network leader, and they battled for local market supremacy with the quality of their local news broadcasts, syndicated features, and homegrown programming.

However, almost all high-growth businesses should assume their success will eventually attract new players. The most compelling prospects for acquisition therefore should be companies that have carved out an attractive niche largely ignored by others. The founders of *Trading Post* and *Auto Trader* did that by offering a more compelling value proposition than the dominant newspaper classified advertising sections. Rather than charge a fat up-front advertising fee, *Trading Post* enticed and earned the loyalty of sellers with its "risk-free" invitation to "advertise free—pay only if you sell." *Auto Trader* captured customers with its "a picture is better than a thousand words" and "we'll take the photo" service. Their success blossomed because newspapers remained largely oblivious to the corrosive impact of their selling propositions and guerrilla marketing tactics. If they noticed them at all, newspaper managers lethargically dismissed the publications as advertising rags that were capturing low-hanging revenue dollars from nonsubscribers and the dregs of their newspaper readership.

The Acquisition Should Have an Economic Franchise or Its Potential

It is always best to acquire an economic franchise instead of just a business. In his 1991 shareholder letter, Warren Buffett underscored the critical differences between the two:

An economic franchise arises from a product or service that: (1) is needed or desired; (2) is thought by its customers to have no close substitute; and (3) is not subject to price regulation. The existence of all three conditions will be demonstrated by a company's ability to regularly price its product or service aggressively and thereby to earn high rates of return on capital. Moreover, franchises can tolerate mis-management. Inept managers may diminish a franchise's profitability, but they cannot inflict mortal damage.

In contrast, "a business" earns exceptional profits only if it is the low-cost operator or if supply of its product or service is tight. Tightness in supply usually does not last long. With superior management, a company may maintain its status as a low-cost operator for a much longer time, but even then unceasingly faces the possibility of competitive attack. And a business, unlike a franchise, can be killed by poor management.[16]

In our increasingly turbulent economic and fast-evolving environment, the search for long-term franchises becomes all the more difficult, as demonstrated by Yahoo!'s ascendancy over Prodigy, Excite, CompuServe, and Altavista in the 1990s, an ascendancy that was severely eroded in the current millennium by Google with its darkening power over Internet search capabilities and its dominance in the affiliated advertising.

From 1975 to 2006, *Auto Trader* and its offspring magazines exhibited the key components of an economic franchise. As efficient advertising media, they offered consumers a remarkably effective means to sell their used cars at prices superior to those offered by car dealers. Although newspapers and shoppers offered classified ads, they could not economically provide the photograph "worth a thousand words" or the "we'll take the photo" personal service. Moreover, both private party and commercial advertisers were discouraged from supporting an interloping competitor because that would have required an inefficient allocation of promotion dollars to support multiple venues.

A disruptive medium—the Internet—made the magazine irrelevant in the new millennium because it could not publish instantaneously or as inexpensively or pervasively and could not provide the full breadth and depth of information represented by the Internet's collection of numerous photos and comprehensive product details. However, during its 30-year history, the *Auto Trader* magazine successfully established its brand, which through innovative development established the basis for the launch and rapid success of AutoTrader.com.

Protected Product, Service, or Content

The concept of an economic franchise assumes a business that has a protected product, service, or content. Those shields function as a barrier to entry that provides the business with both a competitive edge and a defensible differentiation in appealing to consumers. They also represent a foundation from which the owner can capture a profitable market position with potential opportunities for expansion. The drug industry has proprietary drugs with which it can capture protected market share, and Apple has its patents for products such as the iPod and iPad.

In 2011, the defensive value of intellectual property came screaming to the forefront when a consortium of technology companies ponied up $4.5 billion to acquire a cache of patents from the bankrupt Nortel Networks. "The size and dollar value for this transaction is unprecedented, as was the significant interest in the portfolio among major companies around the world," said George Riedel, chief strategy officer and president of business units at Nortel.[17] But the precedent was quickly smashed a few months later when Google agreed to pay $12.5 billion for Motorola Mobility, a company that days earlier had posted a market capitalization of about half that value. Though better known for its cellular phone manufacturing and marketing prowess, Motorola Mobility had a portfolio of 17,000 patents and 7,500 pending patent applications. As the intellectual property expert and market columnist Mike McLean observed:

> In acquiring Motorola Mobility's patents and its recent purchase of more than 1,000 IBM patents, Google is arming itself to not only protect its business, but placing it in a position to be on the offensive. Motorola's [intellectual property] team has plenty of experience dealing with patent assertion in the wireless space and one would

expect Google to make good use of that team in an arena it has recently become all too familiar with—the court room.[18]

The defensive value of intellectual property is obvious to a company such as Google, which remains eager to defend its Android, search, and other core applications. But as McLean implies, there can be similarly valuable offensive values such as those celebrated by the shareholders of Eolas Technologies and Lucent. In 2003, the courts ruled that Microsoft had to pay Eolas $521 million for improperly usurping its Internet browser patent rights, and in 2007, Lucent received an astonishing $1.54 billion judgment against Microsoft.[19]

Recognizable brands, of course, represent another form of protection. Disney evokes a positive image and attracts consumer acceptance and loyalty. Landmark witnessed the power of the *Auto Trader* brand when it originally sought to compete with its alternative *Auto Weekly* brand in cities such as Detroit. Like the Confederate general Nathan Bedford Forrest's misquoted aphorism, Stuart Arnold got there "firstest with the mostest," and that leadership gave his titles a top-of-mind awareness that provided a competitive edge among consumers. Through the subsequent Cox and Landmark partnership, Trader leveraged that edge nationally by adopting the *Auto Trader* brand for Landmark's titles. Others employed similar tactics, such as Starbucks and Dollar Tree as they scooped up a variety of businesses similar to theirs and unified most under a single brand name and operating concept.

The Acquisition Should Be Value-Priced

The famed dean of financial investment theory and practice Benjamin Graham wrote in his classic *Security Analysis*, "An investment operation is one which, upon thorough analysis, promises safety of principal and satisfactory return. Operations not meeting these requirements are speculative."[20] In assessing acquisitions, Graham's dictum should be kept at the forefront of the investment process. Although there is a clear necessity to assume risk in investing, there should be a cold calculation of the probable upside relative to the competitive and operating environment of the prospective acquisition. Billions were invested and lost during the dot-com boom of the 1990s on the basis of wildly enthusiastic projections of what could be rather than what was practical and realistic. Unfortunately for most of their investors, the vast majority of those concepts were the delusional dreams of their starry-eyed progenitors, and the speculating moneymen behind them lost almost everything if they failed to sell out before their crash.

Rather than throwing money at speculative new ventures, it is often better to invest in proven concepts that offer attractive expansion opportunities. Small, already successful businesses demonstrate the validity of their operating concept and model, and if they can be acquired for something less than their intrinsic value and they have the other characteristics of a promising venture, they represent an appropriate investment opportunity. Thorough analysis of its processes and results should provide assurance that a business can grow sufficiently to produce a superior return on the required investment. If the concept can be comfortably expanded geographically or into broader market segments without substantive threat from competitors, there should be a comfortable margin of safety that warrants pursuit.

In assessing value, it is paramount to think like an investor. An investor understands that there are an infinite number of investment opportunities and devotes her energies to ferreting out those which will produce the greatest wealth with sensible risk. A prudent investor understands that he should perform a dispassionate analysis of the realistic prospects for a business, ignoring its alluring but illusory sex appeal. The dazzling opportunities routinely touted by the media and cocktail party acquaintances too often blind investors to the pitfalls, and they are almost certain to come at a steep price that weakens prospects for earning a superior return.

First and foremost, the business should be evaluated on the basis of its ability to produce free cash flow after paying all its bills, funding its capital investments, and paying its taxes. Those cash flows over the foreseeable future should generate a return on investment better than that offered by other realistic alternatives. If they don't offer that promise, the company is overpriced and should not be acquired.

In most circumstances, it is best to invest in opportunities that offer an assured positive cash flow from the start. If a business is not making money at the time of acquisition, it rarely transitions quickly to profitability. In fact, the acquirer most often discovers there are material hidden expenses and threats to revenues that become apparent only after the sale. Those discoveries pinch initial cash flow and place stress on the transition and future expansion. They also erode principal, which Graham has stressed should be safely preserved. Accordingly, while the brave crow that you have to spend money to make money, it is best if that admonition does not apply to funding the core operations after acquisition. If the business was making money before acquisition, it should continue to generate profits on the established core, and those profits can be reinvested to expand. Although such expansion will require future investments, they will remain speculative unless supported by a profitable core.

As Kentucky Fried Chicken and McDonald's absorbed start-up losses during rapid expansion, they were always reassured by the safety of their principal invested in the older operations that continued to generate improving cash flows. When Starbucks chose to acquire and rename George Howell's Coffee Connection chain in Boston, it did so because it understood that the resulting cash flows would produce a higher return than the funds required for a more risky competitive launch. The acquisition not only gave Starbucks an established beachhead among Boston's coffee aficionados, it eliminated the costly consequences of a local coffee price war.

It Should Leverage the Buyer's Experience

The acquirer should also focus on prospects that will leverage his experience and resources. As Fidelity Magellan Fund maven Peter Lynch cautions, a buyer should invest only in businesses that she understands. Personal experience and familiarity provide the basis for understanding the market opportunity, the key ingredients to produce success, the infrastructure required to support the business, and the contacts necessary to cultivate and develop the enterprise. Without those things, the acquirer is unlikely to know everything necessary to assess the business properly, and after acquisition she will be impeded as she learns the lessons necessary to make the best decisions for the business.

Sometimes lack of knowledge necessitates postponement of an acquisition until that knowledge and experience can be developed. Although some individuals will chose to invest in acquiring an MBA in business school, others will accept a job in a company to obtain the knowledge they are missing. Though an accomplished salesman and manager, Howard Schultz knew little about roasting coffee beans and managing a food services company. He therefore persuaded Starbucks' founders to hire him and teach him the business while he worked as their vice president.[21]

As a newspaper man, Conrad Hall was especially familiar with the classified advertising business, and it was therefore a comfortable leap when he concluded that the Winston–Salem *Trading Post* would be an attractive expansion opportunity for Landmark. Similarly, when Trader acquired the Detroit *Employment Guide*, its managers possessed a long familiarity with the recruitment advertising business. Nevertheless, before jumping in with both feet, Trader appointed one of its best managers to supervise that first acquisition and thoroughly study the help-wanted advertising business for almost six months before commencing a full rollup and rollout in that industry segment.

It Should Leverage Existing Resources

The underlying risk of an investment is reduced when the investor has resources that can be tapped by the acquisition to support its development. In addition to lower-cost capital, those resources may include equipment, facilities, distribution channels, promotion and advertising synergies, and administration services.

Often, relationships alone represent the kinds of resources that will produce benefits for an acquisition. A buyer's vendors may provide incentives superior to those of the acquired business, and its professional advisors may recommend tactics that will stimulate growth and reduce costs.

Additionally, relevant knowledge and experience can be a most valuable resource for sharing. When Landmark made its first investment in cable TV, it was confident that it could leverage the broadcasting management and experience of its radio and television stations to accelerate growth, and it used its industry contacts to identify the people who could offer the best insight into the development of that new medium.

It is, however, critical to employ resources that will be compatible with the operating and market environment of the acquisition. When Landmark began investing in targeted publications such as *Auto Trader*, it exploited its familiarity with administering small publishing operations like those of its community newspapers. If it had applied the mindset of a classified ad manager of one of its large metropolitan dailies, the results could have been disastrous for the development of those niche publications. It instead prudently dedicated talent from its community newspaper group, which was accustomed to earning profits on small revenue streams largely unnoticed by its big-city brethren. Its management was accustomed to producing success while slipping stealthily between the toes of the elephants.

In the case of a rollup of like enterprises, the opportunity to integrate similar businesses promises to reduce overhead costs and improve the efficiency of the overlapping infrastructure. NationsBank's prowess at slicing costs by merging back-office functions, eliminating overhead, and streamlining processes was demonstrated as it rolled up notable regional banks such as First Republic of Texas, C&S/Sovran in Georgia and Virginia, Barnett Banks in Florida, and eventually Bank of America, whose name it assumed.[22] Moreover, substantial capital investments may be avoided when businesses can share facilities, systems, and support staff.

Chapter 15

Conclusion

It was a rare event for the Pacific Northwest—a beautiful sunny day—as Robert Beheler walked into the East Portland car dealership. He'd visited it many times before, but today the weather seemed to suggest a particularly propitious moment to achieve his goal. Today he was going to persuade the dealership to commit to an advertising spread in *Auto Mart*. Today he was going to make it past the gauntlet of salespeople, past the used car manager, and finally meet with the general manager.

As he strolled across the showroom floor, he took a deep breath, put his cheeriest smile on his face, and advanced toward the sales bullpen where all the deals were desked. Sure enough, there was the GM standing on the dais several feet above the showroom floor; Beheler walked over confidently, gazed up at the GM, reintroduced himself, and exchanged a few pleasantries. But as always, the GM was preoccupied, displaying obvious lack of interest as he looked down at Beheler.

"What's it going to take to get your business?" Beheler finally asked.

The GM had heard all the pitches before, and with a good measure of disdain he emphatically replied: "A miracle."

"Today is your lucky day," Beheler instantly exclaimed, beaming in response. "I happen to be a miracle worker!"[1]

In the littered history of mergers and acquisitions, the attraction of a miracle worker is indisputable. There are far too many examples of merger mania that appear to be driven simply by the adrenaline rush and euphoria of doing the deal. In the realm of rollups, the enormous effort required to cultivate and complete scores of transactions leaves little time for the daunting task of integration and supervision critical to ensuring that incremental value is generated after a deal's close. Without the operational management talent to implement and direct the integration and development missions, it is no wonder that Steven Harter's Notre Capital Ventures ran into serious difficulties with its almost simultaneous serial rollups of Comfort Systems, US Delivery, Physicians Resource Group, and Metals USA. To address those thorny issues, the talents of a miracle worker would be a blessing.

But a prudent acquirer understands that miracle workers are unlikely to materialize. Moreover, rather than Cinderella's fairy godmother, the purported miracle worker is likely to turn out to be another delusional wannabe, incapable of transforming the seedy pumpkin and the mangy field mice into the investor's magnificent horse-drawn carriage destined for the palace of riches.

A prudent acquirer, however, understands that a well-considered acquisition does not need a miracle worker. Assuming that the transaction makes economic sense according to reasonable projections and sound investment principles, the critical elements required for acquisition success include astute managerial ability and its conscientious application to orchestrate the postclosing consolidations. Those factors are far more critical than the deal-savvy acumen of the rollup architect.

Like all successful merger transactions, rollups require far more than the relatively instantaneous gratification arising from doing the deal. As in any lasting relationship, the wedding represents the easiest and smallest part of a successful marriage. The hard part consumes the vast majority of effort and energy, and a prudent consolidator is one who can be even more passionate and dedicated during the postclosing period: the years during which the sometimes tedious and frustrating process of integration, realization of synergistic benefits, and capitalization on innovative opportunities will occur.

The success of Landmark's and Trader's rollup efforts can be attributed very much to management's compulsion to build successful businesses. Rather than being driven by deal mania, the managers were genuinely obsessed with creating large, nationally based businesses that captured the attention and then the loyalty of consumers. Their efforts and energy therefore were focused on identification and implementation of the best practices that would facilitate achievement of their development goals while addressing the imperatives underlying the segment's critical success factors.

Their success demonstrates that rollups can prove to be an extraordinarily successful strategy for building substantive enterprises that generate a superior return for their investors. Like the numerous other flourishing companies built through mergers, the Landmark and Trader examples provide compelling evidence that a rollup's success is facilitated if it has substantial prospects for the short-term replication through start-ups of the business in additional markets and the foundation of a significant innovative development opportunity; organizations that reap impressive success are the ones that aggressively pursue such replication and innovative development opportunities.

But before such businesses can be replicated and transformed through innovations, successful rollups must be directed by insightful, managerially astute leaders who do the following:

- Maintain focus on the principles of value investing in the selection and completion of transactions
- Emphasize the coordinated and conscientious integration of each acquisition
- Remain devoted to identifying the best practices in each acquisition
- Engender managerial flexibility toward adopting productive changes and best practices
- Motivate adherence to developmental initiatives
- Emphasize recruitment and training of replacement management talent
- Facilitate implementation of productivity measures
- Retain a keen focus on sales, customer service, and efficient operations
- Ensure constant vigilance over costs.

Although it is possible that Trader could have earned a satisfactory return on investment strictly through the conscientious rollup of the small operators in its chosen industry segments, the superior returns arose from its supplementary activities of rollout and innovation. By employing the knowledge gained from its rollup activities, Trader developed the template for the launch of identical businesses in other geographic areas: Its acquisition of a dozen employment publications was leveraged by its independent launch of 44 more *Employment Guide Magazines,* and its acquisition of a handful of free distribution auto guides provided the foundation for the launch of almost 80 more under the national *Auto Mart* brand. Clearly, the returns were catapulted exponentially by Trader's rollout activities.

Trader's returns were increased by implementing innovative processes in the operations it acquired and rolled out. By developing improved automated systems, it dramatically lowered its production and operating costs while creating and delivering more value through both improved quality and enhanced customer service.

But as important as it is for management to have the ability to achieve its operational goals, the critical need for constant innovation remains primary, particularly transformative innovation. To repeat Joseph Schumpeter's 1950 conclusion, the modern world is driven by the "perennial gale of creative destruction" that is "incessantly revolutionizing the economic structure from within, incessantly destroying the old one, incessantly creating a new one."[2]

The paging industry arose to satisfy a compelling need, and its entrepreneurs captured a slice of the good life for themselves when they sold out to the rollup artists, who failed to realize that business would disintegrate as cellular phones and smartphones pushed paging services toward obsolescence.

Wayne Huizenga's Blockbuster Video quickly consolidated a huge share of the video rental business. Its size and national footprint gave it the economies of scale to promote efficiently and negotiate advantageous price concessions from the film studios. It captured value-cost leveraging benefits by developing and adopting advanced systems and software to process and manage the billions of rentals, providing consumers with a superior, convenient experience of speed and reliability. Finally, its expansive inventory of both new releases and classic videos redefined the core expectations of consumers, enhancing its ability to generate revenues and loyalty. But after Huizenga's departure, the company failed to keep pace with the perennial gale of creative destruction. Netflix stole innovative leadership with its comprehensive mailable inventory and the instantaneous gratification offered by streaming downloads. Simultaneously, Coinstar's Redbox captured the lead as the low-cost provider by installing hundreds of thousands of automated kiosks spewing out rentals at $1 per night. Blockbuster's failure to maintain its innovative edge led it from its over $9 billion 1993 market capitalization to bankruptcy and liquidation by 2010.[3]

For most independent operators, it is almost inevitable that the risks of remaining competitive in the ever-evolving marketplace will become so great that the owners conclude it desirable to take their bets off the table. The small entrepreneur sells out to his competitor or a rollup artist, happily pocketing his liquidated bounty.

In the case of Trader Publishing Company, its owners came to a similar juncture. After almost 15 years, the two principals had become fully persuaded of the truth of the adage "same bed, different dreams," a Chinese proverb that distills the essence of what causes the division of most partnerships. Having taken over the reins from his father, Frank Batten, Jr., concluded that Landmark was too dependent on the fate of classified advertising—particularly automotive advertising—and Cox's ownership had grown disillusioned with the prospects of print media, believing it desirable to concentrate more on Internet, cable, and broadcast opportunities. Accordingly, in 2005, the two companies decided that the time was ripe to sell their Trader joint venture. For a stressful six months, the owners and Trader's management team diverted their attention from growth to divestment. Cox enlisted Lehman Brothers, and Landmark appointed Morgan Stanley to advise it during the process; the two investment banking firms joined with Trader's management team to prepare for an auction to sell the $1.3 billion revenue company. Anticipating rabid interest in the company, which had grown at an average compounded annual rate exceeding 15 percent since 1991, the investment bankers predicted high enthusiasm among cash-rich media companies and private equity firms enthralled with the prospect of leveraging their own resources to accelerate Trader's development success. So propitious was the investment environment, they estimated that Trader would fetch between $4 billion and $6 billion, a value of 10 to 15 times the projected 2006 EBITDA.

Then, on the cusp of launching the auction, the partners became preoccupied with their tax and reinvestment dilemma. With their insignificant equity basis in the business, even a sale at the investment bankers' $4 billion low-end estimate would incur a $1.6 billion tax bite, and then they would have to find a reinvestment opportunity capable of delivering Trader's robust returns. But how reasonable would it be to find attractive alternative investments for their after-tax $2.4 billion that were capable of replicating Trader's $400 million annual pretax dividend?

Rather than sell the business, the partners concluded that they should divide the company between the two partners on a tax-efficient basis, with each getting the components he believed most desirable. Though most of Trader's managers were as distraught as the mother pleading to King Solomon to keep her child from being severed in half, the partners arrived at a resolution after six months of intense wrangling: Cox would take the *Auto Trader* and *Auto Mart* classified magazines along with Landmark's stake in AutoTrader.com, and Landmark would retain all of Trader's remaining assets. On September 12, 2006, the deal was finalized, and Landmark renamed its now wholly owned division Dominion Enterprise, which consisted of the publishing and Internet businesses of *For Rent Magazine*, *Harmon Homes*, *Employment Guide*, *Parenting*, and all the ancillary publications of the nonautomotive group (boat, cycle, RV, big truck, and heavy equipment traders).[4]

Within three years after the dissolution of Trader Publishing Company, Cox closed the publishing operations of the previously $400 million revenue *Auto Trader* and $100 million *Auto Mart*, disintegrating victims of the runaway success of AutoTrader.com and other Internet services.

Reallocating their sales and operational resources to AutoTrader.com, Cox essentially doubled down on its Internet bet, dismissing the legacy publishing business it had acquired with Trader's dissolution.

Landmark's course was the opposite. After carefully considering the prospects and economic environment, Frank Batten, Jr., concluded the time was ripe to sell all of its properties, and Landmark's vice chairman, Dick Barry, confirmed Batten's decision on January 3, 2008: "We are exploring strategic alternatives, and that can entail a number of possibilities, one of which is the sale of the company's businesses."[5] The easiest to sell was The Weather Channel, which NBC snapped up for a reported $3.5 billion on September 12, 2008.[6] But the remainder of Landmark's businesses missed the sales window that came crashing down with the new millennium's most devastating financial collapse. Lehman, as the investment banker managing Landmark's sale of Dominion Enterprise, collapsed in ignominy just after the bids had come in, and the bids reflected both the pessimism about media's prospects and the increased investment conservatism of the new era. Representing less than half the values projected a little more than a year earlier, all the offers were rejected by Landmark's ownership, which concluded it would keep its remaining properties except its Nashville WTVF CBS affiliate television station that it had agreed to sell to Bonten Media Group. But by October 15, that deal too was also pulled off the table when Bonten's financing evaporated, another casualty of the 2008 financial collapse.[7]

By the end of 2010, Cox's AutoTrader.com was continuing to post impressive results, with revenues soaring well above $1 billion and attractive profits to boot. Landmark's Dominion Enterprises was posting respectable earnings on recovering revenues of under $1 billion despite having converted almost all its vehicle publications to exclusively Internet platforms, including Traderonline.com, Boats.com, and CycleTrader.com. Also doing well were Dominion's ForRent.com and Homes.com portals. Its Internet site hosting services for realtors, car dealers, power sports, and other segments had maintained considerable profitability despite the business closures experienced in those segments.

The astonishing events of the last few years underscore the truth of Schumpeter's admonition about capitalism's destructive gales of creation. They therefore confirm the imperative that acquirers should maintain a wary eye for the clouds of change while constantly navigating the course of innovation to find safe harbors. Those who lack the confidence, the critical managerial acumen, and the necessary navigational skills are best advised to sell, particularly when the seas of acquisition become frothy from the thrashing battles among big-money sharks attacking attractive opportunities in a ravenous feeding-frenzy. Alternatively, there is always the hope for a miracle worker.

Appendix

History of Trader Publishing Company

Originally organized to develop and operate a nationwide network of classified advertising publications, Trader Publishing Company pursued a business strategy dedicated to creating efficient media to facilitate sales of used merchandise and vehicles among buyers and sellers. In later years, that mission was expanded to include the provision of recruitment advertising and customer relationship management support services among its various client groups, including vehicle dealerships, apartment management companies, real estate agencies, and the hospitality industry.

Tracing its roots to the November 1985 acquisition of the Winston–Salem *Trading Post* and *Wheels & Deals*, the company began as a subsidiary of Landmark Communications, Inc., whose management had concluded that targeted classified advertising publications represented an attractive investment opportunity. Perceiving benefits from consolidation of localized editions under a national organization and brand, it began the rollup of independent publishers throughout the United States. In July 1988, Cox Enterprises' leadership reached the same conclusion and acquired the operations of the *Auto Trader* licensor. In the next 15 months, the two companies completed 25 additional acquisitions that operated 83 classified ad publications.

Because their publications shared a business strategy with minimal market overlap, Cox and Landmark recognized the compelling advantage of merging their respective operations to form Trader Publishing Company as a partnership on April 1, 1991.

Throughout the next decade, Trader expanded the number of localized *Auto Trader* magazines through acquisitions and start-ups, including the spin-out from its core magazine of segmented titles such as *Boat Trader, Big Truck Trader, RV Trader,* and *Cycle Trader.* It also developed nationally distributed titles, including *Old Car Trader, Yacht Trader,* and *Corvette Trader,* and it added to the national group with the acquisition of *Walneck's Classic Cycle Trader.* In 1997, it expanded into traditional consumer magazine and trade journal publishing with the acquisition of *Soundings, Trade Only,* and *Woodshop News.*

Having established itself as the nation's preeminent vehicle and general classified advertising publisher, Trader began seeking new opportunities to sustain growth. Leveraging the experience it gained from three free distribution publications it had acquired in 1989 and 1992, in 1995 Trader launched free *Auto Mart* titles, magazines providing commercial car dealers with supplemental advertising exposure among consumers. To provide distribution of those free titles in grocery stores and other high-traffic outlets, Trader acquired National Media Systems in March 1996, subsequently renaming it Trader Distribution Services, and by 1997 localized *Auto Mart* editions were serving almost every major U.S. market.

Perceiving a need to provide targeted publications to assist employers in their recruitment efforts, Trader acquired the free distribution Detroit *Employment Guide* in January 1997. In the next three years, Trader launched 51 similar publications in new markets and acquired 11 others.

To round out its offering of free distribution titles, in June 2000 Trader acquired United Advertising Publications, Inc., the nation's foremost publisher of real estate magazines, apartment guides, and parenting publications, including *Harmon Homes, For Rent,* and *Parenting.*

The emergence of the Internet led Trader to develop electronic versions of its products, including the launch of Traderonline.com in February 1996. In 1998, Trader acquired CareerWeb.com to facilitate Internet access to its employment database. To create the nation's leading automotive website, Trader contributed the automotive portion of Traderonline.com to the newly independent company AutoTrader.com, L.L.C., in August 1999. Trader continued to develop several leading vehicle advertising portals, including BoatTrader.com, CycleTrader.com, and

AeroTrader.com, among others. With the acquisition of United Advertising Publications, Trader devoted substantial effort to developing ForRent.com, HarmonHomes.com and Parenthood.com.

To leverage its strengths to develop new products, the company launched Trader Ventures in 1999. By 2003, Trader Ventures was operating the largest network of services to provide used car dealerships with point-of-purchase window stickers and data distribution services to promote their inventory on thousands of Internet websites. The division also acquired *Traveler's Discount Guide, Travel Discount Guide, Travel Savers,* and *U.S. Travel Guide,* which are the nation's leading motel discount coupon guides, with online access available through Roomsaver.com.

In 2004, to support its real estate magazines and provide real estate website-hosting services, Trader acquired Homes.com, Inc., and, in the following years, it acquired other real estate services, including Best Image Marketing, Katabat Corp., Advanced Access, and eNeighborhoods. To provide similar web services to its other segments, it subsequently acquired more than a dozen companies, including Dealerskins, XIGroup, and @utoRevenue (auto dealers); PowerSports Network (motorcycle and power sports dealers); RVAmerica (RV dealers); 123Movers (moving companies); and NextDoorNetwork (apartment complexes).

In 2005, Trader's partners, Cox and Landmark, found their interests diverging and concluded that the most efficient way to dissolve the partnership was to divide its assets. In 2006, the partners distributed the *Auto Trader* and *Auto Mart* publishing assets to Cox and almost all the other assets to Landmark. The company's printing plant assets continued to be operated as a joint venture until 2008, when Landmark assumed full ownership.

Throughout its history, Trader grew steadily through acquisition and entrepreneurial expansion in its respective market segments. The following schedule (summarizes those activities.

Trader Publishing Company Acquisition and Publication Start-Up Summary, 1991–2006

	1991*	1992	1993	1994	1995	1996	1997	1998
Number of acquisitions								
Paid classified publications	34			1	3		1	
Free auto guide guides	2	1			2	3		
National magazines	1					1	2	
Employment publications							3	3
Travel publications								
Real estate/apart. guides								
Data collection								
Distribution companies						1		
Internet businesses								1
Direct marketing/other								
Printing plants	1				1			
	38	1	–	1	6	5	6	4
Publications								
Acquired	202			1	14	5	14	2
Start-ups		10	10	48	27	49	32	38

	1999	2000†	2001	2002	2003	2004	2005	2006
Number of acquisitions								
Paid classified publications		1	1	1				
Free auto guide guides								
National magazines	1				1	1		
Employment publications	2	3						
Travel publications		2	1	1				
Real estate/apart. guides		1	3	2	1		1	
Data collection	1	3		8	13	10	6	4
Distribution companies								
Internet businesses	1					2	9	1
Direct marketing/other						1	2	
Printing plants								
	5	10	5	12	15	14	18	5
Publications								
Acquired	3	313	39	12	15	14	1	
Start-ups	26	30	14	34	30	96	57	

*1991 acquisitions include those completed by Cox Enterprises, Inc., and Landmark Communications, Inc., for the period November 1985 to March 1991.

†The 2000 acquisition of United Advertising Publications included 51 *For Rent Magazines*, 185 *Harmon Homes* publications, 26 parenting publications, 10 *Harmon Autos*, and 3 national trade magazines. It is listed as a single acquisition under the "Real estate/apartment guides" category.

Notes

Introduction

1. David Roux, Church Club Panel on Mergers & Acquisitions, October 2007, http://www.youtube.com/watch?v=NC65FJhtDWw, retrieved October 11, 2011.
2. Chris Isidore, "Daimler Pays to Dump Chrysler," CNNMoney.com, May 14, 2007.
3. Devin Leonard, "Mark Cuban Wants a Little R-E-S-P-E-C-T," *Fortune*, October 4, 2007.
4. "Circuit City, Canadian Subsidiary File for Creditor Protection," CBC News, November 10, 2008; "Blockbuster Withdraws Proposal to Acquire Circuit City," Thomson Financial News Limited, July 1, 2008.
5. Warren Buffett, Berkshire Hathaway, Inc., Annual Report, 1994.
6. Robert G. Hagstrom, *The Warren Buffett Way*, Hoboken, NJ, Wiley, 2005, p. 6.
7. Robert Bruner, *Deals from Hell*, Hoboken, NJ, Wiley, 2005, p. 13.
8. Dinara Bayazitova, Matthias Kahl, and Rossen Valkanov, "Which Mergers Destroy Value? Only Mega-Mergers," *Social Science Research Network*, October 23, 2009, p. 1.
9. Andrew Ross Sorkin, "JP Morgan Pays $2 a Share for Bear Stearns," *New York Times*, March 17, 2008, http://www.nytimes.com/2008/03/17/business/17 bear.html, retrieved October 5, 2011. Originally set at $2 per share, the price eventually increased to $10.
10. Annual Report 2008, ABInBev, 2008, p. 5.
11. Annual Report/Form 10-K 2005, eBay, Inc., 2005, p. 95. The structure of the transaction included payment of $1.3 billion cash, 32.8 million shares of eBay common stock (then valued at $1.3 billion), and a performance earn-out bonus with a maximum value of $1.3 billion.
12. Douglas Macmillan, "E-Bay Sells Skype, Keeps 35%," *Bloomberg Business-Week*, September 1, 2009.

13. Peter Bright, "Microsoft Buys Skype for $8.5 Billion: Why, Exactly?" *Wired*, May 10, 2011.

14. Benjamin Graham and David Dodd, *Security Analysis*, New York, McGraw-Hill, 1934, p. 38.

15. Ray Kroc, *Grinding It Out: The Making of McDonald's*, New York, NY, St. Martin's, 1977.

16. Mark Robichaux, *Cable Cowboy: John Malone and the Rise of the Modern Cable Business*, Hoboken, NJ, Wiley, 2002, p. 4; Jeff Pelline, "AT&T to Buy TCI for $48 Billion," CNET News, May 8, 1998.

17. Howard Schultz, *Pour Your Heart into It*, New York, NY, Hyperion, 1997.

18. Tom Witkowski, "Brooks-PRI Pays Price for Rollup Strategy," *Boston Business Journal*, November 29, 2002.

19. Joseph Schumpeter, *Capitalism, Socialism and Democracy*, 3rd ed., New York, Harper & Brothers, 1950, p. 83.

20. Steve Coomes, "Poultry Perseverance: The Old-Fashioned Brand Hatched on a Small Scale by a Kentucky Colonel Has Endured and Flourished on the Strengths of a Finger-Lickin' Formula," *Nation's Restaurant News*, January 28, 2008.

21. Steve Weiss, "The Scoop on the Egg McMuffin: Herb Peterson," *Restaurants & Institutions*, June 15, 1993.

22. Dollar Tree, Annual Report 1996, 1997.

Chapter 1

1. While fictitious, this interchange is reflective of numerous accounts of actual conversations between J. William Diederich and media managers.

2. See a succinct and compelling summary in Bruner, *Applied Mergers and Acquisitions*, Hoboken, NJ, Wiley, 2000, pp. 69–96.

3. Richard Roll, "The Hubris Hypothesis of Corporate Takeovers," *Journal of Business* 59:197–216, April 1986.

4. *Wall Street*, directed by Oliver Stone, 20th Century Fox, 1987.

5. Schumpeter, 1950, pp. 82–84.

6. "Newspaper Audience 2011 by Gender & Age Group," Scarborough USA, February 2010–March 2011; "Satellite Penetration at All-Time High," RBR.com, reporting Nielsen Media Research/NSI data for July 2008.

7. "TCI Will Buy Virginia-Based TeleCable Television," Associated Press, August 9, 1994.

8. Philp Walzer, "Landmark Completes Sale of The Weather Channel to NBC," *Virginian-Pilot*, September 13, 2008.

9. Bambi Francisco, "Happy Anniversary Internet Bubble," MarketWatch.com, March 10, 2005.

10. "Internet Bubble," *Encyclopaedia Britannica Online*, viewed September 16, 2011.

11. For the most part, the apartment rental and parenting publications were consolidated by United Advertising Publications before Trader's acquisition in 2000; Harmon Homes had been rolled up earlier by Hartz Mountain Industries, Inc.

Chapter 2

1. John Coleman Darnell and Colleen Mannassa, *Tutankhamun's Armies*, Hoboken, NJ, Wiley, 2007, pp. 4–6.

2. Leslie D. Manns, "Dominance in the Oil Industry: Standard Oil from 1865 to 1911," in *Market Dominance: How Firms Gain, Hold, or Lose It and the Impact on Economic Performance*, David Rosenbaum, ed., Westport, CT, Praeger, 1998.

3. John J. Clark and Margaret T. Clark, "The International Mercantile Marine Company: A Financial Analysis," *American Neptune* 57(2):137–154, 1997.

4. Robert Durden, *The Dukes of Durham, 1865–1929*, Durham, NC, Duke University Press, 1975, p. 27.

5. Craig Harris, "Arizona Diamondbacks Owner Ken Kendrick Reveals $2.8 Million Secret Honus Wagner Card," *Arizona Republic*, April 16, 2011.

6. Patrick G. Porter, "Origins of the American Tobacco Company," *Business History Review* XLIII(1), 1969:59; Alan M.Brandt, *The Cigarette Century: The Rise, Fall, and Deadly Persistence of the Product That Defined America*, New York, Basic Books, 2007, p. 39.

7. Robert Sobel, *The Entrepreneurs: Explorations within the American Business Tradition*, New York, Weybright & Talley, 1974, p. 236.

8. Ibid., p. 195.

9. David Nasaw, *The Chief: The Life of William Randolph Hearst*, New York, Houghton Mifflin, 2000, pp. 78, 386.

10. Denis Bryan, *Pulitzer: A Life*, Hoboken, NJ, Wiley, 2001.

11. "The LTV Corporation," Funding Universe.com, http://www.fundinguniverse.com/company—histories/The-LTV-Corporation-Company-History.html, retrieved October 1, 2011.

12. Robert Sobel, *The Rise and Fall of the Conglomerate Kings*, New York, Stein and Day, 1984, p. 30.

13. Ibid., pp.127–154.

14. Ibid., pp. 47–76.

15. Ibid., p. 64.

16. Ibid., p. 187.

17. "Bill Daniels Interview," Barco Library, Hauser Oral and Video History Collection, conducted February 10, 1986, and May 13, 1986.

18. Kathryn Harris, "Garstin Joins Top Cable TV Broker Daniels," *Los Angeles Times*, June 30, 1992.

19. Jim Keller, "Jack Crosby Interview," Barco Library, Hauser Oral and Video History Collection, conducted July 30, 1998.

20. "Waste Management, Inc.," Hoover's Company Profiles, December 30, 2010.

21. Ibid.

22. Waste Management, Inc., 2008 Annual Report, pp. 2 and 20. With the great recession of 2008, the company experienced volume declines in its economically sensitive industrial collection segment, and its recycling revenues were hammered by steep market declines in volume and demand. Accordingly, by 2010, its $12.5 billion revenues were still 6.5 percent lower than the 2008 peak and its earnings had dropped 7.8 percent to $963 million. See Waste Management, Inc., 2010 Annual Report, p. 68.

23. Paul Carroll and Chunka Mui, *Billion Dollar Lessons*, New York, Portfolio/ Penguin Group, 2008, p. 60.

24. Debra Sparks, "Poof! And Small Turns into Big," *BusinessWeek*, August 2, 1998, pp. 72–73.

25. "Blockbuster, Inc., Company Profile," Referenceforbusiness.com, http://www. referenceforbusiness.com/history2/93/Blockbuster-Inc.html, September 30, 2011.

26. Dyan Machan, "Crime, Garbage—and Billboards," *Forbes* 156(12):52–54, 1995.

27. Donald L Sexton, "Wayne Huizenga: Entrepreneur and Wealth Creator," *Academy of Management Executive* 14(1):40–48, 2001.

28. Elizabeth MacBride, "New Advisor Aggregators Put the Roll-up Ghosts to Bed, for Now," *Forbes*, February 3, 2011.

29. Paul F. Kocourek, Steven Y. Chung, and Matthew G. McKenna, "**Strategic** Rollups: Overhauling the Multi-Merger Machine," *Strategy+Business*, Second Quarter, 2000.

30. Selena Maranjian, "Should You Avoid Roll-Ups," The Motley Fool, http://www.fool.com/foolu/askfoolu/2002/askfoolu020212.htm, February 12, 2002, retrieved October 11, 2011.

31. Alex Schav, "Unrolling U.S. Office Products," The Motley Fool, http://www.fool.com/LunchNews/1998/LunchNews981103.htm?terms=Roll-ups&vstest=search_042607_linkdefault, November 3, 1998, retrieved October 11, 2011.

32. "U.S.A. Floral Receives Approval to Complete Sale of International Division–Florimex," *Business Wire*, September 10, 2001.

33. Witkowski, 2002.

34. "Brooks Settles SEC Options Case," *MassHigh Tech*, May 20, 2008.

35. "Corporate Express, Inc." *International Directory of Company Histories*. 2002. Retrieved from Encyclopedia.com, http://www.encyclopedia.com/doc/1G2-2845100031. html, October 10, 2011.

36. Carroll and Mui, 2008, p. 62.

37. Ibid., p. 62.

Chapter 3

1. Story related to the author by J. William Diederich.

2. Connie Sage, *Frank Batten: The Untold Story of the Founder of the Weather Channel*, Charlottesville, University of Virginia Press, 2011, p. 38.

3. Frank Batten, *The Weather Channel: The Improbable Rise of a Media Phenomenon*, Cambridge, MA, Harvard University Press, 2002, p. 21.

4. Ibid., p. 34.

5. Ibid.

Chapter 5

1. Chris Isidore, "Daimler Pays to Dump Chrysler," CNNMoney.com, May 14, 2007.

2. See Bruner, 2004, pp. 280–291, 341–346.

3. Jeremy Van Loon, "Daimler Considers Sale of Chrysler: Synergy 'Limited,' Executive Says as Carmaker Cuts 13,000 Jobs," *Ottawa Citizen*, February 2, 2007.

4. Mark Sirower, *The Synergy Trap*, New York, Free Press, 1997, pp. 18–41.

5. John Burr Williams, *The Theory of Investment Value*, Cambridge, MA, Harvard Universiy Press, 1938, pp. 542–543.

6. Merton Miller and Franco Modigliani, "Dividend Policy Growth, and the Valuation of Shares," *Journal of Business* 34:411–433, 1961; Franco Modigliani and Merton Miller, "The Cost of Capital, Corporation Finance, and the Theory of Investment," *American Economic Review* 48:261–297, 1958.

7. Joel M. Stern, *Measuring Corporate Performance*, New York and London: Financial Times LTD, 1975.

8. S. N. Kaplan and R. S. Ruback, "The Valuation of Cash Flow Forecasts: An Empirical Analysis," *Journal of Finance* 50:1059–1093, 1995.

9. Andrew Ang and Jun Liu, "How to Discount Cash Flows with Time — Varying Expected Returns," *Journal of Finance* 69:2745–2783, 2004.

10. By 1997, "acquirers allocated over $20 billion during the past fifteen years for advice about the fair value of the companies they were acquiring." Sirower, 1997, p. 70.

11. Dinara Bayazitova, Matthias Kahl, and Rossen I. Valkanov, "Value Creation for Acquirers: New Methods and Evidence," Social Science Research Network, http://ssrn.com/abstract=1502385, July 24, 2011 version, retrieved October 30, 2011. Studies that find negative average returns to bidders include Ajeyo Banerjee, and James E. Owers, "Wealth Reduction in White Knight Bids," *Financial Management* 21:48–57, 1992; John Byrd, and Kent Hickman, "Do Outside Directors Monitor Managers? Evidence from Tender Offer Bids," *Journal of Financial Economics* 32:195–221, 1992; Henri Servaes, "Tobin's Q and the Gains from Takeovers," *Journal of Finance* 46:409–419, 1991; and Nikhil Varaiya, and Kenneth Ferris, "Overpaying in Corporate Takeovers: The Winner's Curse," *Financial Analysts Journal* 43:64–70, 1987. A comprehensive analysis of 134 surveys and scientific studies between 1979 and 2000 suggests that the majority of large transactions do produce positive returns exceeding the acquirers' cost of capital, although at least a third do not pay; see Bruner (2004), 30–64.

12. Shahin Shojai, "Economists' Hubris — The Case of Mergers and Acquisitions," *Journal of Financial Transformation* 26:4–12, 2009.

13. Warren Buffett, Berkshire Hathaway, Inc., 2010 Annual Report, 2011, p. 28.

14. Michael Moe, *Finding the Next Starbucks*, New York, Portfolio Penguin Group, 2006, p. 18. Moe is the cofounder, chairman, and CEO of ThinkEquity Partners, LLC, and was formerly director of global research at Merrill Lynch.

15. Enrique Arzac, *Valuation for Mergers, Buyouts, and Restructuring*, Hoboken, NJ, Wiley, 2005, p. 15.

16. Ibid.

17. Bruner, 2004, p. 278.

18. Robert Schiller, *Irrational Exuberance*, 2nd ed., Princton, NJ, Princeton University Press, 2005, p. 8.

19. "TCI Will Buy Virginia-Based TeleCable Television," Associated Press, August 9, 1994.

Chapter 6

1. Story related to the author by Jim Shumadine, November 7, 2011.
2. Story related by Dick Barry, October 28, 2011.

Chapter 7

1. A less contemporary version of this story was related to the author as a grad student in 1978 by Dr. R. Lee Brummet, professor of accounting at the University of North Carolina.
2. Pallavi Gogol, "Bank of America Told to Pay Whistleblower $930,000," Associated Press, September 14, 2011; Barry Ritholz, "FHFA Lawsuit vs. Bank of America, Merrill & Countrywide," Boston.com, September 2, 2011, http://finance.boston.com/boston/news/read?GUID=19381607, retrieved October 1, 2011.
3. Dick Barry, interview, October 28, 2011.

Chapter 8

1. Story related to the author by Britt Reid.
2. Maranjian, 2011.
3. Coomes, 2008.
4. U.S.A. Floral Products, Inc., 10-K, December 21, 1997, p. 3.
5. Kocourek, Chung, and McKenna, 2000.
6. Sparks, 1998, pp. 72–73.
7. S. L. Mintz, "Rolling on Down: How Integrated Electrical Services and Comfort Systems USA Succeed Where Other 'Roll-Ups' Flounder," *CFO Magazine*, September 1, 1999.
8. Kocourek, Chung, and McKenna, 2000.
9. Sparks, 1998, pp. 72–73.
10. Ilan Mochari, "Auto-Shop Roll-Up Wrecked in Rush," *Inc.*, January 2001.
11. Kocourek, Chung, and McKenna, 2000.
12. "Republic Industries, Inc. Company History," *Company Profiles*, fundingu niverse.com, retrieved October 3, 2011.
13. Tom Shean, "The Return of the Taxmaster," *Virginian-Pilot*, April 5, 2009.
14. Dean Foust, "Wachovia: Golden West Wasn't Golden," *BusinessWeek*, June 4, 2008.
15. David Yochum, "Roll-Up Trend: Main Street Meets Wall Street," *Houston Business Journal*, January 11, 1998.
16. Ibid.

17. "PhyCor, Inc.," *Gale Directory of Company Histories*, http://www.answers.com/topic/phycor-inc., retrieved October 5, 2011.

18. Sparks, 1998, pp. 72–73.

19. "KFC Corporation," *Gale Directory of Company Histories*, http://www.answers.com/topic/kfc-corporation, retrieved October 5, 2011.

20. Ravenscraft and Scherer, "Mergers, Sell-Offs, and Economic Efficiency," Washington, D.C., Brookings Institution, 1987; D. Mueller, "Mergers and Market Share," *Review of Economics and Statistics* 67(2): 259–267, 1985, and B. E. Eckbo, "Mergers and the Value of Antitrust Deterrence," *Journal of Finance* 47(1): 1–25, 1992.

21. "Starbucks to Buy Seattle's Best Coffee," *Seattle Post-Intelligencer*, April 15, 2003.

22. Gordon MacMillan, "Guardian Media Agrees Deal to Buy Auto Trader Publisher," brandrepublic.com, August 6, 2003.

23. "Waste Management Settles," CNNMoney, November 7, 2001, http://money.cnn.com/2001/11/07/news/waste_mgt/index.htm, retrieved October 4, 2011.

24. Walter Hamilton, "WorldCom Ex-CEO Sentenced for Fraud," *Los Angeles Times*, July 14, 2005.

25. "Mattel, Inc.," Company Histories & Profiles, FundingUniverse.com, http://www.fundinguniverse.com/company-histories/Mattel-Inc-Company-History.html, retrieved October 4, 2011.

26. "Arch Wireless, Inc.," *Gale Directory of Company Histories*, http://www.answers.com/topic/arch-wireless-inc#ixzz1bobHZrqJ, retrieved October 14, 2011.

27. Peter J. Howe, "Arch Wireless to Acquire Metrocall, Westborough Firm Plans Layoffs, Move," *Boston Globe*, March 30, 2004, http://www.boston.com/business/globe/articles/2004/03/30/arch_wireless_to_acquire_metrocall/, retrieved October 14, 2011.

Chapter 9

1. Related by Conrad Hall, describing one of his conversations with a prospective acquisition target.

2. Mochari, 2001.

3. Mintz, 1999.

4. Integrated Electrical Services, Inc., Quarterly Report, June 30, 2011.

5. Graham and Dodd, 2009, p. 38.

6. "Warren Buffett Invests $3 Billion in GE," Associated Press, October 1, 2008.

7. Metals USA, Inc., 10-K, 2001, p. 71.

Chapter 10

1. Story related by Conrad Hall to the author.
2. As related to the author by Macon Brock in an interview, September 29, 2011.
3. Peter McKelvey, "The Ties That Bind in Roll-Up Plays That Work," *Mergers and Acquisition Journal* 33(6):37, June 1, 1999.
4. As related to the author by Macon Brock in an interview, September 29, 2011.
5. Coomes, 2008.
6. As related to the author by Dick Roberts in an interview, October 11, 2011.
7. Kroc, 1977, p. 126.

Chapter 11

1. Story related to the author by Richard Jamin.
2. Coomes, 2008.
3. Related by letter from Mike Nenni to the author, December 1, 2008.

Chapter 12

1. Story related to the author by Britt Reid, October 16, 2011.
2. Dollar Tree, 2002 Annual Report, pp. 11–12.
3. Related to the author by Dick Roberts, October 11, 2011.
4. Mochari, 2001.

Chapter 13

1. Stephen Singular, *Relentless: Bill Daniels and the Triumph of Cable TV*, The Bill Daniels Estate, 2003, p. 44
2. Related to the author by Dick Roberts, October 11, 2011.
3. Ibid.
4. "Wireless Telecommunications Carriers in the US: U.S. Industry Report," *IBISWorld*, September 20, 2011.
5. "1946: First Mobile Telephone Call," Technology Timeline, AT&T Enterprise, http://www.corp.att.com/attlabs/reputation/timeline/46mobile.html, retrieved October 4, 2011.
6. Jim McNair, "Rural Areas Jostle Way into Cellular Market; License Lottery Sparks Questionable Practices," *Fort Lauderdale Sun-Sentinel*, December 12, 1988.
7. "Wireless Telecommunications Carriers in the US: U.S. Industry Report," 2011.

8. Because of the intervening dot-com collapse, the IPO never materialized, and Cox and its partners continued to develop the service into its present status as a highly profitable billion-dollar-revenue stand-alone enterprise that is still without peer in terms of the volume of listings and the quality of the descriptive content and photographs.
9. Clayton Christensen, *The Innovator's Dilemma*, Cambridge, MA: HBS Press, 1997, p. xvii.

Chapter 14

1. Kroc, 1977, pp. 6–7.
2. Robichaux, 2002, p. 7.
3. Schultz, 1997, pp. 25–26.
4. Daniel Pink, "How to Make Your Own Luck," *Fast Company*, June 2003.
5. Warren Buffett, "To the Shareholders," Berkshire Hathaway, Inc., Annual Report, 2007.
6. "Convergent Technologies (Unisys)," Wikipedia.com, http://en.wikipedia.org/wiki/Convergent_Technologies_%28Unisys%29, retrieved October 8, 2011.
7. David Lieberman, "Blockbuster Files for Chapter 11 Bankurputcy, Will Reorganize," *USA Today*, September 23, 2010.
8. Schultz, 1997, pp. 99–109.
9. "Coke Announces Dasani Water," *Beverage Digest*, February 1999.
10. "U.S. Liquid Refreshment Beverage Market: Volume by Segment 2007–2008," Beverage Marketing Corporation, http://www.beveragemarketing.com/?section=news&newsID=111, retrieved October 8, 2011.
11. Valarie Philips, "50 Years of Finger-Lickin' Chicken: 'Pete' Harman Started KFC Right Here in Salt Lake City," *Deseret News*, July 30, 2002.
12. "Barnes & Noble History," http://www.barnesandnobleinc.com/our_company/history/bn_history.html, retrieved October 23, 2011.
13. "Darden Restaurants, Inc.," *Gale Directory of Businesses*, http://www.answers.com/darden+restaurants?cat=biz-fin, retrieved October 9, 2011.
14. "Brinker International," *Gale Directory of Businesses*, http://www.answers.com/topic/brinker-international-inc, retrieved October 9, 2011.
15. Warren Buffett, "To the Shareholders," Berkshire Hathaway, Inc., Annual Report 1993.
16. Warren Buffett, "To the Shareholders," Berkshire Hathaway, Inc. Annual Report 1991.
17. "Nortel Announces the Winning Bidder of Its Patent Portfolio for a Purchase Price of US$4.5 Billion," Nortel Networks press release, June 30, 2011.

18. Mike McLean, "Google and Motorola—A Match Made in Patent Heaven?" *UBM TechInsights—EDN*, September 15, 2011, http://www.edn.com/article/519354-Google_and_Motorola_A_match_made_in_patent_heaven_.php, retrieved October 9, 2011.

19. "The Continued Evolution of Patent Damages Law: Patent Litigation Trends 1995–2009 and the Impact of Recent Court Decisions on Damages," Patent Litigation Study, PricewaterhouseCoopers, 2010.

20. Graham and Dodd, 2009, p. 38.

21. Schultz, 1997, pp. 38–48.

22. Howard E. Covington and Marion A. Ellis, *The Story of NationsBank: Changing the Face of American Banking*, Chapel Hill: University of North Carolina Press, 1993.

Chapter 15

1. Story related to the author by Jeff Moore, October 21, 2011.

2. Schumpeter, 1950, p. 83.

3. "Blockbuster Inc.—Company Profile, Information, Business Description, History, Background Information on Blockbuster Inc.," ReferenceForBusiness.com, 2011.

4. "Cox Enterprises and Landmark Communications Announce Division of Partnership Assets in Trader Publishing Company," Cox Enterprises press release, March 17, 2006; "Dominion Enterprises Completes Company Formation," http://www.dominionenterprises.com/main/newsID/10/do/news_detail, retrieved October 17, 2011.

5. Philip Walzer, "Landmark Considers Possible Sale of Pilot, Weather Channel," *Virginian-Pilot*, January 3, 2008.

6. Philip Walzer, "Landmark Completes Sale of The Weather Channel to NBC," *Virginian-Pilot*, September 13, 2008.

7. Philip Walzer, "Landmark's Sale of Tenn. TV Station Falls Through," *Virginian-Pilot*, October 16, 2008.

Bibliography

"1946: First Mobile Telephone Call," Technology Timeline, AT&T Enterprise, http://www.corp.att.com/attlabs/reputation/timeline/46mobile. html, retrieved October 4, 2011.

ABInbev, Annual Report, 2008.

Ang, Andrew, and Jun Liu, "How to Discount Cash Flows with Time — Varying Expected Returns," *Journal of Finance* 69:2745–2783, 2004.

"Arch Wireless, Inc.," *Gale Directory of Company Histories*, http://www. answers.com/topic/arch-wireless-inc#ixzz1bobHZrqJ, retrieved October 14, 2011.

Arzac, Enrique, *Valuation for Mergers, Buyouts and Restructuring*, Hoboken, NJ: Wiley, 2005.

Banerjee, Ajeyo, and James E. Owers, "Wealth Reduction in White Knight Bids," *Financial Management* 21:48–57, 1992.

"Barnes & Noble History," http://www.barnesandnobleinc.com/our_company/history/bn_history.html, retrieved October 23, 2011.

Batten, Frank, *The Weather Channel: The Improbable Rise of a Media Phenomenon*, Cambridge, MA: Harvard, 2002.

Bayazitova, Dinara; Kahl, Matthias; and Valkanov, Rossen I., "Value Creation for Acquirers: New Methods and Evidence," Social Science Research Network, http://ssrn.com/abstract=1502385. July 24, 2011 version, retrieved October 30, 2011.

Bernstein, Peter, *Capital Ideas: The Improbable Origins of Modern Wall Street*, New York: Free Press, 1992.

"Bill Daniels Interview," Barco Library, Hauser Oral and Video History Collection, conducted February 10, 1986, and May 13, 1986.

"Blockbuster, Inc., Company Profile," Referenceforbusiness.com, http://www.referenceforbusiness.com/history2/93/Blockbuster-Inc.html, September 30, 2011.

"Blockbuster, Inc.—Company Profile, Information, Business Description, History, Background Information on Blockbuster Inc.," Reference ForBusiness.com, 2011.

"Blockbuster Withdraws Proposal to Acquire Circuit City," *Thomson Financial News Limited*, July 1, 2008.

Brandt, Alan M., *The Cigarette Century: The Rise, Fall, and Deadly Persistence of the Product That Defined America*, New York, Basic Books, 2007.

Bright, Peter, "Microsoft Buys Skype for $8.5 Billion. Why, Exactly?" *Wired*, May 10, 2011.

"Brinker International," *Gale Directory of Businesses*, http://www.answers.com/topic/brinker-international-inc, retrieved October 9, 2011.

"Brooks Settles SEC Options Case," *MassHigh Tech*, May 20, 2008.

Bruner, Robert, *Applied Mergers and Acquisitions*, Hoboken, NJ: Wiley, 2004.

Bruner, Robert, *Deals from Hell*, Hoboken, NJ: Wiley, 2005.

Bryan, Denis, *Pulitzer: A Life*, Hoboken, NJ, Wiley, 2001.

Buffett, Warren, "Acquisition Criteria," Berkshire Hathaway, Inc., 2010 Annual Report, 2011.

Buffett, Warren, "To the Shareholders," Berkshire Hathaway, Inc., Annual Report, 1991.

Buffett, Warren, "To the Shareholders," Berkshire Hathaway, Inc., Annual Report, 1993.

Buffett, Warren, "To the Shareholders," Berkshire Hathaway, Inc., Annual Report, 1994.

Buffett, Warren, "To the Shareholders," Berkshire Hathaway, Inc., Annual Report, 2007.

Byrd, John, and Kent Hickman, "Do Outside Directors Monitor Managers? Evidence from Tender Offer Bids," *Journal of Financial Economics* 32:195–221, 1992.

Carroll, Paul, and Chunka Mui, *Billion Dollar Lessons*, New York: Portfolio/Penguin Group, 2008.

Christensen, Clayton, *The Innovator's Dilemma*, Cambridge, MA: HBS Press, 1997.

Chrysler Corp., 1997 Annual Report, 1998.

"Circuit City, Canadian Subsidiary File for Creditor Protection," CBC News, November 10, 2008.

Clark, John J., and Margaret T. Clark, "The International Mercantile Marine Company: A Financial Analysis," *American Neptune* 57(2): 137–154, 1997.

"Coke Announces Dasani Water," *Beverage Digest*, February 1999.

"The Continued Evolution of Patent Damages Law: Patent Litigation Trends 1995–2009 and the Impact of Recent Court Decisions on Damages," Patent Litigation Study, PricewaterhouseCoopers, 2010.

"Convergent Technologies (Unisys)," Wikipedia.com, http://en.wikipedia.org/wiki/Convergent_Technologies_%28Unisys%29, retrieved October 8, 2011.

Coomes, Steve, "Poultry Perseverance: The Old-Fashioned Brand Hatched on a Small Scale by a Kentucky Colonel Has Endured and Flourished on the Strengths of a Finger-Lickin' Formula," *Nation's Restaurant News*, January 28, 2008.

"Corporate Express, Inc." *International Directory of Company Histories*. 2002. Encyclopedia.com: http://www.encyclopedia.com/doc/1G2–2845100031.Html, retrieved October 10, 2011.

Covington, Howard E., and Marion A. Ellis, *The Story of NationsBank: Changing the Face of American Banking*, Chapel Hill: University of North Carolina Press, 1993.

"Cox Enterprises and Landmark Communications Announce Division of Partnership Assets in Trader Publishing Company," Cox Enterprises press release, March 17, 2006.

"Darden Restaurants, Inc.," *Gale Directory of Businesses*, http://www.answers.com/darden+restaurants?cat=biz-fin, retrieved October 9, 2011.

Darnell, John Coleman, and Colleen Mannassa, *Tutankhamun's Armies*, Hoboken, NJ: Wiley, 2007.

Dollar Tree, Annual Report 1996, 1997.

Dollar Tree Annual Report 2002, 2003.

Drucker, Peter, *Managing for the Future*, New York: Plume/Dutton Signet, 1992.

Durden, Robert, *The Dukes of Durham, 1865–1929*, Durham, NC: Duke University Press, 1975.

eBay, Inc, Annual Report/Form 10-K 2005, 2006.

Eckbo, B. E., "Mergers and the Value of Antitrust Deterrence," *Journal of Finance* 47(1):1–25, 1992.

Foust, Dean, "Wachovia: Golden West Wasn't Golden, *BusinessWeek*, June 4, 2008.

Francisco, Bambi, "Happy Anniversary Internet Bubble," MarketWatch.com, March 10, 2005.

Gogol, Pallavi, "Bank of America Told to Pay Whistleblower $930,000," Associated Press, September 14, 2011.

Graham, Benjamin, and David Dodd, *Security Analysis*, 6th ed., New York: McGraw-Hill, 2009.

Hagstrom, Robert G., *The Warren Buffett Way*, Hoboken, NJ: Wiley, 2005.

Hamilton, Walter, "WorldCom ex-CEO Sentenced for Fraud," *Los Angeles Times*, July 14, 2005.

Harris, Craig, "Arizona Diamondbacks Owner Ken Kendrick Reveals $2.8 Million Secret Honus Wagner Card," *Arizona Republic*, April 16, 2011.

Harris, Kathryn, "Garstin Joins Top Cable TV Broker Daniels," *Los Angeles Times*, June 30, 1992.

Howe, Peter J., "Arch Wireless to Acquire Metrocall, Westborough Firm Plans Layoffs, Move," *Boston Globe*, March 30, 2004, http://www.boston.com/business/globe/articles/2004/03/30/arch_wireless_to_acquire_metrocall/, retrieved October 14, 2011.

Integrated Electrical Services, Inc., Quarterly Report, June 30, 2011.

"Internet Bubble." *Encyclopædia Britannica. Encyclopædia Britannica Online,* September 23, 2011.

Isidore, Chris, "Daimler Pays to Dump Chrysler," CNNMoney.com, May 14, 2007.

Kapan, S. N., and R. S. Ruback, "The Valuation of Cash Flow Forecasts: An Empirical Analysis," *Journal of Finance* 50:1059–1093, 1995.

Keller, Jim, "Jack Crosby Interview," Hauser Oral and Video History Collection, Barco Library, July 30, 1998.

"KFC Corporation," *Gale Directory of Company Histories,* http://www.answers.com/topic/kfc-corporation, retrieved October 5, 2011.

Kocourek, Paul F., Steven Y. Chung, and Matthew G. McKenna, "Strategic Rollups: Overhauling the Multi-Merger Machine," *Strategy+Business,* Second Quarter, 2000.

Kroc, Ray, *Grinding It Out: The Making of McDonald's,* New York, St. Martin's, 1977.

Leonard, Devin, "Mark Cuban Wants a Little R-E-S-P-E-C-T," *Fortune,* October 4, 2007.

Lieberman, David, "Blockbuster Files for Chapter 11 Bankruptcy, Will Reorganize," *USA Today,* September 23, 2010.

"The LTV Corporation," FundingUniverse.com, http://www.fundinguniverse.com/company-histories/The-LTV-Corporation-Company-History.html, retrieved October 1, 2011.

MacBride, Elizabeth, "New Advisor Aggregators Put the Roll-up Ghosts to Bed, for Now," *Forbes,* February 3, 2011.

Machan, Dyan, "Crime, Garbage—and Billboards," *Forbes* 156(12): 52–54, 1995.

Macmillan, Douglas, "E-Bay Sells Skype, Keeps 35%," *Bloomberg Business-Week,* September 1, 2009.

MacMillan, Gordon, "Guardian Media Agrees Deal to Buy Auto Trader Publisher," brandrepublic.com, August 6, 2003.

Manns, Leslie D., "Dominance in the Oil Industry: Standard Oil from 1865 to 1911, in *Market Dominance: How Firms Gain, Hold, or Lose It and the Impact on Economic Performance*, David Rosenbaum, ed., Westport, CT, Praeger, 1998.

Maranjian, Selena, "Should You Avoid Roll-Ups?" The Motley Fool, http://www.fool.com/foolu/askfoolu/2002/askfoolu020212.htm, February 12, 2002, retrieved October 11, 2011.

"Mattel, Inc.," Company Histories & Profiles, FundingUniverse.com, http://www.fundinguniverse.com/company-histories/Mattel-Inc-Company-History.html, retrieved October 4, 2011.

McKelvey, Peter, "The Ties That Bind In Roll-Up Plays That Work," *Mergers and Acquisition Journal* 33(6), June 1, 1999.

McLean, Mike, "Google and Motorola—A Match Made in Patent Heaven?" *UBM TechInsights—EDN*, September 15, 2011, http://www.edn.com/article/519354-Google_and_Motorola_A_match_made_in_patent_heaven_.php, retrieved October 9, 2011.

Metals USA, Inc., 10-K, 2001.

Miller, Mertin, and Franco Modigliani, "Dividend Policy Growth, and the Valuation of Shares," *Journal of Business*, 34:411–433, 1961.

Mintz, S. L., "Rolling on Down: How Integrated Electrical Services and Comfort Systems USA Succeed Where Other Roll-Ups Flounder," *CFO Magazine*, September 1, 1999.

Mochari, Ilan, "Auto-Shop Roll-Up Wrecked in Rush," *Inc.*, January 2001.

Modigliani, Franco, and Merton Miller, "The Cost of Capital, Corporation Finance, and the Theory of Investment," *American Economic Review* 48:261–297, 1958.

Moe, Michael, *Finding the Next Starbucks*, New York: Portfolio Penguin Group, 2006.

Mueller, D. "Mergers and Market Share," *Review of Economics and Statistics* 67(2): 259–267, 1985.

Mufson, Steven, "Bank of America Still Feeling Drag from Purchase of Mortgage Firm Countrywide," *Washington Post*, December 3, 2010.

Nasaw, David, *The Chief: The Life of William Randolph Hearst,* New York: Houghton Mifflin, 2000.

"Newspaper Audience 2011 by Gender & Age Group," *Scarborough USA,* February 2010–March 2011.

"Nortel Announces the Winning Bidder of Its Patent Portfolio for a Purchase Price of US$4.5 Billion," Nortel Networks press release, June 30, 2011.

Pelline, Jeff, "AT&T to Buy TCI for $48 Billion," CNET News, May 8, 1998.

Philips, Valarie, "50 Years of Finger-Lickin' Chicken: 'Pete' Harman Started KFC Right Here in Salt Lake City," *Deseret News,* July 30, 2002.

"PhyCor, Inc.," *Gale Directory of Company Histories,* http://www.answers.com/topic/phycor-inc., retrieved October 5, 2011.

Pink, Daniel, "How to Make Your Own Luck," *Fast Company,* June 2003.

Porter, Patrick G., "Origins of the American Tobacco Company," *Business History Review* XLIII(1): 59–76, 1969.

"Republic Industries, Inc., Company History," *Company Profiles,* funding universe.com, retrieved October 3, 2011.

Ravenscraft, D., and F.M. Scherer, "Mergers, Sell-Offs, and Economic Efficiency," Washington, D.C., Brookings Institution, 1987.

Ritholz, Barry, "FHFA Lawsuit vs. Bank of America, Merrill & Countrywide," Boston.com, September 2, 2011, http://finance.boston.com/boston/news/read?GUID=19381607, retrieved October 1, 2011.

Robichaux, Mark, *Cable Cowboy: John Malone and the Rise of the Modern Cable Business,* Hoboken, NJ: Wiley, 2002.

Roll, Richard, "The Hubris Hypothesis of Corporate Takeovers," *Journal of Business* 59:197–216, April 1986.

Roux, David, Church Club Panel on Mergers & Acquisitions, October 2007, http://www.youtube.com/watch?v=NC65FJhtDWw, retrieved October 11, 2011.

"Satellite Penetration at All-Time High," RBR.com, reporting Nielsen Media Research/NSI data for July 2008.

Schav, Alex, "Unrolling U.S. Office Products," The Motley Fool, http://www.fool.com/LunchNews/1998/LunchNews981103.htm?terms=Roll-ups&vstest=search_042607_linkdefault, November 3, 1998, retrieved October 11, 2011.

Schiller, Robert, *Irrational Exuberance*, 2d ed., Princeton, NJ: Princeton University Press, 2005.

Schultz, Howard, *Pour Your Heart into It*, New York: Hyperion, 1997.

Schumpeter, Joseph, *Capitalism, Socialism and Democracy*, 3rd ed., New York: Harper and Brothers, 1950.

Servaes, Henri, "Tobin's Q and the Gains from Takeovers," *Journal of Finance* 46:409–419, 1991.

Sexton, Donald L., "Wayne Huizenga: Entrepreneur and Wealth Creator," *Academy of Management Executive* 15(1):40–48, 2001.

Shean, Tom, "The Return of the Taxmaster," *Virginian-Pilot*, April 5, 2009.

Shojai, Shahin, "Economists' Hubris—The Case of Mergers and Acquisitions," *Journal of Financial Transformation* 26:4–12, 2009.

Singular, Stephen, *Relentless: Bill Daniels and the Triumph of Cable TV*, The Bill Daniels Estate, 2003.

Sirower, Mark, *The Synergy Trap*, New York: Free Press, 1997.

Sobel, Robert, *The Entrepreneurs: Explorations within the American Business Tradition*, New York: Weybright & Talley, 1974.

Sobel, Robert, *The Rise and Fall of the Conglomerate Kings*, New York, Stein and Day, 1984.

Sparks, Debra, "Poof! And Small Turns into Big," *BusinessWeek*, August 2, 1998, pp. 72–73.

"Starbucks to Buy Seattle's Best Coffee," *Seattle Post-Intelligencer*, April 15, 2003.

Stern, Joel M., *Measuring Corporate Performance*, New York and London: Financial Times LTD, 1975.

"TCI Will Buy Virginia-Based TeleCable," Associated Press, *Los Angeles Times*, August 9, 1994.

USA Floral Products, Inc., 10-K, December 21, 1997.

"U.S.A. Floral Receives Approval to Complete Sale of International Division–Florimex," *Business Wire*, September 10, 2001.

"U.S. Liquid Refreshment Beverage Market: Volume by Segment 2007–2008," Beverage Marketing Corporation, http://www.beverage marketing.com/?section=news&newsID=111, retrieved October 8, 2011.

Van Loon, Jeremy, "Daimler Considers Sale of Chrysler: Synergy 'Limited,' Executive Says as Carmaker Cuts 13,000 Jobs," *Ottawa Citizen*, February 2, 2007.

Varaiya, Nikhil, and Kenneth Ferris, "Overpaying in Corporate Takeovers: The Winner's Curse," *Financial Analysts Journal* 43:64–70, 1987.

Vlasic, Bill, and Bradley Stertz, *Taken for a Ride: How Daimler-Benz Drove Off with Chrysler*, New York, William Morrow, 2000.

Wall Street (film), directed by Oliver Stone, 20th Century Fox, 1987.

Walzer, Philip, "Landmark Completes Sale of The Weather Channel to NBC," *Virginian-Pilot*, September 13, 2008.

Walzer, Philip, "Landmark Considers Possible Sale of Pilot, Weather Channel," *Virginian-Pilot*, January 3, 2008.

Walzer, Philip, "Landmark's Sale of Tenn. TV Station Falls Through," *Virginian-Pilot*, October 16, 2008.

"Warren Buffett Invests $3 Billion in GE," Associated Press, October 1, 2008.

"Waste Management, Inc.," Hoover's Company Profiles, December 30, 2010.

"Waste Management Settles," CNNMoney, November 7, 2001, http://money.cnn.com/2001/11/07/news/waste_mgt/index.htm, retrieved October 4, 2011.

Weiss, Steve. "The Scoop on the Egg McMuffin: Herb Peterson," *Restaurants & Institutions*, June 15, 1993.

Williams, John Burr, *The Theory of Investment Value*, Cambridge, MA, 1938.

"Wireless Telecommunications Carriers in the US: U.S. Industry Report," *IBISWorld*, September 20, 2011.

Witkowski, Tom, "Brooks-PRI Pays Price for Rollup Strategy," *Boston Business Journal*, November 29, 2002.

Yochum, David, "Roll-Up Trend: Main Street Meets Wall Street," *Houston Business Journal*, January 11, 1998.

Index

CPSIA information can be obtained
at www.ICGtesting.com
Printed in the USA
BVHW040851130519
547751BV00020B/60/P